Social Work and Social Policy

Advancing the Principles of Economic and Social Justice

Edited by

Ira C. Colby
Catherine N. Dulmus
Karen M. Sowers

WILEY

JOHN WILEY & SONS, INC.

Library of Congress Cataloging-in-Publication Data:
Social Work and Social Policy : Advancing the Principles of Economic and Social Justice / Ira C. Colby, Catherine N. Dulmus, Karen M. Sowers.
    pages cm
  Includes bibliographical references and index.
  ISBN 978-1-118-17699-3 (pbk : alk paper) 1. Social service. 2. Social policy. I. Colby, Ira C. (Ira Christopher), editor of compilation. II. Dulmus, Catherine N., editor of compilation. III. Sowers, Karen M. (Karen Marlaine), editor of compilation.
  HV40.S617673 2013
  361–dc23

                                                                                            2012026667

Printed in the United States of America

10 9 8 7 6 5 4 3 2 1

Contents

Preface   vii

About the Editors   x

Contributors   xi

Chapter 1   **Social Welfare Policy as a Form of Social Justice   1**
Ira Colby

Introduction   1

Social Welfare Policy Defined   5

The Relationship Between Justice Theory and Social Welfare
    Policy   6

Social Work Values and Policy   8

The Traditional Conceptual Framework of Social Welfare   9

Crafting Justice-Based Policy   12

Conclusion   15

Key Terms   16

Review Questions for Critical Thinking   16

Online Resources   17

References   17

Chapter 2   **Reconceptualizing the Evolution of the American
    Welfare State   21**
Bruce Jansson

Introduction   21

Some Daunting Challenges Facing Historians of the American
    Welfare State   21

Nine Eras   28

Topics for Further Research   56

Where Next?   60

Key Terms   61

Review Questions for Critical Thinking   62

Online Resources   62

References   62

Chapter 3   **Human Security and the Welfare of Societies   65**
Jody Williams

Introduction   65

The Need to Redefine Security for the 21st Century   68

Human Security: Its Fundamentals and Its Roots   70
Is There a Future for a Human Security Framework?   75
Conclusion   77
Key Terms   78
Review Questions for Critical Thinking   78
Online Resources   79
References   79

Chapter 4   **Social Policy From a Global Perspective   81**
Robin Sakina Mama

Introduction   81
Globalization   82
Globalization as It Relates to Policy   86
Globalization and Ethics   87
Globalization, Policy, and Social Work Practice   88
Key Terms   89
Review Questions for Critical Thinking   89
Online Resources   89
References   90

Chapter 5   **Social Justice for Marginalized and Disadvantaged Groups: Issues and Challenges for Social Policies in Asia   93**
Joseph Kwok

Introduction   93
Social Justice: An Asian Perspective   95
Social Justice and Social Harmony   96
Social Policy   98
An Asian Context on Social Policy and Social Justice   99
An Asian Perspective on Social Policy Development   101
Social Enterprise and Social Capital   107
Conclusion   112
Key Terms   113
Review Questions for Critical Thinking   113
Online Resources   113
References   114

Chapter 6   **Welfare Reform: The Need for Social Empathy 117**
Elizabeth A. Segal

Introduction 117
A Brief History of Welfare Reform 119

Temporary Assistance for Needy Families 120
The Success of Welfare Reform 121
Who Receives Welfare? 122
Why Welfare Reform Has Failed 123
Inherent Contradictions in Welfare Reform 125
Values Conflicts 125
The Gap in Experiencing and Understanding Poverty 127
Social Empathy 128
Where Do We Go From Here? The Future of Welfare in America 130
Key Terms 131
Review Questions for Critical Thinking 131
Online Resources 131
References 131

Chapter 7   **Not by the Numbers Alone: The Effects of Economic and Demographic Changes on Social Policy 135**
Michael Reisch

Introduction 135
Economic Globalization 136
Poverty, Inequality, and Unemployment 139
Demographic Changes: Racism and Immigration 145
Implications for Social Policy 150
Welfare Reform as a Policy Illustration 151
Conclusion 153
Key Terms 154
Review Questions for Critical Thinking 154
Online Resources 154
References 154

Chapter 8   **The U.S. Patriot Act: Implications for the Social Work Profession 165**
Stan Stojkovic

Introduction 165
The U.S. Patriot Act: Significant Activities and a New System of Justice 167
The U.S. Patriot Act and the Social Work Profession 173
Conclusion 177
Key Terms 178
Review Questions for Critical Thinking 178
Online Resources 178
References 179

Chapter 9   **Social Justice in a World of Anywhere Access? 181**
Paul R. Raffoul

Introduction 181
Globalization 183
Societal Acceptance and Utilization of Technology 184
Use of Social Media 184
Information Access and Authenticity 186
Ensuring Diversity and Cultural Differences 187
Influencing the Development of Social Policy 187
Unintended Consequences of Technology and Social Policy 188
A Look Ahead to the Year 2022 189
Key Terms 191
Review Questions for Critical Thinking 191
Online Resources 191
References 191

Author Index 193
Subject Index 197

Preface

Social welfare policy can be true magic in the sense that outcomes have the potential to dramatically change lives, open new possibilities, strengthen communities, and, ultimately, realize social justice for all people. However, social welfare policy can also be an agent of oppression that stifles growth, perpetuates myths and prejudices, and leads to institutional discrimination (see Table 1). American history is filled with failed policies as well as successful initiatives. Yet we are perplexed when what we see as being valued and needed is viewed by others as repressive and beyond the scope of government.

No one policy text can provide a complete or full picture detailing the complexities of the social policy world. This text, however, brings together several significant social policy experts to share their unique perspectives. Purposefully, this work does not reflect a traditional policy textbook approach. Yes, many additional social issues could have been included, but our purpose is that the reader consider key issues that face policy makers (e.g., elected officials and agency administrators), and from there develop strategies to create fair and just social policies.

This book is designed as a beginning social welfare policy textbook for undergraduate and graduate students in social work programs. The text provides a broad overview of social welfare policy in the United States and an introduction to global policy issues. This book addresses the Council on Social Work Education (CSWE) required competencies for accreditation. Specifically, the book addresses the following required accreditation competencies:

- Educational Policy 2.1.4—Engage diversity and difference in practice
- Educational Policy 2.1.5—Advance human rights and social and economic justice
- Educational Policy 2.1.8—Engage in policy practice (know the history and current structures of social policies and services; the role of policy in service delivery)
- Educational Policy 2.1.9—Respond to the contexts that shape practice

We are struck that many of the confounding issues that are discussed today are similar to those that plagued social services 100 and 200 years ago. We also see the influences of the ever-changing technological world. Today we speak of a global community, not an international world; global implies more evening between nation states in the north, south, east, and west; geographic borders are diminished as people are able to communicate directly with each other in real time. Clearly, technology continues to take on a more dominant role in social services. Although we are excited about what seems to be the daily new version of a laptop, iPad, iPhone, or software, we are equally perplexed with the unexpected ethical issues that result in a world of social media. How do we ensure that our privacy and rights are protected, in particular in this post-9/11 world?

Table 1   Examples of Positive and Negative Social Policies

Positive Social Policy		Negative Social Policy	
Medicare	One of the largest health insurance programs in the world that provides a modified form of universal health insurance to the elderly as well as many disabled people.	Arizona Immigration Law: Support Our Law Enforcement and Safe Neighborhoods Act	Includes provisions that add state penalties that are related to enforcing immigration law, such as harboring or transporting illegal immigrants, trespassing, employer sanctions, human smuggling, and alien registration documents.
Head Start Program	Provides significant educational, health, economic, and quality-of-life benefits to Head Start students, their families, and the communities in which they live.	Aid to Families with Dependent Children	Limited financial assistance to female-headed households, which unintentionally encouraged males to be absent.
Social Security	While poverty was once far more prevalent among the elderly than among other age-groups, the poverty rate among seniors is similar to that of working-age adults and much lower than that of children; Social Security is often mentioned as a likely contributor to the decline in elderly poverty.	Temporary Assistance to Needy Families	Limits lifetime assistance to poor families to five years.
Earned Income Tax Credit	Viewed as a powerful anti-poverty tool, with research showing that this program is the single most important factor in lifting people out of poverty.	Reduction of Funding to Supplemental Nutrition Program (SNAP)	U.S. House of Representatives Agriculture Committee voted (in April 2012) to reduce SNAP by $33 billion; in Texas alone, 300,000 families will receive reduced benefits

Each chapter begins with a reflective piece in which the editors share their thoughts and poses general, overarching questions. Of course, the reader is encouraged and expected to develop his or her own additional questions. Questioning opens the door for critical thinking and building different "what if?" scenarios. At the end of each chapter, there are suggested key terms, online resources, and discussion questions. Again, these are simply tools to encourage you to build on the author's particular thesis: Search through various websites, do your own data mining, open yourself to diverse opinions, form your own opinions, and propose policy solutions.

First and foremost, this work is not meant to be a politically correct text, nor is it written with the expectation that the reader will agree with each and every point or position taken. The editors and authors expect you to develop your own positions, although they should be built from a critical thinking frame of reference; commentary rooted in and constrained by political ideology leads nowhere and results in dysfunctional policy development.

Policy work requires the practitioner to be as fully versed as possible in the issue at hand. Understanding differing perspectives is essential if one hopes to find a solution or at least a workable compromise. As you read these chapters, try a simple exercise—visit divergent think tanks, such as the Cato Institute (www.cato.org) or the Hoover Institute (www.hoover.org), comparing their findings with those of the Brookings Institution (www.brookings.edu) or the Center on Budget Policy and Priorities (www.cbpp.org); understanding differences will help clarify and solidify your own perspective on an issue. Using think tanks in such a way creates your personal point-counterpoint debate.

We firmly believe in the power of ideas, perspectives, and philosophies. We recognize that there are many ways to climb a mountain, but the selection of the best path requires that we seek information and plan the best route. We recognize that in the current political, ideological hardened environment, finding common ground is difficult. As we have seen in the U.S. Congress since 2010, politically rooted intransigence yields minimal results; the idea of finding common ground through compromise is lost. We expect you and all of our social work colleagues to lead a new way in policy thinking and work, one that will result in positive change firmly rooted in the basic precepts of social justice.

Ira C. Colby
Catherine N. Dulmus
Karen M. Sowers

About the Editors

Ira C. Colby, DSW, is Dean of the Graduate College of Social Work at the University of Houston, in Houston, Texas. Dr. Colby has served on, chaired, or held elective positions in several national social work associations, including past president of the Council on Social Work Education, and he serves on several journal editorial boards. Dr. Colby has served as principal investigator on many research projects, accumulating approximately $8 million in external funding; he has authored more than 60 publications and presented more than 70 papers at national and international forums. He has been recognized with several awards, including an Honorary Doctorate of Humanics from Springfield College, his baccalaureate degree institution, induction as a Fellow into the National Academies of Practice, the Distinguished Alumni Award of the Virginia Commonwealth University, and an Honorary Professorship at the East China Technological University in Shanghai.

Catherine N. Dulmus, PhD, LCSW, is Professor, Associate Dean for Research, and Director of the Buffalo Center for Social Research at the University at Buffalo and Research Director at Hillside Family of Agencies in Rochester, New York. She received her baccalaureate degree in Social Work from Buffalo State College in 1989, a master's degree in Social Work from the University at Buffalo in 1991, and a doctoral degree in Social Welfare from the University at Buffalo in 1999. As a researcher with interests that include community-based research, child and adolescent mental health, evidence-based practice, and university-community partnerships, Dr. Dulmus' recent contributions have focused on fostering interdependent collaborations among practitioners, researchers, schools, and agencies critical in the advancement and dissemination of new and meaningful knowledge. She has authored or coauthored several journal articles and books and has presented her research nationally and internationally. Before obtaining the PhD, her social work practice background encompassed almost a decade of experience in the fields of mental health and school social work.

Karen M. Sowers, PhD, is Dean and Beaman Professor in the College of Social Work at University of Tennessee, Knoxville. She is the University of Tennessee Beaman Professor for Outstanding Research and Service. Dr. Sowers received her baccalaureate degree in Sociology from the University of Central Florida and her master's degree and doctoral degree in Social Work from Florida State University. Dr. Sowers serves on several local, national, and international boards. Dr. Sowers is nationally known for her research and scholarship in the areas of international practice, juvenile justice, child welfare, cultural diversity, and culturally effective intervention strategies for social work practice, evidence-based social work practice, and social work education.

Contributors

Ira C. Colby, DSW, ACSW, LCSW
Graduate College of Social Work
University of Houston
Houston, Texas

Bruce Jansson, PhD
School of Social Work
University of Southern California
Los Angeles, California

Joseph Kin Fun Kwok, RSW, PhD, BBS, JP
Hong Kong, China

Robin Sakina Mama, PhD
Department of Social Work
Monmouth University
West Long Branch, New Jersey

Paul R. Raffoul, PhD
Graduate College of Social Work
University of Houston
Houston, Texas

Michael Reisch, MSW, PhD
School of Social Work
University of Michigan
Ann Arbor, Michigan

Elizabeth A. Segal, PhD
School of Social Work
Arizona State University
Phoenix, Arizona

Stan Stojkovic, PhD
Helen Bader School of Social Welfare
University of Wisconsin—Milwaukee
Milwaukee, Wisconsin

Jody Williams
Nobel Peace Laureate
International Campaign to Ban Land Mines
Graduate College of Social Work
University of Houston
Houston, Texas

Chapter 1
Social Welfare Policy as a Form of Social Justice

Ira Colby

> How might you engage in activities that will influence values that result in policy choices and outcomes that reflect your values?

Introduction

Social justice is organized on a continuum of philosophies that range from conservative and individualistic in nature to the liberal, communal viewpoint. In other words, just as President Barack Obama subscribes to a particular model of social justice, so too did former President George W. Bush. We must recognize that we may disagree with one particular philosophy, but that does not negate the fact that every person has her or his particular perspective of social justice. A social policy is a direct, public expression of the dominant, accepted model of social justice. For example, the maximum SNAP (Supplemental Nutritional Assistance Program, aka "food stamps") payment was $526 for a three-person family between October 2011 and September 2012; this translates to approximately $17 per day. Do you feel this is a fair and just amount? Or, is this too much financial support that only encourages dependency? Or, is this amount too low given the costs to purchase a basic nutritionally sound diet? Can the United States afford to increase funding to SNAP? Some might say "no" because of the growing deficit and national debt. Yet others might say "yes" because we are choosing to fund SNAP at a lower level while funding other programs at higher levels. In other words, policy outcomes involve choices made through political decisions based on the dominant values.

The core mission of the social work profession is the promotion of social, economic, and political justice for all people. Communities built on the principles of justice provide its members with opportunities to fully participate and share benefits in a fair and equitable manner. Although this is a noble ideal, the reality is very different, as disparities continue to plague people and nations around the world.

In 1978, more than 130 nations met under the leadership of the World Health Organization (WHO) at the International Conference of Alma-Ata, and addressed one global social issue—health care. The group envisioned that by the year 2000 a global effort would result in health care for all people. The conference's report forthrightly stated, "Inequality in the health status of people, particularly between developed and developing countries, as well as within countries, is politically, socially, and economically unacceptable" (Declaration of Alma-Ata, 1978).

In 2000, the United Nations adopted the Millennium Declaration that resulted in eight development areas with the ultimate purpose to eliminate extreme poverty, hunger, illiteracy, and disease by 2015 (United Nations, 2000 and United Nations, 2011a).

Clearly, there have been—and continue to be—significant global efforts, with laudable goals, to close the gaps between the rich and poor. Even so, the gulf that separates the so-called haves and have-nots remains wide and deep, reported as follows:

- WHO points to progress that has been made in achieving the health-related Millennium Development Goals, yet in 2010, they found that 115 million children under 5 years of age worldwide are underweight (World Health Organization Statistics, 2011a, p. 12).

- UNAIDS writes that "The year 2011 marks 30 years of AIDS. In that time, AIDS has claimed more than 25 million lives and more than 60 million people have become infected with HIV. Still, each day, more than 7,000 people are newly infected with the virus, including 1,000 children" (United Nations, March 2011b, p. 1).

- In 2011, 43 percent of American households, approximately 127.5 million people, are considered to be "liquid-asset poor" (Eichler, 2012).

- The WHO reports that, in 2008, noncommunicable diseases continued to increase to 36 million persons, up from 35 million in 2004 (World Health Organization, p. 9).

- Measles, one of the leading causes of child death, dropped by 78 percent worldwide between 2000 and 2008; yet, in 2008, there were 164,000 measles deaths globally—nearly 450 deaths every day or 18 deaths every hour (World Health Organization, 2011b, p. 1).

- The World Bank reports that extreme poverty—living on $1.50 or lower per day—dropped worldwide to 22 percent of the developing world's population or 1.29 billion people, compared to 43 percent in 1990 and 52 percent in 1981 (World Bank, 2012, p. 1).

The human, economic, and societal costs of ill health and poverty are immense. Millions of people unnecessarily die prematurely from preventable and curable diseases, while poverty continues to anchor people in social ills that are unimaginable. With relatively little costs for simple interventions, people could live longer, more productive lives. But for millions of people worldwide, in the north and south, in the east and west, justice and fairness remain unattainable and are mere abstracts in their world. Data on many indicators, such as poverty, educational attainment, literacy, safe housing, clean water, life expectancy, and violence, lead to a common conclusion: True justice is far from being realized.

Social workers confront horrific problems on a daily basis that reflect the broad range of social issues that plague and threaten the lives of people and weaken our civil structures. Central to the social work profession's mission is its work with and on behalf of the most vulnerable, at-risk, and marginalized persons in our communities. Reamer (1993) writes that social workers confront the most compelling issues of our time by working with clients, and from these individual and collective experiences a unique perspective grows (p. 195). Social workers are able to translate this practice wisdom into a powerful tool to influence public policy. Simply stated, practice informs policy by shaping its form and structure. By including policy practice in one's work, according to Hagen (2000), social workers are able "to serve clients more effectively and to promote justice at all government levels" (p. 555).

Policy creates a community's context of justice in how it approaches the provision of social services. Public and private organizations, nonprofit and voluntary associations implement policies, which in turn are "experienced by individuals and families" (Jansson, 1999, p. 1). Similarly, policy is vital to the social worker by specifying the type and level of service the practitioner is able to provide. Policy is a formal statement articulating rules and regulations that reflect values, beliefs, data, traditions, discussions, debates, and compromises of the body politic. Policy carries out multiple functions, ranging from crafting the broad framework in which a program or service evolves to detailing the available services.

Social welfare policies, which are a subset of the broader social policy arena, focus on issues that are controversial and the epicenter for many debates. Discussions on radio call-in shows and television panel shows are replete with welfare matters, ranging from immigration and border issues to women's health care and reproductive rights. The 2012 presidential primary race was filled with attacks on social issues and policies directed to amend the growing inequalities faced by the young and old and, in particular, women. Sadly, the tenor of the arguments and controversies themselves are not new. Throughout American history, political leaders have staked out their positions relating to welfare, such as the following:

- Benjamin Franklin: "I am for doing good for the poor, but I differ in opinion about the means.... The more public provisions were made for the poor, the less they provided for themselves and the poorer they became.... On the contrary, the less that was done for them, the more they did for themselves." (*The Writings of Benjamin Franklin*)

- President Franklin Roosevelt: "The Federal Government must and shall quit this business of relief. I am not willing that the vitality of our people be further sapped.... We must preserve not only the bodies of the unemployed from destitution but also their self-respect, their self-reliance and courage and determination." (State of the Union address)

- President John F. Kennedy: "Welfare...must be more than a salvage operation, picking up the debris from the wreckage of human lives. Its emphasis must be directed increasingly toward prevention and rehabilitation.... Poverty weakens individuals and nations." (Woolley and Peters)

- President Lyndon B. Johnson: "Unfortunately, many Americans live on the outskirts of hope—some because of their poverty, and some because of their color, and all too many because of both. Our task is to help replace their despair with opportunity. This administration today, here and now, declares unconditional war on poverty in America. I urge this Congress and all Americans to join with me in that effort." (public papers)

- President Ronald Reagan: "I have never questioned the need to take care of people who, through no fault of their own, can't provide for themselves. The rest of us have to do that. But I am against open-ended welfare programs that invite generation after generation of potentially productive people to remain on the dole; they deprive the able-bodied of the incentive to work and require productive people to support others who are physically and mentally able to work while prolonging an endless cycle of dependency that robs men and women of their dignity." (RonaldReagan.com)

The social work profession, through its professional membership associations, has a long history of engaging in policy development to provide justice-based social welfare policies. As Haynes and Mickelson (2000) write, "although social workers have been influential in the political arena, politics has not consistently been a central arena for social work practice. Consequently, a historic and ongoing dynamic tension exists" (p. 2). A common refrain among social workers is that "I just don't have the time for policy work." This is certainly understandable for the individual who is assigned a caseload of 30 clients in a public agency or in a setting that is underfinanced and underresourced.

For some, the primacy of their work is the client's immediate situation, and time is not available to inform and advocate for justice-based social policies. There are others who feel that policy practice has little to do with their daily work. Policy is viewed as irrelevant and with little connection to the client's life situation. This unfortunate perspective hinders the social work profession's efforts to create positive social change, leading to a just society for all people. The growing practice wisdom and accumulating evidence goes untapped and, as a result, creates an unnecessary barrier for policy practice. For whatever reason, many trees seem to get in the way, but the commonly held belief among social workers that policy work belongs elsewhere is a self-planted tree that must be cut down.

Social Welfare Policy Defined

There is no one overriding definition of social welfare policy that scholars, policy makers, or practitioners refer to on a consistent basis. The lack of one agreed-upon definition results in frustration and a pessimistic perspective, such as Popple and Leighninger (1990), who believe that welfare is a very difficult concept to clearly define as "it is difficult, confusing, and debated" (p. 26). There are numerous sources for definitions, however, the most common reference materials including the *Social Work Dictionary* (Barker, 2003) and various editions of the *Encyclopedia of Social Work* (see, for example, Dear, 1995 and Morris, 1986). Textbooks and journal articles also offer a variety of definitions. A sample of the various definitions illustrates the diversity in the definitions, ranging from all-encompassing to narrowly focused descriptors.

- Social welfare policy is anything the government chooses to do, or not to do, that affects the quality of life of its people. (DiNitto & Dye, 1983, p. 2)
- The explicit or implicit standing plan that an organization or government uses as a guide for action (Barker, 2003, p. 330)
- Establishes a specific set of program procedures (Baumheier and Schorr, 1977, p. 1453)
- Includes all public activities (Zimmerman, 1979, p. 487)
- Considers resource distribution and its effect on "peoples' social well-being" (Dear, 1995, p. 2227)
- Primarily understood as cash and in-kind payments to persons who need support because of physical or mental illness, poverty, age, disability, or other defined circumstances (Chatterjee, 1966, p. 3)
- Pattern of relationships that develop in society to carry out mutual support function (Gilbert & Specht, 1974, p. 5)
- Human concern for the well-being of individuals, families, groups, organizations, and communities (Morales & Sheafor, 1989, p. 100)
- Collective interventions to meet certain needs of the individual and/or to serve the wider interests of society (Titmuss, 1959, p. 42)
- A system of social services and institutions, designed to aid individuals and groups to attain satisfying standards of life and health, and personal social relationships that permit them to develop their full capacities and promote their well-being in harmony with the needs of their families and community (Friedlander, 1955, p. 140)

- A nation's system of programs, benefits, and services that help people meet those social, economic, educational, and health needs that are fundamental to the maintenance of society (Barker, 1995, p. 221)

These definitions reflect a specific philosophy or view of welfare. Close examination reveals three common themes:

1. Social welfare includes a variety of programs and services that result in specific, targeted client benefit.
2. Social welfare, as a system of programs and services, is designed to address the needs of people. The needs are wide-ranging; on the one hand, they may be all-encompassing, including economic and social well-being, health, education, and overall quality of life; conversely, needs may be narrowly targeted, focused on one issue.
3. The primary outcome of social welfare policy is to improve the well-being of individuals, groups, and communities. Helping those people address their specific needs benefits society at large.

The Relationship Between Justice Theory and Social Welfare Policy

All welfare policies are extensions of justice theories and reflect particular principles on the human condition. David Miller (p. 1, 2005) poses the central question related to justice and welfare:

> What constitutes a fair distribution of rights, resources and opportunities? Is it an equal distribution, in which case an equal distribution of what? ... Or is it a distribution that gives each person what they deserve, or what they need? Or a distribution that gives everyone an adequate minimum of whatever it is that matters?

Miller's questions focus on *distributive justice* — that is, how will benefits be allocated to a community? Will they be equal, disproportional, or possibly need-based? The key issues in distributive justice are often framed by moral and legal positions, which can polarize groups to support or oppose a particular policy. The potential answers to Miller's queries rest within specific justice theories.

Reflecting an individual's, group's, or organization's values and beliefs, justice theories create a rationale to support particular policy initiatives. Recognizing and understanding the various, often competing justice theories is central in creating a successful policy change strategy; such understanding requires the social work profession, as Morris writes (1986), "to take into account not only its own beliefs and values, but those held by a large number of other non advocate citizens" (p. 678).

John Rawls' (1971) theory of justice most closely reflects the principles and beliefs of the social work profession, but the core premise regarding resource distribution and property ownership expressed by Robert Nozick (1974) is counter to the profession's values.

Rawls (1971) believes that birth, status, and family are matters of chance, which should not influence or bias the benefits one accrues; true justice allows a society to rectify its inequities, with the end result yielding fairness to all its members. All social goods—liberty, power, opportunities, income, and wealth—are to be equally distributed only if the unequal distribution of these goods favors the least-advantaged members of a community. Rawls contends that the inequality of opportunity is permissible if it advantages those who have been set aside. For example, a university's admission criteria that benefits one racial or gender group over another is acceptable if that group has been or remains disadvantaged. Rawls' theory proposes a *minmax* approach that essentially maximizes the place of the least advantaged. Using the concept of the "veil of ignorance," Rawls reasons that if a person would not know the impact of a policy on him or herself, then one will not advantage one group over another. For example, two people really like the same piece of cake, and one is asked to cut it so each person may have a slice. Not knowing which slice one may receive, he or she will probably make the slices as even as possible. To do otherwise, the person may end up with the smaller slice. The dual beliefs that a transaction's result is for the greater good while advantages and set-asides for those who have been marginalized are appropriate reflect core social work values.

Nozick (1974) argues a free-market libertarian model that advocates for individuals to be able to keep what they earn. Redistribution of social goods is not acceptable and violates a key premise that a person should be able to retain the "fruits of their labor." Taxation is not tolerable and forces workers to become slaves of the state, with a certain amount of their work-related benefits going to the state for its use. For Nozick (1974), "the less government approach" is the best model and asks, "if the state did not exist would it be necessary to invent it? Would one be needed, and would it have to be invented" (p. 3)? Libertarianism asserts that the state's role should be confined essentially to security and safety issues—police/fire protection, national defense, and the judicial system. Matters related to public education and social welfare, among others, are the responsibility of the private sector. Faith-based organizations, nonprofit social services, nongovernmental organizations, and private for-profit groups should provide welfare services. Services would be structured within a free-market model to encourage efficiency and effectiveness and eliminate redundancy and fiscal waste. The government's role is minimal at best, with individuals left free to do as they wish with their own lives and property. No formal institution can or should interfere with an individual's control of his or her life; the role of the state is to protect from and retaliate against those who use force against an individual (Roth, 1997, pp. 958–959).

Rawls' theory supports the development of a progressive and active welfare state. Policies create a system of redistribution of resources and advantages for those who have been historically and currently set aside.

Nozick's minimalist approach provides only for welfare in the mindset of safety and security for the individual. The government should not be involved in meeting basic human needs or providing any system of support and care; these activities are left to the private, voluntary sectors.

Social Work Values and Policy

The importance of policy is viewed in the profession's organizing documents. From ethical codes for practice to accreditation standards, various national and international bodies clearly spell out the domain of social policy being central in the curricula. For example, the American-based Council on Social Work Education (CSWE) and the National Association of Social Workers and the major international associations—International Association of Schools of Social Work (IA), International Federation of Social Workers (IF), and International Council on Social Welfare (IC)—each through their respective accreditation and/or practice protocols, direct attention to steadfastly embrace content around policy's central role in the profession's life (Council on Social Work Education, 2008; International Association, 2012; International Council, 2012; International Federation, 2012).

The 2008 Council on Social Work Educational Policy and Accreditation Standards (EPAS), the organizing document for baccalaureate and master's-level social work education, identifies 10 core competencies for social work practice. Although some of the competencies support policy practice through research and critical thinking, Educational Policy 2.1.1 specifically states that social workers "Engage in policy practice to advance social and economic well-being and to deliver effective social work services" (Council on Social Work Education, 2008, p. 6).

The National Association of Social Workers' Code of Ethics (1999) notes in its preamble, "Fundamental to social work is attention to the environmental forces that create, contribute to, and address problems in living" and specifically directs its members in Standard 6.02 to "facilitate informed participation by the public in shaping social policies and institutions" (NASW).

The joint Code of Ethics for IA and IF states that social workers have a duty to bring to the attention of their employers, policy makers, politicians, and the general public situations where resources are inadequate or where distribution of resources, policies, and practices are oppressive, unfair, or harmful (International Federation).

Inclusion of social welfare policy in education and practice extends to social workers and programs around the world. The International Council on Social Welfare, for example, specifically promotes worldwide activities on policy advocacy and research (International Council). In nation-states worldwide, there are numerous examples of policy work advocated by the International Council. Canadian social work education, for example, requires the study of Canadian welfare policy in accredited social work programs (Canadian Association of Schools of Social Work, 2004, p. 9); an "accredited social worker" in Australia must have knowledge and the ability for analysis of and impact with policy development (Australian Association of Social Workers, 2004, p. 3); in 2004, the International Association of Schools of Social Work and the International Federation of Social Workers adopted the "Global Standards for the Education and Training of the Social Work Profession," which includes social policy as a core area of study (IASSW, 2012, p. 7).

Worldwide, the promotion, development, and cultivation of effective policy in micro and macro arenas cross geographic borders and cultural divides. Social welfare policy is envisioned to be a powerful tool that can realize the aspirations of an entire society as well as the dreams and ideals embraced by a local community group, family, or individual.

Macro social welfare policy provides a framework and means to strengthen larger communities. As an instrument of change, social welfare policy can reduce or eliminate a particular issue that impacts at-risk and marginalized population groups, such as children, families, seniors, and people of color. Conversely, social policy may exacerbate or penalize a particular population group.

Micro social welfare policy directly influences the scope of work provided by the practitioner. Program eligibility, the form of services provided, a program's delivery structure, and funding mechanisms are outcomes of micro social welfare policy. Ineffective social policy creates frustrating practice obstacles. Typical of the barriers created by policy are eligibility criteria that limit client access to services, regulations that do not allow for case advocacy, and increased caseloads supported with minimal resources and capped time limits.

The Traditional Conceptual Framework of Social Welfare

Social welfare policies are outgrowths of values, beliefs, and principles, and they vary in their commitments and range of services. For example, the primary public assistance program targeting poor families, Temporary Assistance to Needy Families (TANF), is time-limited and does not include full, comprehensive services. Social Security retirement, however, provides monthly retirement income that is based on the worker's lifelong financial contributions through payroll deductions. Essentially, TANF reflects the centuries-old belief that the poor are the cause of their life situation, and public assistance only reinforces their dependence on others. Retirees, who worked and contributed to the greater good through their payroll taxes, are able to make a just claim for retirement benefits.

The range of social welfare policies is best conceptualized through the classic work of Wilensky and Lebeaux (1965), *Industrial Society and Social Welfare*, in which they attempt to answer a basic question: Is social welfare a matter of giving assistance only in emergencies, or is it a front-line activity that society must provide? Their analysis included two important concepts that continue to frame and influence social welfare discussions: residual social welfare and institutional welfare.

A cautionary note is in order: Not all programs and services are easily classified as one or the other; some programs have both institutional and residual attributes. The Head Start program, for example, is institutional in nature but is means tested and restricted to a particular segment of the population. One solution is to expand the classic residual–institutional dichotomy to a residual–institutional continuum. A program's position on the continuum is determined by its eligibility criteria and the breadth and depth of its services.

The dichotomy between residual and institutional welfare imitates the inherent differences found in justice theories expressed by Rawls and Nozick. Effective policy practice requires understanding and assessing the various justice theories that interact with and influence the development of a policy position.

Residual Welfare

Residual welfare views social welfare in narrow terms and typically only includes public assistance or policies related to the poor. Residual services carry a stigma; are time-limited, means-tested, and emergency-based; and are generally provided when all other forms of assistance are unavailable. Welfare services come into play only when all other systems have broken down or proven to be inadequate. Public assistance programs reflect the residual descriptions and include, among others, TANF, Food Stamps, Supplemental Security Income, General Assistance, and Medicaid.

The residual conception of social welfare rests on the individualistic notion that people are responsible for themselves and government intervenes only in times of crisis or emergency. Eligibility requires that people exhaust their own private resources, which may include assistance from the church, family members, friends, and employers, and requires people to prove their inability to provide for themselves and their families.

Social services are delivered only to people who meet certain defined criteria. The assessment procedure, commonly referred to as *means testing*, requires people to demonstrate that they do not have the financial ability to meet their specific needs. A residual program also mandates recertification for program participation every few months, typically three or six months. The recertification process is designed primarily to ensure that clients are still unable to meet their needs through private or personal sources.

People who receive residual services are generally viewed as being different from those who do need public services and are part of the majority group. These recipients are viewed as failures because they do not emulate the ideals of rugged individualism, a cornerstone ideal of American society, which asserts that people take care of their own needs, they are self-reliant, and they work to provide for themselves and their families. Clients in residual programs are often stereotyped by the larger society. They are often accused of making bad decisions, requiring constant monitoring because of their inherent dishonesty, and being lazy. In short, people in residual programs carry a stigma best described as "blaming the victim," which Ryan

(1976) writes is applied to most social problems and people who are "inferior, genetically defective, or morally unfit; the emphasis is on the intrinsic, even hereditary, defect" (p. 7).

Institutional Welfare

The second conception of social welfare described by Wilensky and Lebeaux (1965) is *institutional* social welfare. This definition of social welfare is much more encompassing than the residual definition and extends to services that support all people. This framework recognizes the community's obligation to assist individual members because the problems are viewed not as failures, but as part of life in modern society. Services go beyond immediate and basic need responses to emergencies. Assistance is provided well before people exhaust their own resources, and preventive and rehabilitative services are stressed.

Therefore, an institutional program, as opposed to a residual program, is designed to meet the needs of all people. Eligibility is universal, no stigma is attached, and services are regular front-line programs in society. Institutional programs are so widely accepted in society that most are not viewed as social welfare programs at all. Social insurance programs, veterans programs, public education, food and drug regulations, and Medicare are institutional by nature.

Broadening the View of Social Welfare Policy

Richard Titmuss (1965) argued that social welfare was much more than aid to the poor and in fact represented a broad system of support to the middle and upper classes. In his model, social welfare includes three separate but very distinct pieces: *fiscal welfare* — tax benefits and supports for the middle and upper classes; *corporate welfare* — tax benefits and supports for businesses; and *public welfare* — assistance to the poor. Titmuss ostensibly was arguing that social welfare reflects an institutional perspective.

Abramovitz (1983) applied the Titmuss model to American social welfare and identified a "shadow welfare state" for the wealthy that parallels the social service system that is available to the poor. She concluded that the poor and wealthy alike benefit from government programs and tax laws that raise their disposable income. In other words, were it not for direct government support — whether through food stamps or through a childcare tax exemption — people would have fewer dollars to spend and to support themselves and their families. As with Titmuss, Abramovitz extended social welfare well beyond services to the poor to encompass a wide range of programs and services that support the middle and upper classes.

The Titmuss and Abramovitz position requires accepting the premise that corporate and fiscal welfare are the same as public welfare. If this position is accepted, then all activities are considered institutional. The belief is that welfare, no matter its form, provides a direct subsidy that benefits the individual with secondary positive benefits extending to the greater community. For example, homeowners are able to claim a tax deduction for interest paid on home loans. The deduction encourages home ownership (e.g., by lowering an individual's net taxable income) and supports the home-building industry by encouraging the construction of new housing stock, which in turn requires suppliers to provide goods for the new construction. As more homes are built, more people are hired to build the homes, more supplies are needed, and the cycle continues. Rather than providing a tax deduction, the government could just as easily write a monthly or annual check to the homeowner to subsidize their housing. Titmuss and Abramovitz would argue that the tax deduction is every bit a welfare expenditure, just as a Section 8 housing voucher is for the poor.

One could also argue that corporate and fiscal welfare requires a direct financial and work input from the recipient; that is, the benefit is determined on the amount and degree of effort invested by the individual. The argument continues that public welfare recipients are not required to make a similar contribution. This position reflects an "equity and privilege" model—what one receives is directly related to and proportional to what one contributes or invests. The resulting subsidy is a privilege extended only to those who participate in the program and supports the greater good. This position would argue that a homeowner should receive a tax benefit because purchasing a home supports the greater good; conversely, Section 8 housing does not contribute to the greater good and a community's economic base.

The bottom line with corporate support or welfare, whichever way one frames the subsidy, is that it costs the U.S. government significant revenue. Data suggests that the use of tax deductions and corporate tax breaks costs the United States significant dollars. Dzieza (2012), for example, specifically identifies the General Electric Corporation and Wells Fargo as not paying any federal taxes, while 83 percent of the top 100 publicly traded companies had tax shelters in 2009. All told, the various tax subsidies resulted in an estimated $100 billion loss in tax revenues.

Crafting Justice-Based Policy

Policy practice, notes Jansson (1999), allows the profession to promote its values and the well-being of clients while countering opposition to proactive social welfare (p. 10). The objective of policy practice is simple and straightforward: to change policy.

Haynes and Mickelson (2000) write that "all social work is political" (p. 23). Although some may disagree with this assertion, policy practice clearly takes place within a political environment. Policies are made at the various levels of government (i.e., local, state, and national), by boards of directors of nonprofit agencies and voluntary associations, and by CEOs of for-profit agencies. No matter the setting in which a policy emerges, it is the end result of a series of political decisions—who is included in and excluded from services, what services are provided, how the services are provided, and who provides the services reflect some of the political decisions that are addressed by policy. Given that policy is developed within a political environment, no one should be surprised that a policy is more often than not based on a political philosophy or ideology, while disregarding objective information and evidence. It is common for a policy to be organized around ambiguous evidence, even though there has been a systematic review (Boaz and Pawson, 2005, p. 175). Such is the nature of the political process. The nagging question is how can effective policy emerge if the political environment disregards objective evidence?

Critical Thinking

Critical thinking is the overarching skill set necessary for successful policy work, and as Bok (2006) notes, its development and refinement is one of the central purposes of higher education (p. 67). Critical thinking is a systematic process that allows information to be considered and options to emerge in such a way that result in clear policy. Defined as "reasonable and reflective thinking focused on deciding what to believe or do" (Fisher, 2001, p. 7), *critical thinking* creates and improves a current condition or situation. The use of logic and reasoning are cornerstones in the critical thinking process.

A policy position is the direct application of critical thinking. It requires analyzing and organizing facts, developing opinions based on the facts, arguing the position and considering alternatives, all leading to solving specific problems. Paul and Elder (2007) write that critical thinking is "self-directed, self-disciplined, self-monitored, and self-corrective" (p. 4). A rational and structured thinking process is important in organizing and distilling facts from myth and allows for clear, objective solutions to emerge.

Critical thinking allows and encourages essential questioning while systematically challenging one's own biases and beliefs. Philosophical and ideological positions are tested with the objective to discover new truths rather than to reinforce existing egocentric thinking. Paul and Elder (2007) illustrate egocentric thinking with the following statements (p. 9):

- *It is true because I believe it.*
- *It is true because we believe it.*
- *It is true because I want to believe it.*
- *It is true because I have always believed it.*
- *It is true because it is in my self-interest to believe it.*

These egocentric statements rely on personal bias and prejudice. Policy that reflects this narrow laissez-faire thinking process only reinforces preconceived notions and hinders proactive change that is able to strengthen a community.

Critical thinking grows from evidence-based practice. The skilled practitioner recognizes that egocentric thinking is a common refrain, but by using practice evidence challenges the predisposed position. Evidence and reasoning provide pathways to solutions. Injecting political considerations is necessary in the analysis, but it, rather than the collected evidence, can not become the primary reference point and driver in the process. A successful critical thinking process will yield several alternatives, some of which are better, stronger, and certainly more justice oriented than others.

Traditional critical thinking methods are controlled processes that allow little room to react impulsively. Successful critical thinking must be flexible and allow for creative thinking, whose process is dynamic, vibrant, and intuitive. Flexibility, brainstorming, visioning, and metaphorical relationships are central in stimulating curiosity and furthering consideration of differing perspectives. Creative thinking balances the somewhat rigid critical thinking process by enabling a free flow of ideas and recognizing that some biases are impossible to disregard or subordinate.

Critical thinking is fraught with challenges. First and foremost is to recognize when one's personal views influence and color the collection and interpretation of evidence and lead to a series of foregone conclusions. Rawls (1971) proposed a "veil of ignorance," which would shroud the person from all external variables and allow for an objective and fair result. Unfortunately, the human condition does not allow one to completely abdicate one's values and beliefs. Decisions, no matter how systematic, are not made in a valueless vacuum. Recognizing when one is disregarding evidence is paramount in critical thinking. The ability to minimize or set aside one's beliefs is most difficult but required.

A second challenge to critical thinking revolves around the collection of evidence. The advent and accessibility of the World Wide Web has opened the doors to a variety of data, information, and analyses of issues. The advantages, while many, can be overshadowed by the enticement of readily available information, which, if left unattended, will result in faulty policy work. First and foremost, the reliability and validity of Web sources must always be questioned: Just because information is posted on a Web page does not mean it is legitimate. A second issue deals with information overload. The ease of information accessibility can be overwhelming. For example, Googling "social welfare policies in Texas" in March 2012 resulted in 17.5 million sites collected in .21 seconds (Social Welfare in Texas, 2012). Critical thinking requires disciplined analysis of the Web, the ability to discern good information from bad, and ensuring that creativity is applied while seeking accurate useful information.

A third challenge to critical thinking deals with process. Information must be assessed and distilled in a thoughtful and reflective manner in order for alternatives to emerge. First and foremost, the proposed policy must be justice based and provide the maximum benefit for the community while advantaging those who are marginalized and set aside in a community. Achieving this objective requires time and simply cannot be rushed. Unfortunately, in today's world, time is considered a luxury and not valued as a requisite for work. Individuals are connected to their workplace 24/7; the written memo is virtually nonexistent, having been replaced by e-mails that can be sent from anyplace, any time of day or night; turnaround time for reports has been shortened because of the need for quick information. Successful critical thinking is threatened by absence of process and the need for fast, rapid, and swift decisions.

Conclusion

Today's social problems are complex matters that impact all people, no matter their age, race, gender, ethnicity, or social status. These issues create significant barriers to creating just communities. Although the issues seem overwhelming, social concerns in one form or another will always be part of our landscape. This is not meant to be a pessimistic observation but reflects the unique aspects of the human condition. Roth (1997) writes that

> Social issues . . . would not exist if human beings knew everything, understood all the consequences of their actions, never made mistakes, always agreed with one another about what to do, and put exactly the right policies into practice. (vol. 1, p. xii)

Thomas Friedman, in his work *The World Is Flat: A Brief History of the Twenty-first Century* (2005), argues that the world is now more interconnected than at any time in its history. Lowering of trade and political barriers, coupled with the technical advances of the digital revolution, made it possible to do business instantaneously with people anywhere in the world at any time.

The U.S. Census Bureau estimated that in Spring 2012, the world's population is projected to be slightly more than 7 billion (U.S. Census Bureau, 2012); according to the *Encyclopedia of Language and Linguistics* (Brown, 2006), more than 33,000 languages are spoken around the world. All nations, totaling 242 in 2012, embrace their own defining characteristics, beliefs, and traditions; the number of countries will continue to change and grow in the future. Between 1900 and 1950, approximately 1.2 countries were created each year; from 1950 to 1990, 2.2 nations were organized each year; and in the 1990s, the number of new nations organized jumped to 3.1 countries annually (Enriquez, 2005).

No one can expect to gain even a rudimentary knowledge of the many nations of the world, each with its own language and culture. Nor can we foresee which cultures and languages will be important or exist in the middle of the 21st century. Similarly, no one can predict with steadfast assurance and accuracy future events in local, national, or international arenas.

Today we live in a different, more open world with fewer geographic or social borders to control human interactions. No matter who we are or where we live, all people are touched by distant wars, terrorist threats, hurricanes, typhoons, tsunamis, Middle East oil shortages, bank failures, housing foreclosures, human trafficking, irreversible destruction of our environment coupled with the threats caused by global warming, widespread and pervasive poverty, new and deadly diseases, trade wars, and the daily threat posed by the world arsenal of nuclear weapons. All of these events draw governments into new collaborative intergovernmental relationships, and all of these new patterns of behavior influence the development of social policy.

We also cannot ignore the power and impact of *social media*, which seemed to catapult itself with full force on the world in 2011. Its use and influence in shaping the 2011 so-called Arab Spring and the way it became a key communication vehicle for the U.S.-based Occupy Wall Street movement clearly showed that people can make significant change in policy and governmental actions. Social media's power contributed to corporations changing their policies, as evidenced when Bank of America cancelled its plans to charge customers an additional fee for debit card purchases (Bernard, 2011).

Stoesz (2000) critically charged that the future is "bleak" for liberals unless they become "more versatile in (their) policy repertoire" (p. 622). The same could be said for conservatives and moderates. Stoesz is correct that the social work profession must incorporate a critical thinking, multidimensional approach that is firmly rooted in justice theory if it is to be a central player in the policy-making process. Social workers, including educators, must tap into the power of social media while becoming well-versed in the data compiled by national and international organizations. If the social work profession continues to rely on political, philosophical, or ideological dogma, then the broad and significant social and economic discrepancies that currently exist will only become further entrenched.

Fair policy is achievable by the melding of practice wisdom with objective, critical thinking guided by justice theory that mandates we promote the interests of the least advantaged.

Key Terms

institutional	*social justice*	*social media*
residual	*critical thinking*	

Review Questions for Critical Thinking

1. Are the United Nations Millennium Goals realistic? Identify three barriers for the full and complete implementation of the UN resolution.
2. How is "corporate welfare" the same as and different from "public welfare"?
3. How can *social media* influence a current U.S. social welfare issue?
4. To what extent does the U.S. system of social welfare programs and services reflect John Rawls' position on justice?
5. To what extent should individual social workers be concerned and/or involved with the public policy-making process?

Online Resources

Online Social Justice: www.onlinesocialjustice.com/sites-on-the-web/

International Association of Schools of Social Work: www.iassw-aiets.org

International Council on Social Welfare: www.icsw.org

International Federation of Social Workers: http://ifsw.org/

World Health Organization: www.who.int/en/

References

Abramovitz, M. (1983). Everyone is on welfare: "The role of redistribution in social policy" revisited. *Social Work, 28* (6), 440–445.

Australian Association of Social Workers. (2004). *Continuing professional educational policy*. Retrieved on December 2, 2006 from www.aasw.asn.au/adobe/profdev/CPE_policy_2006.pdf

Barker, R. (1995). *The social work dictionary* (3rd ed.). Washington, DC: NASW Press.

Barker, R. (2003). *The social work dictionary* (5th ed.). Washington, DC: NASW Press.

Baumheier, E. C., & Schorr, A. L. (1977). Social policy. In J. Turner (Ed.), *Encyclopedia of social work* (17th ed., pp. 1453–1463). Washington, DC: NASW Press.

Bernard, T. S. (November 1, 2011). In retreat, Bank of America cancels debit card fee. *New York Times*.

Boaz, A., & Pawson, R. (2005). The perilous road from evidence to policy: Five journeys compared. *Journal of Social Policy*, *34*, 175–194.

Bok, D. (2006). *Our underachieving colleges: A candid look at how much students learn and why they should be learning more*. Princeton, NJ: Princeton University Press.

Brown, K. (2006). *Encyclopedia of Language and Linguistics* (2nd ed.). Amsterdam: Elsevier.

Canadian Association of Schools of Social Work. (2004). *CASSW standards for accreditation*. Ottawa, Ontario: Author.

Chatterjee, P. (1966). *Approaches to the welfare state*. Washington, DC: NASW Press.

Council on Social Work Education. (2008). *Educational policy and accreditation standards*. Alexandria, VA: Author.

Dear, R. B. (1995). Social welfare policy. In R. L. Edwards & J. G. Hobbs, *Encyclopedia of social work* (19th ed., Vol. 3, pp. 2226–2237). Washington, DC: NASW Press.

Declaration of Alma-Ata, International Conference on Primary Health Care, Alma-Ata, USSR, September 6–12, 1978. Retrieved on December 4, 2006 from www.who.int/hpr/NPH/docs/declaration_almaata.pdf

DiNitto, D., & Dye, T. (1983). *Social welfare politics and public policy* (2nd ed.). Englewood Cliffs, NJ: Prentice-Hall.

Dzieza, J. (February 25, 2012). 8 Ridiculous Tax Loopholes: How Companies Are Avoiding the Tax Man. *The Daily Beast*. Retrieved on February 27, 2012, from www.thedailybeast.com/articles/2012/02/25/8-ridiculous-tax-loopholes-how-companies-are-avoiding-the-tax-man.html

Eichler, A. (January 31, 2012). Working poor: Almost half of U.S. households live one crisis from the bread line. *The Huffington Post*. Retrieved on February 5, 2012 from www.huffingtonpost.com/2012/01/31/working-poor-liquid-asset-poverty_n_1243152.html

Enriquez, J. (2005). *The untied states of america: Polarization, fracturing, and our future*. New York, NY: Crown.

Fisher, A. (2001). *Critical thinking: An introduction*. New York, NY: Cambridge University Press.

Friedlander, W. (1955). *Introduction to social welfare*. New York, NY: Prentice Hall.

Friedman, T. (2005). *The world is flat: A brief history of the twenty-first century*. New York, NY: Farrar, Straus, & Giroux.

Gilbert, N., & Specht, H. (1974). *Dimensions of social welfare policy*. Englewood Cliffs, NJ: Prentice Hall.

Hagen, J. (2000). Critical perspectives on social welfare: Challenges and controversies. *Families in Society, 81*, 555–556.

Haynes, K., & Mickelson, J. (2000). *Affecting change: Social workers in the political arena* (4th ed.). Boston, MA: Allyn and Bacon.

International Association of Schools of Social Work. (2012). Global standards for the education and training of the social work profession. Retrieved on February 2, 2012, from www.iassw-aiets.org

International Council on Social Welfare. (2012). What we do. Retrieved on February 2, 2012, from www.icsw.org/intro/whatdowedoe.htm#policy

International Federation of Social Workers. (2012). Code of Ethics. Retrieved on March 5, 2012, from http://ifsw.org/policies/code-of-ethics/

Jansson, B. (1999). *Becoming an effective policy advocate: From policy practice to social justice*. Pacific Grove, CA: Brooks Cole.

Miller, D. (2005). Justice and boundaries. Speech presented at the Centre for the Study of Social Justice Conference, November 26, 2005, Nuffield College, Oxford. Retrieved on December 1, 2006, from http://social-justice.politics.ox.ac.uk/materials/launch/dmiller_session1.pdf

Morales, A., & Sheafor, B. (1989). *Social work: A profession of many faces* (5th ed.). Boston, MA: Allyn and Bacon.

Morris, R. (1986). Social welfare policy: Trends and issues. In A. Minahan (Ed.), *Encyclopedia of social work* (18th ed., Vol. *2*, pp. 664–681). Silver Spring, MD: National Association of Social Workers.

National Association of Social Workers. (1999). *Code of ethics of the National Association of Social Workers*. Washington, DC: Author.

Nozick, R. (1974). *Anarchy, state, and utopia*. New York, NY: Basic Books.

Paul, R., & Elder, L. (2007). *The miniature guide to critical thinking: Concepts and tools* (4th ed.). Dillon Beach, CA: Foundation for Critical Thinking.

Popple, P., & Leighninger, L. (1990). *Social work, social welfare, and American society*. Boston, MA: Allyn and Bacon.

Public Papers of the Presidents of the United States: Lyndon B. Johnson, 1963-64 (Volume I, entry 91, pp. 112–118). (1965). *Washington*, DC: Government Printing Office.

Rawls, J. (1971). *Theory of justice*. Cambridge, MA: Harvard University Press.

Reamer, F. (1993). *The philosophical foundations of social work*. New York, NY: Columbia University Press.

RonaldReagan.com, the official site. Retrieved on December 10, 2006, from www
.ronaldreagan.com/secondterm.html.

Roth, J. K. (1997). *Encyclopedia of social issues* (Vol. 4). New York, NY: Marshall
Cavendish.

Ryan, W. (1976). *Blaming the victim* (rev. ed.). New York, NY: Vintage Books.

Social welfare in Texas. (2012). Retrieved on March 2, 2012, from www.google.com.

State of the Union address, Franklin Delano Roosevelt. This Nation.com. Retrieved
on November 5, 2006, from www.thisnation.com/library/sotu/1935fdr.html

Stoesz, D. (2000). Renaissance. *Families in Society: The Journal of Contemporary
Human Services*, *81* (6), 621 – 628.

The writings of Benjamin Franklin, London: 1757 – 1775, *Volumes 1 – 5*. Retrieved
on November 5, 2006, from www.historycarper.com/resources/twobf3/price
.htm

Titmuss, R. (1959). *Essays on the welfare state*. New Haven, CT: Yale University
Press.

Titmuss, R. (1965). The role of redistribution in social policy. *Social Security Bul-
letin*, *28* (6), 34 – 55.

United Nations. (2000). Resolution adopted by the General Assembly [without
reference to a Main Committee (A/55/L.2)], 55/2, United Nations Millennium
Declaration. Retrieved on January 5, 2012, from www.un.org/millennium/
declaration/ares552e.pdf

United Nations. (2011a). *Millennium Development Goals Report 2011*. New York,
NY: United Nations.

United Nations. (March 2011b). Uniting for universal access: Towards zero new
HIV infections, zero discrimination and zero AIDS-related deaths. *Report of
the Secretary-General*. Retrieved on November 5, 2011, from www.unaids.org/
en/media/unaids/contentassets/documents/document/2011/A-65-797_English
.pdf

U.S. Census Bureau. (2012). World POPClock projection. Retrieved on March 3,
2012, from www.census.gov/population/popclockworld.html

Wilensky, H., & Lebeaux, C. (1965). *Industrial society and social welfare*. New York,
NY: Free Press.

Woolley, J., & Peters, G. *The American Presidency Project* [online]. Santa Barbara,
CA: University of California (hosted), Gerhard Peters (database). Available from
www.presidency.ucsb.edu/ws/?pid = 8758

World Bank. (February 2012). New estimates reveal drop in extreme poverty
2005 – 2010. Retrieved on February 15, 2012 from http://econ.worldbank.org/
WBSITE/EXTERNAL/EXTDEC/0,,contentMDK:23129612~pagePK:64165401~
piPK:64165026~theSitePK:469372,00.html

World Health Organization. (2011a). *World health statistics*. Geneva, Switzerland:
WHO Press.

World Health Organization. (2011b). *Measles fact sheet*. Retrieved on November 5,
2011, from www.who.int/mediacentre/factsheets/fs286/en/

Zimmerman, S. L. (1979). Policy, social policy, and family policy. *Journal of Marriage and the Family*, *41*, 467 – 495.

Chapter 2
Reconceptualizing the Evolution of the American Welfare State

Bruce Jansson

> As you read this chapter, ask yourself if you think it is important to understand history, not just to know some dates or be familiar with certain key persons. Some might say that history repeats itself and, therefore, we should be knowledgeable of the past. Mark Twain, however, allegedly said, "History does not repeat itself, but it does rhyme."

Introduction

The American welfare state has become a pivotal feature of American civilization. Spending on human resources consumed 69 percent of the federal budget in 2010, not including spending by states and local government and not including tax expenditures such as the Earned Income Tax Credit (U.S. Office of Management and Budget, 2012). It includes thousands of pages of regulations that govern the implementation of its many programs and that protect the public's safety from environmental, housing, drug-related, and other hazards. It employs tens of thousands of persons.

Yet analyzing the welfare state's history poses daunting challenges for scholars. This article provides a survey of its development while posing questions for further research in its concluding section. It suggests that historians and social-policy theorists need to reconceptualize the evolution of the American welfare state by moving in new directions.

Some Daunting Challenges Facing Historians of the American Welfare State

Before it is even possible to analyze the evolution of the American welfare state, key conceptual issues must be addressed. We discuss six of these challenges as follows.

Expanding the Welfare State's Parameters

Some scholars have defined the welfare state in relatively narrow terms as consisting primarily of those programs that focus on traditional social work concerns, such as mental health, welfare, maternal health, and child welfare programs (Axinn & Levin, 1982; Leiby, 1978; Trattner, 1979). I call these "the traditional histories" in subsequent discussion, which I contrast with my own history of the American welfare state (Jansson, 1988, 2005).

This relatively narrow definition risks ignoring considerable portions of the welfare state if we define it as including a wide range of policies that are relevant to the social, psychological, and economic well-being of citizens. Not only do these policies span a wide range of substantive issues, but they also include tax policies that shape the distribution of wealth in the United States, budget policies that determine what policies receive priority, policies geared toward preventive as well as curative goals, policies at all levels of government, and policies that shape interactions between public and private sectors.

The welfare state's substantive programs include a wide range of programs that address social and economic problems and needs of citizens, such as (a) *institutions* that house persons with specific kinds of social problems or criminal offenses, including persons with mental problems, children who are orphaned or who are deemed to have been neglected or abused, and prisons; (b) means-tested *safety-net programs* for the poor (Food Stamps, Medicaid, Supplementary Security Income or SSI, Section 8 housing vouchers and subsidies); (c) *universal social programs* (Medicare, Social Security, and Unemployment Insurance); (d) *regulations* (food, drug, housing protections; civil rights laws for persons of color, women, mentally ill persons, persons with disabilities, the elderly, LGBT persons, and others); (e) *protections for persons in specific organizations* (such as work-safety conditions for workers, safety and medical care for persons in mental institutions, nursing homes, and convalescent homes, and safety and care for children in childcare and in their homes); (f) *opportunity-enhancing programs* (such as operations of educational programs and student scholarships, job-training programs, the junior-college system, land distribution, and economic-development programs); (g) *social and medical services* (such as mental-health, social-service, and medical services); (h) *preventive services* (such as public-health, early-detection, outreach, sex-education, and preschool programs); (i) *cultural and recreational programs* that include libraries, internet-access programs, public entertainment through Public Television, and the public national, state, and county parks; and (j) *family supplementing programs* that include childcare, foster care, and adoption programs.

These programs also include *community-building programs*, such as creation of specific development zones where businesses receive tax concessions to locate in them. They include local *zoning and land-use policies* that influence where homeless persons can live and where halfway homes can be located. They include *criminal law*, which determines, for example, what drugs are criminalized and the penalties criminals will suffer. They include *civil law*, which determines, for example, grounds for divorce and the obligations of divorced persons to each other and to their children. They include a large body of legal rules by local, state, and federal courts that shape the procedures and regulations of the American welfare state.

The American welfare state requires resources to operate its many programs, so funding sources must be considered as part of the welfare state, including (a) *government spending* (authorizations and appropriations of federal, state, and local governments); (b) *government tax expenditures* (organizations' and persons' tax deductions, exclusions, deferrals, or tax credits when filing their tax forms with federal and state governments with respect to mortgage interest deductions, corporate funding of employees' health insurance, funds placed in pension accounts by citizens, and citizens' charitable contributions); (c) *tax credits* (childcare tax credits and the Earned Income Tax Credit); (d) *payroll taxes* principally for Social Security, Medicare, and Unemployment Insurance; (e) *consumer payments* (such as out-of-pocket costs by enrollees in Medicare and Medicaid); and (f) *private philanthropy*, which includes a network of foundations and private donors that gave resources to an array of health and welfare institutions in 2007.

Traditional histories of the American welfare state emphasize curative programs that were established to help persons suffering from family, mental, income, health, and other problems, placing less emphasis on preventive preschool, education, and public health programs. In some eras, such as the 19th century, Americans pioneered land distribution and public education initiatives that were intended to promote opportunities for a wide range of Americans. Histories should not only chronicle these programs but also ask why they have failed to promote greater equality during specific eras — and why they were more effective in other eras, such as during the four decades after 1930 when social and economic inequality decreased as compared to prior and subsequent periods.

Traditional histories focused on relationships of the welfare state with a relatively small number of vulnerable populations — such as women, persons of color, or welfare recipients. Yet many vulnerable populations have emerged during the American historical experience, and each of them is inextricably linked to the regulations and programs of the American welfare state. I proposed five (often overlapping) groups that include at least 14 vulnerable populations: (a) *economic vulnerable populations* (such as poor persons); (b) *racial vulnerable populations* (such as African Americans, Latinos, Asian Americans, and Native Americans); (c) *sociological vulnerable populations* that have been placed in restrictive roles (such as women and the elderly); (d) *nonconformist populations* that are widely viewed as violating social norms (such as persons on welfare, gay men and lesbian women, persons who have been incarcerated, mentally ill persons, and persons with physical disabilities); and (e) *model vulnerable populations* (such as Jewish Americans and members of some white ethnic groups) (Jansson, 2005). To these groups might be added *immigrants* in specific eras, because members of different waves of immigrants have experienced — and continue to confront—profound prejudice, such as Irish Americans in the 19th century, Eastern Europeans and Italians from the Civil War to 1920, and Latinos in the contemporary period.

When discussing vulnerable populations, however, it is important not to ignore social class. Members of different waves of immigration, for example, were not only members of specific ethnic or racial groups, but often were relatively poor. European historians place far more emphasis on social class than do American historians and social scientists, who should devote more attention to disentangling the separate and combined influence of race and class in creating and sustaining such social problems as poverty, poor health, and mental illness (Kawachi, Daniels, & Robinson, 2005).

The American welfare state is possibly the most complex one in the world. Unlike ones that are primarily funded and directly by a central government, the American welfare state is shaped by the intersection of different levels of government and funding streams; courts; and not-for-profit, for-profit, and public entities. If we examine contemporary health policy in any major city, all of these factors determine the kinds and quality of medical services that low-income persons receive.

These complex jurisdictional arrangements are products of the unique way in which the American welfare state evolved from local to state to federal governments from the colonial era to the present. If the local and state agencies and programs *were* the American welfare state up until 1932 for all intents, the federal government *then* strengthened its role over the succeeding decades while often requiring states and localities to contribute fiscally and administratively to federal programs. The roles of states became somewhat strengthened in the 1980s, when many programs were devolved to them from the federal government during the presidency of Ronald Reagan.

Complex relationships exist, as well, between public, not-for-profit, and for-profit sectors. If not-for-profit agencies assumed major roles prior to the New Deal, they were relegated to lesser roles with the emergence of major government social spending during the New Deal and subsequently, but they still remained an important feature of the welfare state through extensive contracts and grants from government agencies. Hardly existing before the New Deal, for-profit agencies grew rapidly in the six decades following the New Deal in medical, nursing home, childcare, and other areas—often receiving considerable reimbursements and contracts from public agencies.

Courts have assumed a far larger role in shaping the American welfare state than in many other nations. The American Constitution, with its various amendments and its Bill of Rights, was the source of many rulings concerning privacy, confidentiality, due process, relationships of federal and state governments, and fairness in the welfare state's myriad programs and regulations. Litigation is endemic to the American welfare state's evolution, both in historical eras and in the present.

Traditional histories of the American welfare state focused on the development of official programs and regulations. Yet many social needs have been met in American history not by public authorities, but by an array of welfare-state surrogates, such as political machines in big Eastern and Midwestern cities (which provided jobs and welfare), private philanthropy, self-help groups, and faith-based initiatives, such as the social welfare activities of Catholic and Protestant churches (Walch, 1993). Families assumed major welfare functions, such as the extensive hiring of relatives and development of business enterprises by Jewish and Asian immigrant families.

It is important to understand the nature and extent of these welfare-state surrogates, because they often acted *as* a welfare state in the colonial era, the 19th century when the United States hardly possessed an official welfare state, and up to the present. Even today, most persons with mental health problems, for example, use informal sources of care or simply do without care from any source (Davis, 2007).

The American welfare state interacted in complex ways with these nonpublic initiatives. In the early part of the 19th century, religious services were often mandated for inmates of poorhouses, mental asylums, and prisons. Sometimes public authorities funded not-for-profit subsidiaries of churches that refrained from proselytizing as they freely used public resources for their charity. More recently, such fundamentalist presidents as George W. Bush have subsidized faith-based charities directly with (apparently) only vague requirements that they not proselytize—initiatives that are currently under review by the U.S. Supreme Court to see if they violate the constitutional separation of church and state.

Historians of the American welfare state need to be more attuned to the actual resources that were devoted to it. Some of them, such as Skocpol (1995) when discussing pensions for Civil War veterans and Mothers Pensions in the Progressive era, suggest that these were major policy initiatives when, in fact, they were supported by negligible resources. Even New Deal and Great Society initiatives were often backed by surprisingly small resources — with substantial allocations (aside from tax expenditures) only emerging in the 1970s (Jansson, 2001; Skocpol, 1995).

I contend, then, that historians of the American welfare state's evolution need to markedly broaden its parameters. Indeed, we need multiple histories that focus upon the evolution of various components of the American welfare state as well as ones that integrate them into a unified analysis.

Placing the Welfare State in Its Full Context

If traditional histories risk unduly narrow parameters on the substantive content of the American welfare state, they tend, as well, not to analyze a range of contextual factors that have shaped its evolution. They correctly analyze such cultural factors as American punitive orientations toward poor persons and racism and the inheritance of poor-law traditions from Europe by early settlers, but they place less emphasis on the role of the two major parties in supporting or opposing welfare reforms, the critical role of presidents, the role of military spending in constricting the domestic discretionary budget, special interests such as health insurance and drug companies, demographic factors, and immigration. The temperance, abolitionist, Know-Nothing, tenant farmer, and fundamentalist movements receive relatively little attention.

Nor did traditional histories aim to place the American welfare state in a comparative context. Why did it grow more slowly than European states in the wake of World War II when Americans became relatively conservative even as Europeans were greatly increasing domestic spending? In what specific ways is the American welfare state unique?

The rapid globalizing of the world in recent decades, as reflected by escalating movements of populations and capital across international boundaries, provides another reason for viewing the American welfare state in a global perspective. From the colonial period onward, Americans depended on immigration to provide them with a labor force sufficient to move the frontier westward—and then to provide workers for its emerging industry in the wake of the Civil War. The nation's dependence on foreign capital in the 19th century was similar to the contemporary dependence of developing nations on capital inflows, and it exacerbated economic volatility in the United States with important repercussions for social policy. The depression of 1893, like many deep recessions that preceded it, provided the backdrop for the progressives' reform movement at the start of the 20th century and was partly linked to the nation's primitive banking system and its reliance on other nations for capital.

Many major social problems in the United States are linked to globalization, such as losses of jobs, migration of populations into the United States from developing nations, and movement of cocaine and other drugs across national boundaries. If international treaties do not require American corporations that purchase or manufacture goods abroad to meet minimum wage and work-safety conditions, then they will be tempted to place even more jobs abroad—and to continue to use the threat of movement of their operations abroad to force American workers to accept lower wages.

New histories of the American welfare state need to devote more space to analyzing American social welfare initiatives abroad. How did the United States interact with the United Nations? How much foreign aid was funded in different eras, and how was it used? Why was the United States so tardy in committing resources to the global AIDS epidemic even though the Central Intelligence Agency once called it the most serious threat to the national security of the United States? How did the United States gain control of the World Bank and the International Monetary Fund—and often use them to make developing nations cut domestic spending, even when this policy undermined their efforts to address their social and economic problems (Stiglitz, 2002)?

Rethinking Which Time Periods to Prioritize

Historians also face the challenge of segmenting the welfare state's history into useful chronological segments. Traditional histories have used such periods as the colonial period, the Civil War era, the Progressive era, the New Deal, and the Great Society.

Selection of a relatively small number of eras risked ignoring key events, however. I supplemented them with periods of conflicting policy tendencies, such as when Democratic presidents confronted Republican Congresses or when President Richard Nixon confronted a Democratic Congress, in periods like 1945–1952, 1961–1963, 1969–1980, and 1992–2000. I also added conservative periods when relatively few social policies were adopted by the federal government and when some substantial policy pull-backs took place, such as periods like 1868–1900 (the Gilded Age), 1920–1932 (with its three conservative presidents), 1941–1944 when Congressional conservatives ended the New Deal work programs, 1952–1960 when President Dwight Eisenhower failed to propose new social programs although he approved substantial augmentation of Social Security, 1980–1992 when Presidents Ronald Reagan and George H. W. Bush cut back or rescinded social policies, and 2000–2008 when President George W. Bush mostly focused on counterterrorism and the War with Iraq after the destruction of the World Trade Center on September 11, 2001 (Jansson, 2005).

My choice of these segments had merit for a chronological analysis of the evolution of the American welfare state, but a case can be made, instead, to identify key historical periods when important choices were made that shaped the nature of the American welfare state, including its formation, its relationship with important developments in the broader society (such as the frontier, the Civil War, the early period of industrialization, and urbanization), its development during societal crises like depressions and wars, its relations with such nongovernmental entities as corporations and religious institutions, and its relationships with state and local government. Moreover, eras could be selected when the American welfare state made a strong push forward with respect to regulations, services, and programs that provided "hard" benefits like cash and food. They could also be selected because important issues or concepts emerged during them even if they were not fully realized, such as when President George W. Bush sought to privatize substantial portions of Medicare, Medicaid, and Social Security by using tax concessions to induce citizens to create private savings accounts to be used for pensions and health care.

These criteria suggest that eight segments were particularly critical to the construction of the American welfare state, including the early formative period in the colonial era; the era of localism, morality, and frontier opportunity in the early and middle portions of the 19th century; the confluence of massive social problems and a primitive welfare state during and after the Civil War; the Progressive era when regulations first appeared; the New Deal and its immediate aftermath when public policy developed non-market alternatives; the Great Society when federal social services were greatly augmented; the 1970s when funding priorities of the American welfare state markedly changed; and the 1980s through 2008 when Presidents Ronald Reagan and George W. Bush sought to retrench, devolve, and privatize the American welfare state. By contrast, policy developments from 1877 to 1900 and during the presidencies of Harry Truman, Dwight Eisenhower, George H. W. Bush, and Bill Clinton appear less important to the basic nature of the American welfare state, even if some important policies emerged during them.

Nine Eras

I draw upon the preceding discussion to suggest some ways that our understanding of developments in each of the nine eras might be advanced through new scholarship.

The Emergence of a Primitive Welfare State in the Colonial Period

A comparative perspective already illuminates discussion of the colonial period in traditional histories, particularly with respect to the importing of the Elizabethan Poor Laws to the colonies. Yet, early European settlers to the colonies, principally from England and Germany, were more European than American in the period preceding the American Revolution (Wood, 1992), bringing to the colonies not just the Elizabethan Poor Laws but many ideas drawn from societies that were evolving from feudal to capitalist nations—and from state religions toward greater toleration.

European immigrants who came to the colonies in the 17th and 18th centuries were imbued with conflicting tendencies because they experienced this period of transition in Europe (Jansson, 2005). They came from societies with a hierarchy of social statuses, social elitism, tolerance of the poor, deference, and localism that was characteristic of medieval society. Early colonial settlers were used to European societies where virtually everything was tightly regulated, including the establishment of businesses in local towns, labor policies, and the location and expansion of towns. The policy known as *mercantilism* gave national authorities the right to support specific kinds of industries and to build infrastructure to facilitate economic growth. Local and state authorities could even regulate the price of bread—the commodity most central to the diet of peasants. Even the ability of persons to migrate internally within societies was strictly regulated by laws of settlement.

Yet they came from societies where medieval policies and social arrangements that had prevailed in Europe for centuries were under sharp attack from intellectuals and business interests, not to mention peasants who were dispossessed from the land into urban areas. If intellectuals espoused free markets, democratic systems of government, and deregulation, business interests attacked the taxes and regulations that were placed on them by central authorities—and both intellectuals and business interests often sought greater power for the Parliament (in England) as compared to the monarchy.

Social policies in Europe were embroiled in increasing controversy. Poor-law institutions had a two-sided character. Sometimes they were implemented punitively, such as treating impoverished vagabonds harshly. Yet some poorhouses, possibly building on medieval notions that churches were places of nonjudgmental refuge that helped poor persons and vagabonds, were remarkably supportive of persons in need, even giving out clothing and food to broad numbers of persons (Snell, 1985).

The early settlers came to the American colonies, then, with a curious mélange of concepts and practices. On the one hand, they had ideas akin to ones passed down to them from feudal society, with John Adams even wanting the American president to be called a monarch—and many of them did not want to rebel from England. Many of them viewed the governance of colonies by Governors appointed by English monarchs as acceptable, as well as the many regulations established by these Governors. On the other hand, many of them were often deeply critical of medieval society and, in fact, wanted to create a utopian alternative based on widespread ownership of land, relatively free markets, toleration of religious sects, and relatively limited government—as the writings of Thomas Jefferson strongly suggest. As they neared the American Revolution in 1776, criticism of the Crown became more strident (Wood, 1992).

It is not surprising, then, that American social policy in the colonial period is not easy to characterize, unlike during the 19th century, when relatively harsh views toward the poor and vagabonds emerged. The attention of the settlers was not, in any event, focused on social policy for poor persons, but on their grand experiment to construct a society where preventive social policies would be paramount. As expressed by Thomas Jefferson and others, the colonists wanted to create a society dominated by small landowners in a rural society (Peterson, 1975). Colonial authorities and the land companies licensed by the Crown would sell vast tracts of land to these settlers, who would disperse onto this land, often in unsettled areas (except for Native Americans).

If we broaden our definition of the welfare state to include such preventive programs, then the heart of the colonial welfare state was not its small collection of poorhouses and prisons, but its land distribution policies and involvement of many of its settlers in a market economy. Even indentured servants—a huge portion of the colonial population—intended to use their accumulated savings to purchase land even if they continued a specific trade in rural towns.

The American Revolution reinforced the notion that Americans were creating a new kind of social order that would differ from the social strata and growing cities of European nations. Virtually everyone hoped to be an entrepreneur on small tracts of land, often coupling agriculture with small enterprises such as making hats. If some Europeans still had reservations about the emerging capitalist order, Americans came mostly to assume that capitalism, entrepreneurship, and (land) speculation would lie at the heart of their society. Social classes would still exist, but most citizens (it was hoped) would live on the land in relative prosperity.

Considerable research suggests that the actual life of many settlers sharply diverged from this bucolic view (Nash, 1976). Many persons did *not* own land, including indentured servants, persons in growing towns, and laborers. Slaves and Native Americans hardly shared in Jefferson's utopia.

An American penchant for denial may have been a key facet of the emerging American culture that would forestall important social legislation in coming centuries.

Economic and geographic realities in the colonies also precluded the development of social programs. Aside from some large landowners, the bulk of the population was nearly destitute, whether on the frontier or in towns, and was in no position to pay considerable taxes (Sachs, 2005). The Crown confiscated much of their meager tax revenues before the Revolution. Having fought the American Revolution to evade "taxes without representation," Americans showed an aversion to taxes in general from the outset of their Republic. Desperate for resources to retire debt, to wage war against Native Americans, and to construct some public improvements, Washington and the Congress levied a tax on whiskey only to encounter a rebellion that Washington had to *personally* quell by leading federal troops into Pennsylvania (Smith, 1993).

Nor did federal and state governments possess the capability of developing substantial social programs. The Constitution gave the federal government specific enumerated powers that mostly related to establishing a currency, retaining a militia, conducting foreign policy, and regulated interstate commerce, but it was mute on social welfare issues. (Several vague clauses, such as one that gave the federal government the power to advance "the general welfare" and a clause giving it the power to regulate interstate commerce, would later provide a foundation for social welfare functions, but mostly not until the Progressive era and the 1930s). Even as late as 1937, however, President Franklin Roosevelt feared the Supreme Court would nullify much of his New Deal on grounds that it lacked a Constitutional basis. So paranoid were many citizens about even the limited Constitutional power for the federal government that they insisted that a Bill of Rights be added to the Constitution to limit the power of the central government in 1791.

The disinclination to vest the federal government with significant power in domestic affairs was further accentuated by the growing chasm between federalists like Washington, John Adams, and Alexander Hamilton on the one hand and anti-federalists like Jefferson and his allies on the other hand (Smith, 1993). Jefferson and his allies won a landslide victory over Adams in 1800 that legitimized a weak central government equipped only to act on its narrow enumerated powers. The die was set for the next 132 years, when the federal government would have a negligible role in social welfare policy except for a brief period during and after the Civil War and for veterans—and except for land distribution policies on the frontier. This striking eradication of governmental roles was in marked contrast to European societies, where central governments retained significant policy roles into the 19th century even if large welfare states did not emerge in them until just after World War II.

Even with only a relatively poor and small population, the emerging nation had powerful special interests in the colonial period. Huge cotton-selling firms in New York City had a vested interest in preserving slavery, which provided them with the material to send to England.

Large landowners existed in many states, often exploiting their labor. Construction firms eagerly vied for contracts to build highways and canals in a developing nation.

Often lacking resources to purchase sufficient food and other goods, urban low-income populations sometimes rioted. Riots occurred in rural areas, too, as persons battled over the title to specific lands.

Nor were colonial leaders even remotely prepared to deal with the egregious violations of human rights that were rampant with respect to slaves and Native Americans, not to mention women. Such rights as the freedoms of speech and religion in the Bill of Rights, as well as the right to vote, were widely viewed as applicable only to white male citizens, not slaves, Native Americans, or women. The Constitution institutionalized slavery by mentioning it, directly or indirectly, more than 13 times, even declaring slaves to count as only three-fifths of a person when computing how many Representatives slave-holding states should have. Not wanting slave states to become a majority in the Congress, Northern framers of the Constitution were able to forbid its extension into the still-unsettled Northwest territories, but no serious effort was made to forbid slavery itself, even if Congress finally ended the slave trade in 1808.

No longer protected by the Proclamation Line of 1763 that the British had established to place boundaries on white settlers' intrusion onto their lands, Native Americans encountered an endless stream of settlers in succeeding decades who laid claim to their lands, receiving only delayed assistance from treaties with the federal government that "guaranteed" them land on the frontier—land that was often taken from them when yet another wave of settlers and treaties pushed them farther westward.

Segregated not physically but in terms of their role in society, women were mostly expected to be mothers who would not intrude on male prerogatives in professions, business, or government. Often rendered destitute because they could not even inherit property, women were relegated to a second-class status until well into the 20th century.

It can be argued, then, that traditional histories with their focus on Elizabethan Poor Laws place too little emphasis on many social welfare policies of the colonial period, including Constitutional provisions, land distribution, slavery, confiscation of Native Americans' land, aversion to taxes, dislike of central government, and conflict between federalists and antifederalists led by Thomas Jefferson. The new nation was overwhelmingly rural, with few fiscal resources and with only primitive social welfare institutions such as a few poorhouses and prisons. Unlike European societies, Americans mostly did away with policy functions of central governments as the views of Thomas Jefferson supplanted those of the federalists, leaving the United States with a capitalist economy supplemented by only primitive roles for government.

Christian Morality and Frontier Opportunity, 1800–1860

Welfare and child welfare policies—or the centerpiece of traditional histories—were *also* surpassed in size by land-distribution policies and were part of a larger quest to impose Christian morality on the American public. With additional resources needed to construct them and with a hardening view of destitute persons, the nation built many poorhouses in the Early Republic as they placed a negative construction on unemployed persons, who they increasingly associated with the Irish and other immigrants in a pattern that would become even more marked in the later decades of the 19th century. In this era of institutions, many states also constructed mental institutions, sometimes at the behest of Dorothea Dix's monumental crusade to rescue the mentally ill from poorhouses.

The poorhouses and other institutions can also be viewed as part of a larger moral crusade to rescue the emerging, and very Christian, nation from sin. As the work of Boyer (1978) suggests, Christian revivalism and morality pervaded the Early Republic. If Jefferson had idealized the emerging society as a society of small landowners who would lead upstanding lives, an array of persons added religion to this utopian concept. They would purge the nation of such sins as laziness, criminality, vagrancy, truancy, disobedience to parents, poor school performance, alcoholism, and (even) mental illness. Such moralists viewed virtually *every* social problem as a manifestation of immorality that could be prevented or arrested only by conversion to Christianity and inculcation of good habits.

No better way could be found to inculcate morality—and even Christian morality—into persons with presumed social problems than institutions, where every second of their waking hours could be regulated. It was common in poorhouses and mental institutions of this era to begin and end the day with religious services—with hard work and discipline enforced for the remaining portions.

The endemic morality of this era found expression, too, in an array of community settings that often had a preventive focus. The Sunday School movement was a huge crusade to reach poor children, where thousands of middle-class volunteer teachers provided highly structured religious and moral instruction to as many as 400,000 low-income urban children by 1835 (Boyer, 1978). Convinced that "the very first drink is a long step toward Hell," temperance crusaders sought to restrict licenses to taverns, limit retail sales of alcohol, imprison sellers and users of alcohol, and to persuade legislators in various states to declare it an illegal substance. They had persuaded 13 states by the 1850s to prohibit the sale of alcohol (Tyrell, 1979).

Another interesting variation in applied morality took place when Charles Brace, who founded the private Children's Aid Society of New York, sought to rescue a growing population of street children (Mennel, 1973). Convinced that institutions deprived them of their innate creativity, he and his associates shipped more than 90,000 of these children to frontier families from 1853 to 1895, where he hoped they would learn the virtues of hard work. No less than other reformers, he sought to imbue these street children with virtues such as industriousness and personal discipline, only on the frontier rather than in institutions.

The linking of social problems with lack of morality was fraught with peril because many persons, then and now, develop myriad social problems not because they are amoral, but because of environmental, economic, physiological, sociological, developmental, familial, and other factors. When they are stigmatized with "bad character," they are probably less likely to surmount these problems than if they are given positive and, where possible, evidence-based assistance—or where empowerment strategies are used. The connection with Christianity also posed problems that would resurface in the contemporary period when efforts by the administration of George W. Bush to give resources to faith-based agencies and churches were challenged through the courts.

Even as America was waging a moral crusade against various perceived moral problems, it was also greatly expanding the social experiment it had begun in the colonial era: giving massive numbers of people opportunities to help them gain upward mobility. It expanded its relatively open-door policy to immigrants mostly from Europe and Russia by admitting millions of persons, and made it relatively easy for them to obtain citizenship. It opened millions of acres of frontier lands for purchase at federal land auctions. It provided federal military protection to settlers from attacks by Native Americans. It tolerated the illegal squatting by many settlers on vacant but unpurchased land—and then enacted legislation on numerous occasions to allow many of them to purchase it (Rohrbough, 1968).

The United States launched yet another experiment when it implemented Jefferson's dream of universal free public education from the first through the eighth grade (before the Civil War) and then through high school (after the Civil War)—unprecedented policies in world history with access to education still restricted to upper elites in most nations. It gave white males the right to vote, including many immigrants from Europe.

The magnitude of these social experiments of massive immigration, relatively easy access to citizenship for Caucasian persons, distribution of vast lands on the frontier, access to public education, and the right (for white males) to vote were unprecedented in world history (Jansson, 2005). Many indigenous American citizens joined the westward movement, often selling their land to obtain funds to purchase land farther West. These social experiments—arguably the heart of the American welfare state at that time—took place in a mostly agricultural society, even though small towns and cities grew in number.

The universal acceptance of capitalism as the way to organize the nation's economy, which had already emerged in the colonial period, was unique in world history, where bartering and semi-feudal relationships still existed in much of the world. Americans had already subscribed to the notion of a (capitalistic) footrace where citizens—given land, education, and the vote—would create their own opportunities.

Much was wrong in this seeming paradise, and the society lacked the resources, institutions, or the will to do much about it (Sellers, 1991). Extreme poverty often existed on the frontier as settlers scrambled to survive winters and struggled to grow crops. Agricultural markets experienced booms and busts. Speculators often got special deals from federal land officers, allowing them to purchase huge holdings. Railroads were given extravagant amounts of free or cheap land in return for construction of lines heading West. Frontier life was often violent. A significant population of vagabonds, who lacked land or other possessions, emerged in the Early Republic. As parents headed West or succumbed from the epidemics that swept cities because of a lack of sanitation and food inspections, large numbers of children fended for themselves on the streets—the harbinger of the homeless problem in later periods of American history (Halloran, 1989).

The human tragedies experienced by slaves and Native Americans in the colonial period vastly increased in the Early Republic. Far from remaining in the original Southern states, plantation owners moved vast numbers of slaves westward to Mississippi, Louisiana, and Texas—and aspired to new territories in areas that became the states of Missouri, Kansas, and Nebraska. Native Americans were removed from their lands on a massive scale and succumbed to diseases brought to them by settlers.

Nor did women's lot appreciably improve, despite the remarkable and prescient ideas and actions of such feminists as Susan B. Anthony and Elizabeth Cady Stanton. Unmarried women could work, but mostly as housekeepers or nannies. Married women remained constricted by the doctrine of "separate spheres" that relegated them to household chores and child-rearing duties, leaving positions in business, agriculture, and the professions to white males (Harris, 1978).

Governments at local, state, and federal levels remained primitive by contemporary standards. Lacking a civil service, they were often corrupt. They lacked resources to tackle social problems even if they had wished to address them. Remarkably, Dorothea Dix convinced the Congress to enact legislation to use some federal proceeds from federal land sales to help subsidize mental hospitals in various states, only to suffer a stinging veto from President Franklin Pierce in 1854, who declared,

> I cannot find any authority in the Constitution for making the federal government the great almoner of public charity throughout the United States.... Can it be controverted that the great mass of the business of government—that involved in the social relations . . . the mental and moral culture of men . . . the relief of the needy or otherwise unfortunate members of society—did not in practice remain with the States?
>
> (Axinn & Levin, 1982)

The Confluence of Massive Social and Economic Problems in the South, Southwest, and West With a Primitive Welfare State During and After the Civil War

When the framers legitimated slavery in the Constitution, they unwittingly set the stage for a Civil War. Unable to ban slavery because they would have needed a two-thirds majority in the Congress to amend the Constitution, Northerners tolerated it—until Southerners tried to create new slave-owning states in areas that became Nebraska and Kansas (Appleby,

1992). When Abraham Lincoln was elected president in 1860 on the platform of *not* allowing new states that allowed slavery, Southerners feared that he might actually seek an end to slavery, and they bolted the Union by attacking a Northern fort in South Carolina.

The resulting Civil War and its aftermath posed fundamental social welfare issues that the nation was ill-prepared to answer: If slavery were abolished, what would happen to the freed slaves in terms of their economic survival, not to mention other social and civil rights? How would the rights of African Americans be protected in the South? How would Northerners prevent the reemergence of a white power structure in the South dedicated to oppressing African Americans?

Only the federal government possessed the resources, legal authority, and policing power to protect the freed slaves from Southern whites, and only the federal government could generate the resources needed to provide education and give job skills to a slave population that had been systematically deprived of education and resources.

The president and Congress finally eradicated slavery with passage of the 13th Amendment to the Constitution in 1865. As important, Northern troops occupied the South with a huge contingent of Northern troops that clamped down on egregious acts of violence against African Americans. Empowered by the Military Reconstruction Act of 1867 to serve as the protector of civil rights, Northern military forces allowed aggrieved African Americans to obtain redress from them rather than local courts. It seemed, too, that the Freedman's Bureau, created in 1865 and lodged in the War Department, would be a vehicle for addressing some social and economic needs of the freed slaves. The legislation creating it even promised 40 acres of abandoned or confiscated land to every male refugee, and it was charged with providing education and welfare to freed slaves.

Events after the Civil War soon suggested, however, that the primitive welfare state of the nation, consisting mostly of scattered poorhouses and related institutions, as well as a liberal land and immigration policy for Caucasian Europeans, would prove totally inadequate to the task of assisting freed slaves. In deep debt after the War, the federal government lacked needed resources. It lacked the will to develop needed programs to help the freed slaves when Lincoln was succeeded by President Andrew Johnson, an unabashed Southerner who tried to dissolve the Freedman's Bureau and who pardoned vast numbers of Confederate officials so that they could seek election in Southern states to public office — even appointing many of them to the Freedman's Bureau. Johnson's policies encouraged Southern whites to enact "Black Codes" in some jurisdictions that limited African Americans' right to free assembly and speech, even subjecting them to whipping for discourteous behavior.

When Johnson was soon replaced by General Ulysses Grant in 1866 in repudiation of Johnson's pro-South positions, the federal government became far more sympathetic to the rights of freed slaves. It enacted the 14th Amendment in 1868, which rescinded the Constitutional provision that African Americans counted as only three-fifths of a person, required that all citizens be given "equal protection" under the law, and stipulated that all people be accorded the protection of due process. The 15th Amendment in 1870 established universal suffrage of all adult males, and Civil Rights Acts enacted in 1870 and 1875 limited the ability of states to enforce discriminatory legislation and outlawed segregation in public facilities and schools. Congress even declared infringements of the civil rights of people to be a federal offense in the Ku Klux Klan Act of 1872.

These laws protecting the civil rights of African Americans would prove ineffective, however, if they were not enforced—either by the armed occupation of the South or by federal courts. Seething at their loss of power and often imbued with racism, many Southern whites had resorted to guerilla warfare against African American leaders immediately in the wake of the Civil War, and they continued it even after the onslaught of federal legislation that protected the rights of freed slaves.

Ominously, as well, the termination of the Freedman's Bureau in 1872 demonstrated that the Congress and President Grant did not truly understand that the nation needed to supplement civil rights with programs that would address the social and economic needs of freed slaves. How could a mostly illiterate population with no resources, land, and equipment survive in the South without massive assistance? An estimated one-fourth of freed slaves died in the aftermath of the War, whether from starvation, disease, or exposure.

In perhaps the most important event after the Civil War, Northern Democrats who represented the interests of the white Southern elite exacted a promise from Northern Republicans to withdraw Northern troops from the South in exchange for supporting Republican Rutherford Hayes when the vote in the Electoral College had become stalemated. Minus Northern troops to protect them and lacking the weapons, resources, and organization of white Southerners, African Americans were soon ousted from public offices and denied suffrage through the imposition of literacy tests and poll taxes on them. They were further intimidated by widespread public lynching.

Southern legislatures soon enacted Jim Crow laws that undid protections of the civil rights legislation enacted after the Civil War. In a final insult, the Supreme Court chose not to heed the Civil Rights Acts of 1870 and 1875 in *Plessy v. Ferguson* (1896), when it ruled that an African American male could be required to sit in separate railroad cars from Caucasians, setting the stage for imposition of segregation in virtually every aspect of Southern society including public schools. In its ruling, moreover, the Court ruled that civil rights could be enforced *only* with respect to the discriminatory acts of individuals rather than those of state and local governments, which legitimated the Jim Crow laws.

An array of factors worked in tandem to bring about these tragic results. Having never exercised *federal* power on a large scale prior to the Civil War, it is remarkable that a Northern-dominated Congress was even able to enact sweeping civil rights legislation—or that it even approved and funded a military occupation of the South for 12 years after the War—or that it even created the Freedman's Bureau. Lacking traditions to support and sustain large social programs, Americans were also imbued with views of the former slaves that discouraged positive assistance to them.

Northerners often viewed the freed slaves' plight as resulting from their lack of morality, believing that slavery had made them a lazy and promiscuous people who would fare poorly in a freed condition *unless* they received moral education (Friedman, 1982). The schools of the Freedman's Bureau focused on such education, much like the Sunday School movement of the antebellum period. If they mostly needed moral education, why give them practical skills, credit, land, equipment, horses, and housing needed to survive in rural regions? Possessing considerable racism, Northerners did not support helping large numbers of freed slaves to move to Northern cities to compete for the many jobs in the emerging industrial order. Nor did they confiscate sufficient lands of former slave owners to help former slaves, and they allowed speculators and Northerners to purchase most of the confiscated land rather than giving it to freed slaves. Nor did Northerners even think to place large numbers of freed slaves on remaining federal lands on the frontier, partly because they coveted this land for themselves.

In similar fashion, the nation would prove unable to address the same needs of large numbers of Spanish-speaking persons in the Southwestern and Western lands secured by the American conquest of Mexico in 1848. While the United States agreed in the Treaty of Guadalupe Hidalgo to honor the civil rights of these persons, Western settlers forced them from their land by intimidation and force, as well as through the courts — and intimidated or forbade them from voting. They became low-paid workers for mining, ranching, and farming interests (McWilliams, 1968).

The Civil War and the conquest of Mexico created social, economic, and human-rights problems, then, that the nation lacked the ability to understand or to address. Rather than helping freed slaves and conquered peoples in the American Southwest and West, courts often undermined their rights. The nation desperately needed the social programs and regulations of an advanced welfare state to cope with these huge social and economic problems, but it could only develop temporary and rudimentary remedies in the South — and virtually none whatsoever in the Southwest and West.

The Regulatory Response of Progressives to Urban Problems

If the nation lacked the capability to address the major social problems of the South, Southwest, and West, it proved ill-prepared, as well, to deal with the problems of an urbanizing and industrializing society that evolved in the four decades following the Civil War. It primarily chose to address them through regulations rather than substantial social programs, but they were, nonetheless, a major step toward the assertion of governmental powers to address social needs.

Traditional histories of the American welfare state place too much emphasis on the very small social programs created during the Progressive era such as Mothers' Pensions. In fact, only 46,000 women were helped by these programs by 1919 (Gordon, 1994). Traditional histories fail to emphasize sufficiently the true innovation of the Progressive era: the enactment of many regulations, particularly in local and state jurisdictions.

Facilitated by cheap labor from millions of immigrants as well as considerable foreign capital, the United States urbanized and industrialized at rates that were unprecedented in world history in the wake of the Civil War. Industrialists had virtually a monopoly on power. Unions hardly existed. Subject to few regulations, industrialists subjected their workers to dangerous working conditions and paid them meager wages. To forestall efforts by government to control them and to obtain contracts to build the infrastructure of American cities, they bribed lawmakers at all levels of government. With virtually no social or economic programs other than an array of social welfare institutions and an emerging network of hospitals, the nation had no strategy for addressing the victimization and problems of the industrial workforce that it had largely imported from abroad.

It is understandable that Americans instinctively resorted to *regulations* rather than social policies to address its social problems. Once enacted, they required few resources to implement at a time when the federal government devoted only 5.5 percent of its gross domestic product (GDP) to public spending, compared with 25.5 percent for France (Jansson, 2005). "Setting rules" was congruent with the moral culture of the United States, which often equated social ills with wrongdoing by landlords, industrialists, politicians, purveyors of spoiled food, and others—wrongdoing that could be curtailed if rules were established that prohibited specific actions like subjecting workers to fire hazards or selling contaminated food. They also reflected actual experiences of most Americans, with dangers imposed on them by harmful actions of an array of powerful persons (Thelen, 1975).

In the so-called Progressive era that extended roughly from 1900 until the American entry into World War I in 1917, Americans enacted a host of regulations at local, state, and federal levels. We take for granted regulations that place requirements on industry, landlords, employers, and institutions like schools, such as safe working conditions, safe housing conditions, minimum wages, and achievement standards for schools. We know that tens of thousands of pages of administrative regulations exist for federal and state programs. Civil rights protections exist for many vulnerable populations in federal and state jurisdictions. Many public-service programs must have grievance procedures for those clients who believe they were treated unfairly. Companies must allow employees to decide by secret ballot if they wish to unionize. Large health systems must give advance notice of their intention to downsize operations or specific facilities—and hold public hearings before acting.

Yet virtually no regulations existed in the United States in 1900, with dire consequences: Food was often tainted; housing was dilapidated and in danger of burning; workers were exposed to workplace dangers; women were involuntarily placed into prostitution; unlicensed professional workers were required to work 12 or more hours per day; and children were placed in employment. The civil rights of persons from many vulnerable populations were flagrantly violated. Persons who were injured at their places of employment often received no restitution.

The need for regulations was greater than during the pre–Civil War period, because Americans no longer mostly lived on farms or in small towns as a result of the rapid industrialization of the United States between 1865 and 1900. Many of the 10 million immigrants who came to the United States between 1865 and 1890—and another 18 million who followed them in the next 30 years—worked in industrial settings. Their hours of work were unregulated, as was their pay. So unsafe were their machines that 35,000 workers died per year and 536,000 were injured per year in the Progressive era (Weinstein, 1975). Now living in congested areas, citizens were more vulnerable to epidemics such as cholera caused by lack of sanitation. Speculators built vast housing tracts that were unregulated by fire codes or other standards. Absent drug-safety regulations, many persons died or were harmed by taking unsafe drugs.

The progressive movement was the first urban reform movement in the United States. Its leaders often were relatively affluent Caucasian persons during a period of relative prosperity. As exemplified by Theodore Roosevelt and Jane Addams, they were outraged by the political power and arrogance of so-called robber barons who had created huge mega-industries and monopolies in the Gilded Age—only to often use their extraordinary resources to subjugate workers and to bribe politicians to give them lucrative concessions and to forestall regulations on their enterprises. While sometimes harboring some prejudice toward immigrants, progressives were often disgusted by their sheer poverty, poor living conditions, and victimization by employers.

Progressives, too, were often motivated by Christian morality. They were inflamed by spectacular accounts of the greed of industrialists by muckraking journalists. Locked out of the professions and employment when married, many women found social reform to be a fulfilling activity.

Progressives came from both Democratic and Republican parties. Republican President Theodore Roosevelt, who acceded to office in 1902 with the assassination of President William McKinley, courageously took on the corporate tycoons in his first term by siding with workers in some strikes and demanding dissolution of some monopolies. Reform continued when he was elected president in 1904, slowed when William Taft, a conservative Republican, was elected president in 1908, but resumed with the election of Democrat Woodrow Wilson in 1912 over Roosevelt, who ran in that year as the nominee of the Progressive Party—a third party established in 1912 because Taft defeated Roosevelt in their competition to become the Republican presidential nominee.

While they focused on regulations, progressives also obtained some notable reforms that became precedents for subsequent reforms in the New Deal. They got many states to enact "mothers' pensions" for single (usually widowed) mothers and their children, but this welfare program was extremely small and poorly funded—and granted benefits only to women who were deemed to be moral. They got workmen's compensation enacted in most states so that injured workers received a payment rather than having to pursue lengthy litigation that had usually been won by employers—but the payments were extremely low. They were able to establish a Children's Bureau in Washington, D.C., but it mostly focused on research on the status of women and children.

Progressives did not, then, create a robust welfare state but focused mostly on regulations. These regulations were hardly a panacea since governments often lacked the capacity and sometimes the will to implement them, particularly when special interests placed adverse pressure on them. Nor were they a substitute for major social programs that provide an array of benefits to persons.

Progressives mostly avoided the egregious violations of civil rights for persons of color across the nation. Many of them, including President Roosevelt, subscribed to the notion that people of color possessed inferior intelligence as compared to Anglo Saxons (Dyer, 1980). African Americans were commonly lynched in the South, Latinos worked in extreme poverty in mostly agricultural and ranching areas after being displaced from the land by white settlers, and Asian Americans experienced marked prejudice in the West even as they developed ingenious irrigation systems for farming Western lands. Women were finally granted the vote in 1920 with ratification of the 19th Amendment to the Constitution, but they were mostly excluded from business, law, and other professions except for nursing, social work, and teaching at secondary levels.

As in the 19th century, then, the United States had only a primitive welfare state in the Progressive era, despite the enactment of important regulations. Historians need to place far more emphasis on survival strategies of vulnerable populations in an era when they received scant assistance from local, state, or federal governments, except for an emerging set of regulations.

Addressing Destitution in the New Deal With Federal Social Programs

If progressives secured myriad regulations but enacted few social programs, reformers in the New Deal obtained many governmental social programs and some additional regulations. Unlike the Progressive era, which was a time of relative prosperity, the New Deal was triggered by the catastrophe known as the Great Depression, which began with the stock market crash of 1929 but lasted for more than a decade until an upsurge of military manufacturing restored economic growth by 1941 as the nation neared entry into World War II. So crushing was this depression—which often brought unemployment to rates of 25 percent of the adult workers—that even conservatives had to support many of Roosevelt's initiatives to avert massive destitution and even starvation, as well as policies to help senior citizens cope with economic uncertainty.

No one could have guessed from the election of 1932 that Roosevelt would develop unprecedented reforms. He not only downplayed reforms in his campaign addresses, except for vague references to possible reforms, but he advocated cutting spending and balancing a federal budget in substantial deficit. He promised hope and unspecified innovation, but not much more. When he won the election with a landslide—as well as the election of 1936—he had a power base that proved instrumental to developing his reforms.

Roosevelt encountered substantial opposition to his reforms throughout the decade, but particularly from 1937 onward. Conservative Southern Democrats controlled most Congressional committees and teamed with conservative Republicans increasingly as the 1930s progressed. Roosevelt was uncertain whether the Supreme Court would declare most of his reforms to be an unconstitutional exercise of federal authority until 1937, only after he had threatened to pack the court with liberal justices by getting Congress to enlarge it by allowing him to add a new justice each time a justice failed to retire within six months of his 70th birthday. Because the nation only had a small federal income tax levied on the most affluent 5 percent of citizens and because federal excise and import taxes lagged during the Great Depression, federal revenues halved from $4 billion to $2 billion in 1932—meaning Roosevelt had virtually no resources for social reforms. Trade unions, mostly limited in 1933 to skilled laborers, often possessed conservative leaders until their ranks were swelled by unskilled labor later in the decade.

It became immediately clear, however, that Roosevelt would not be a passive observer of the nation's misfortune. He created in the first year of his presidency many programs to help destitute and unemployed persons, including the Federal Emergency Relief Administration (FERA) to develop a national welfare program for unemployed persons to be largely funded by the federal government, as well as its offshoot the Civilian Works Administration (CWA), which would create mostly un- or semi-skilled jobs with some of the FERA funds in the various states—replacing the CWA with the Works Progress Administration (WPA) in 1934. He started the Public Works Administration (PWA) to fund public works projects that required technical expertise, such as dams, airports, and flood-control projects. He started the Civilian Conservation Corps (CCC) to provide jobs for young men in conservation projects. Later in the decade, he established the National Youth Administration (NYA) to subsidize the college education of youth and to establish a range of work projects for them.

He also sought to reform the economic system in the first year of his presidency by establishing the Federal Deposit Insurance Corporation (FDIC) to protect banks from insolvency by insuring deposits—following this with the Securities and Exchange Commission (SEC) in 1934 to forestall undue speculation by investors and stockbrokers. He enacted the National Recovery Administration (NRA) to avert the vicious cycle of price slashing and laying off workers by getting business leaders in various economic sectors, such as steel, coal, and mining industries, to agree on process and to establish production quotas for each company. He established the Agricultural Adjustment Agency (AAA) to accomplish similar goals in the agricultural sector, where thousands of farmers had gone bankrupt and often evicted sharecroppers and tenant farmers from their land. He also enacted the Tennessee Valley Administration (TVA) to stimulate economic development in a huge geographic area by initiating a network of dams and generating plants, selecting electricity to power cooperatives and dams, reforesting huge tracts, and building flood-control projects.

Roosevelt resorted to a clever strategy to fund these domestic initiatives. Having promised to restore a balanced federal budget in his campaign of 1932, he found a way to appear *not* to increase deficits while increasing federal spending to fund his reforms. His solution was to divide the budget into "regular" and "emergency" portions, respectively funding the ongoing portions of the budget (such as the Post Office and other ongoing federal agencies) and his New Deal social programs (Jansson, 2001). He balanced the regular budget with great fanfare in 1933 by making draconian cuts in veterans' benefits and other ongoing programs, while funding the emergency budget with deficits that were to be funded by selling bonds to investors at home and abroad. These deficits, he argued, would only be temporary, because his relief and work-relief programs would be terminated when the Great Depression lifted. This strategy allowed him to claim to be a fiscal conservative even while considerably increasing the national deficit. Even conservatives feared to oppose this ruse, however, because they realized that many persons in their districts were destitute—and usually support annual appropriations for New Deal programs nearly unanimously.

Roosevelt's reforms continued with enactment of the Social Security Act in 1935 with its old-age pension program and unemployment insurance programs mostly funded by payroll deductions, as well as an assortment of means-tested welfare programs, including Aid to Dependent Children (ADC), later changed to Aid to Families with Dependent Children (AFDC) in 1950; Old Age Assistance (OAA); and Aid to the Blind (AB supplemented with Aid to the Disabled or AD in 1950). (With enactment of these welfare programs, the FERA was terminated.) If Roosevelt portrayed his work-relief programs as temporary programs, he described the Social Security Act as a permanent reform—as well as the Fair Labor Standards Act of 1938, which established a national minimum wage, abolished child labor, and set maximum weekly hours of work. The New Deal also enacted the Wagner-Steagall Housing Act in 1937, which established a federal public housing program. In addition to these programs, the New Deal implemented an array of emergency food, medical, and housing programs that were widely viewed as temporary ones to avert malnutrition, exposure, and disease.

Critics of the New Deal have correctly identified flaws and omissions in these various reforms, such as the failure to set national benefit standards for ADC, OAA, and AB or to set minimum wage standards for domestic workers or farm workers. When viewed from the perspective of preceding American history, however, Roosevelt's reforms can only be seen as remarkable achievements. If progressives had mostly focused on regulations, Roosevelt established the first major federally funded social programs in the United States—and supplemented them with an array of regulations over wages, union organizing, and prices.

As important as these reforms were, Roosevelt also created an ongoing power base that would prove instrumental in expanding the American welfare state during the rest of the 20th century. If voting in national elections prior to 1932 had mostly been dictated by ethnicity and regional factors, it was considerably shaped by social class from 1932 until the 1960s, with blue-collar Catholic and ethnic white voters disproportionately voting for Democratic candidates. African Americans, who had mostly voted Republican after the Civil War because the Republican Party led by Abraham Lincoln had abolished slavery, switched to the Democratic Party because Roosevelt helped many of them survive the Great Depression with his various work-relief and welfare initiatives. Jewish voters also aligned with the Democratic Party—an allegiance that was cemented when President Harry Truman strongly supported the establishment of Israel in the wake of World War II.

Roosevelt also brought organized labor into the Democrats' fold. He was, at first, critical of the militant tactics of unions supporting unskilled workers in the mining industry and automobile plants, such as the sit-down strikes of automobile workers. He gained their strong support, however, when he helped get the so-called Wagner Act enacted in 1935, which placed the National Labor Relations Board in the Department of Labor and gave it the power to mandate and monitor elections of employees at specific companies. The bulk of campaign funds for Roosevelt's 1936 campaign came from organized labor. As many unions grew rapidly during the organizing of war industries in World War II, American unions became larger and more affluent, allowing them to become even larger contributors to Democratic candidates and the Democratic Party, as well as persuading many of their members to vote Democratic (Brody, 1980).

Americans' support for an enlarged American welfare state declined rapidly later in the decade, however. Many citizens came to view Roosevelt as seeking too much power in a nation that had only known a weak federal government. Republicans charged that he sought to create a kind of political machine that used work and welfare benefits to entice voters to support his regime. When he proposed to pack the Supreme Court in 1937 with liberal justices to avert vetoes of his domestic legislation, he inadvertently strengthened these fears.

His social-reform movement was further slowed by the lifting of the Great Depression as war preparations for World War II bolstered the economy. Roosevelt increasingly devoted his energies to war preparations. Once the nation was at war, conservatives aggressively attacked his work-relief programs on grounds they were no longer essential. With his attention on the war effort and wanting a bipartisan coalition to wage it, Roosevelt did not oppose the termination of many of the New Deal's work and relief programs, with most of them rescinded by the end of 1942. Yet pension, unemployment, and welfare programs of the Social Security Act, Fair Labor Standards Act, public housing, and the Wagner Act remained as permanent elements of the American welfare state.

Roosevelt strengthened the power of the federal government in yet another important way during World War II. Although the federal income tax had been made constitutional in 1913, it hardly collected any revenues because it was restricted to only the most affluent 5 percent of the American population in the New Deal (Leff, 1984). Desperately needing resources to finance the War, Roosevelt met a firestorm of opposition when he proposed extending the income tax to most Americans—with 15 state legislatures threatening to rescind the 16th Amendment. He nonetheless got a broad-based federal income tax enacted, which became pivotal to the financing and subsequent growth of the American welfare state in succeeding decades.

The New Deal also initiated complex jurisdictional arrangements between local, state, and federal governments. Social Security pensions were administered by the federal government, but federal welfare and work-relief programs, as well as public housing programs, required states to contribute funds and to assume major administrative roles.

Although the New Deal created many programs that gave work and welfare to Americans, it failed to develop programs that gave them social and educational services—or civil rights in the case of persons of color and other vulnerable populations. Intent on not angering Southern Democrats, who were a key part of his coalition and who chaired most Congressional committees, Roosevelt blinked when it came to anti-lynching legislation, even when it was favored by Congressional liberals.

Important as work-relief and relief programs were during the New Deal, traditional histories overstate their size. Federal government spending in the New Deal consumed on average less than 10 percent of the GDP as compared to about 20 percent in 2007, and the federal government collected revenues that totaled only 7.7 percent of the GDP in 1941 as compared to roughly 20 percent in 2007 (Jansson, 2001). Only a small percentage of unemployed persons benefited from relief and work-relief programs. Historians should, therefore, place far more emphasis on survival strategies used by persons suffering from economic destitution in this era, because relatively few of them received major assistance during the worst economic catastrophe in American history. With unemployment rates sometimes soaring to 75 percent, survival strategies of persons of color deserve particular attention.

The Growth of Public Social Services and Personal Rights

The United States emerged from World War II with only a modest welfare state and minimal public investments in it. Domestic spending by the federal government was deeply cut by conservatives in the wake of World War II—and then fought a losing battle against military spending during the 1950s as the Cold War escalated. (Military spending consumed roughly 75 percent of the federal government's budget in the 1950s.)

Medical and social services, as well as legislation to protect the civil rights of many vulnerable populations, were almost completely lacking from the welfare repertoire of the federal government, except for the medical programs of the Veterans Administration. The lack of medical services for retirees became an important issue in the 1960 presidential campaign between Democrat John F. Kennedy and Republican Richard M. Nixon—since the federal government only funded the small, means-tested Kerr-Mills medical program for a small number of low-income retirees. Having decided not to enact national health insurance after World War II, the nation had turned to employers to fund insurance for their employees voluntarily, but many of them decided not to provide it even when they were allowed to deduct its costs from corporate income taxes. Tens of millions of working Americans were left with no health insurance, and their ranks were swollen by retirees whose employer-provided health insurance had lapsed when they retired.

Sensitized to mental health by the illness of his sister, Kennedy came to realize, too, that many mentally ill persons lacked services in the community, particularly because many of them had been released from mental institutions due to the recent advent of psychotropic drugs. Increasing attention, too, was given to the plight of low-income persons whose schools were often dilapidated and poorly staffed, and who faced insensitive and fragmented services. Low-income children rarely received preschool education unlike more affluent persons who purchased it from nongovernmental nursery schools. Sometimes displaced from jobs by technology, workers could rarely locate effective job-training programs. Senior citizens lacked community services that might help them stay in their homes rather than being forced into nursing homes or becoming a burden on their children.

Particularly in the South and Southwest, persons of color suffered flagrant violation of their civil rights in the 1950s. Disabled persons, gay men and lesbian women, women, and Native Americans suffered discrimination in their places of work and in their communities. The Civil Rights Movement provided the catalyst for many of the reforms of the 1960s as the Great Depression had catalyzed reforms in the 1930s. Northerners, watching violent reprisals against nonviolent demonstrations by African Americans in the South as the white power structure opposed a growing grassroots civil rights movement led by such leaders as Martin Luther King Jr., became sensitized to the lack of personal rights of Southern African Americans. They witnessed, as well, scores of uprisings across the nation in inner-city African American communities throughout the nation from 1964 through 1968.

Political developments also facilitated social reforms. When Vice President Lyndon B. Johnson succeeded President Kennedy after his assassination in late 1963, he pledged to enact legislation that Kennedy had proposed but failed to secure Congressional approval for, including civil rights, anti-poverty, and medical legislation. Johnson's landslide victory over Republican Barry Goldwater in 1964 gave him large Democratic majorities in Congress. He possessed prodigious political skills from his many years as Senate Majority leader, and he wanted to establish a domestic legislative legacy that would exceed even Franklin Roosevelt's accomplishments.

Before he was assassinated, President Kennedy secured the enactment of the Manpower Development and Training Act of 1961 and the Mental Retardation and Community Mental Health Centers Act of 1964. President Johnson obtained in his first year of office the Economic Opportunity Act (the so-called War on Poverty), the Food Stamps Act, and the Civil Rights Act of 1964.

With his strong majority in Congress, Johnson secured the enactment in his second year in office with public health insurance for elderly persons (Medicare), a means-tested health program for poor persons of all ages (Medicaid), the Elementary and Secondary Education Act, creation of the Department of Housing and Urban Development and expanded public and subsidized housing programs, the Civil Rights Act of 1965, and the Older Americans Act—as well as many smaller measures.

Johnson's reform momentum was undermined by his own policies. He enacted the largest tax cut in the nation's history in 1964, which severely cut federal revenues, and he had to promise Congressional Southern conservatives, in return for their support of this tax cut, not to incur deficits in the remaining years of his presidency. When he then chose to hugely increase troop commitments to the Vietnam War in 1965, he lacked resources to fund his Great Society and encountered growing opposition to reform from Congressional conservatives who remembered his pledge not to incur deficits.

If Johnson had inherited his reform coalition from President Franklin Roosevelt, he split in ways that would haunt liberals for the remainder of the 20th century (Jansson, 2001). His involvement in the Vietnam War split Democrats into pro- and anti-war factions and accentuated the disillusionment of many white blue-collar Democrats in the North and white Southern Democrats who had been uneasy with Johnson's civil rights legislation, as well as the number of Great Society reforms that they often believed disproportionately and excessively helped persons of color. The term "white backlash" appeared as early as 1964 and described this growing alienation of many Democrats from their party, opening the door to the exodus of many of them to the Republican Party in the last three decades of the 20th century.

Johnson suffered extraordinary political losses in the last two years of his presidency, putting an end to his reform momentum. Already angered by his reforms, conservatives of both parties fought to cut funding for his reforms and to prevent him from enacting additional ones. Facing almost certain defeat if he sought his party's nomination for another term in office, he chose not to seek another term, allowing Vice President Hubert Humphrey to become the Democratic contender for the presidency in 1968.

Kennedy's and Johnson's contributions to the American welfare state were nonetheless substantial, not only by adding social and medical services to the American welfare state, but also by extending civil rights to African Americans and to women, who were included in provisions of the 1964 Civil Rights Act. The civil rights legislation of 1964 and 1965 unleashed many civil rights measures in its wake. Women had already obtained partial coverage by the Equal Pay Act of 1963 and had obtained a ban on gender-based discrimination in Title VII of the Civil Rights Act of 1964, as well as a court ruling by the Supreme Court in 1965 that overturned Connecticut's law that made possession of contraceptives a crime. Women's advocacy groups persuaded President Johnson to include women in the scope of his 1965 executive order that required affirmative action programs to bring equal opportunity for persons of color in programs funded by federal, state, and local governments, establishing a precedent that the term *sex* or *gender* would appear whenever the phrase "race, creed, color, or national origin" appeared in legislation or executive orders.

The policy gains of African Americans directly extended to Latinos and Asian Americans, who were included in provisions banning discrimination on the basis of race, as well as efforts to deny them voting rights. The Chicano movement, led by many leaders including Cesar Chavez, sought to empower Mexican agricultural laborers who had been excluded from provisions of the Wagner Act, finally getting state legislation in California that gave them the right to vote to be unionized often under the United Farm Workers. The Latino community was active in voter registration drives, efforts to pressure the Equal Employment Opportunity Commission to investigate job discrimination against Latinos, and efforts to extend the Civil Rights Act of 1965 to cover Latinos' voting rights.

Mobilization of disabled persons, gay men and lesbian women, and senior citizens was also triggered in part by successes obtained by African Americans. The drive to give gay men and lesbian women more rights was intensified after a riot in Greenwich Village after the police raided the Stonewall Inn in 1969. Gay men and lesbian women wanted to change the diagnostic categories of the American Psychiatric Association that defined *homosexuality* as a form of mental illness. They sought protections against job discrimination in schools and other places. They pressured local, state, and federal governments to combat the AIDS epidemic in the early and mid-1980s, which initially focused on gay males in major American cities with devastating consequences (D'Emilio, 1983).

Through grassroots protests and with the assistance of Surgeon General C. Everett Koop, punitive and neglectful policies of the federal government gradually shifted toward treatment and prevention, even as increasing numbers of gay persons of color—as well as women in African American and Latino communities—contracted the disease.

Gay men and lesbian women had been routinely thrown out of the military forces prior to 1993, but they finally obtained a compromise agreement in the administration of Bill Clinton that allowed them to remain in the military under a "Don't Ask, Don't Tell" policy, which proved to be a discriminatory solution even if it allowed many closeted gays and lesbians to remain in the military. Gay men and lesbian women fought to obtain court rulings and legislation in various states to allow them to form civil unions or marriages like heterosexual couples—unions that would not only legitimate their partnerships but also give them various tax, insurance, and other benefits widely available to heterosexual couples. They sought anti-discrimination laws in local and state jurisdictions with respect to housing and jobs with considerable success.

Partly influenced by a surge in disabled persons among veterans in the wake of the Vietnam War, leaders of the disability community obtained passage of the Rehabilitation Act of 1973, whose section 504 prohibited discrimination against people with disabilities primarily in jobs funded with public funds, and then the Americans with Disabilities Act in 1990, which barred discrimination in all workplaces, housing, transportation systems, and public accommodations.

Often placed on reservations or living in extreme poverty in American cities, Native Americans benefited from Great Society policies that emphasized supports to their culture rather than assimilation; brought many social service, economic, and housing programs to their reservations; and sought tribal participation in their governance. The Indian Self-Determination and Education Assistance Act gave tribes the authority to assume responsibility for administering federal programs of the Departments of Interior and Health, Education, and Welfare.

When it enacted the Immigration Act of 1924, the United States shifted from a relatively open immigration policy to a closed and discriminatory one that gave preference to people from northern Europe as compared to Mexico, Central America, and Asia. Enactment of the Immigration Act of 1965 abolished these quotas by allowing annual admission of 170,000 immigrants from the Eastern Hemisphere and 120,000 from the Western Hemisphere in a "sharp ideological departure from the traditional view of America as a homogeneous white society" (Takaki, 1989). Even more Asian and Central American immigrants were allowed to enter after the Indochina Migration and Refugee Assistance Act of 1975 and the Refugee Act of 1980 were enacted.

So-called undocumented immigrants who worked in the United States for extended periods and paid taxes were often victimized by prejudice and deportation, even though they produced major economic benefits for the United States in agricultural, tourist, restaurant, and other industries—and paid Social Security and other taxes. The Immigration Reform and Control Act of 1986 granted asylum to 3 million undocumented workers if they could prove they had worked in the United States for at least three years, and levied penalties on employers who knowingly hired undocumented workers.

Millions of additional undocumented immigrants came to the United States in the two decades after 1986 because of the huge economic disparities among the United States, Mexico, and developing nations. As many as 10 million immigrants spread across the nation in search of employment. They were often exploited by employers, lived in substandard housing, lacked access to health care aside from emergency conditions, and feared deportation. Large numbers of them perished as they sought to enter the United States across deserts on the Southern border with Mexico. Mexican President Vicente Fox in 2001 and President George W. Bush in 2004 developed proposals to grant three-year work visas to immigrants for hard-to-fill jobs and to provide amnesty for more immigrants, but they were both unable to persuade Congress to approve immigration reforms despite massive demonstrations in 2006 and 2007 by Latinos.

In addition to official policies, *each* of these vulnerable populations launched important consciousness raising, empowerment, and advocacy projects. Women's groups, for example, worked to redress job discrimination, obtain more humane treatment of rape victims in local hospitals and courts, obtain funding for women's shelters, challenge specific instances of discrimination in places of work through lawsuits, get local and state laws to seek payments from divorced or absent fathers, and obtain legislation to outlaw sexual harassment in workplaces. Women's advocacy groups and public interest attorneys had remarkable success in obtaining huge monetary damages from large corporations for failure to promote or reimburse women sufficiently as compared to male employees.

The Great Society differed from the New Deal not only in the substantive content of its reforms, but in their intended permanency. Programs of the Great Society remained mostly intact in succeeding decades even if their funding was slashed in conservative periods such as during the presidency of Ronald Reagan in the 1980s. Yet budget allocations to the Great Society were remarkably Spartan—and the expansion of social services and civil rights did not sufficiently address the economic needs of vulnerable populations.

The Rapid Expansion of Hard Benefits, 1968–1980

The portion of the American welfare state that was funded by entitlements and annual appropriations finally became a major priority for Americans in this period (Jansson, 2005)—with their expenditures rising from $158 billion in 1970 to $324 billion in 1980 (in 1980 dollars).

These increases in domestic spending took place, remarkably, during the conservative Republican presidencies of Presidents Richard Nixon and Gerald Ford, as well as the conservative presidency of Democrat Jimmy Carter. Various factors led to this surprising result, including the Democrats' majorities in Congress throughout this period, the huge growth of Medicare and Medicaid, a small peace dividend when the Vietnam War ended, and the runaway inflation of the 1970s that swelled federal tax revenues. (Inflation pushed many persons into higher federal tax brackets even when their real wages did not increase.)

Increases in domestic spending occurred, moreover, as a result of the unusual politics of the Nixon presidency from 1968 until he left office in 1974. Determined not to let Democrats dominate the domestic agenda so that he could convert the Republican Party from a minority to a majority one, Nixon resolved both to introduce his own domestic reforms *and* to claim partial credit for many reforms introduced by the Democrats. Critical of the emphasis on social and medical services in the Great Society, Nixon wished to emphasize "hard benefits" that gave persons cash, in-kind benefits, and jobs, as well as transfers of federal revenues to states (Jansson, 2001).

Nixon startled the Congress when he proposed the Family Assistance Plan (FAP) in 1969, a sweeping revision of welfare policy. Caught in a crossfire between liberals and conservatives, FAP was not enacted, but Congress approved passage of the Supplementary Security Program (SSI) instead, which combined existing welfare programs for the elderly (OAA), the disabled (DA), and the blind (BA) into a single program with national funding and administration. Although the Food Stamps Program had been enacted in 1964, it had remained a relatively small program in the 1960s because of its cumbersome application process, its local eligibility policies, its optional adoption by states, and its partial funding by states. Nixon and the Congress nationalized Food Stamps, giving it uniform eligibility and benefits and making it a mandatory program for states. The President and Congress indexed Social Security benefits so they would automatically rise with inflation in 1972. The Congress and President Ford enacted the Earned Income Tax Credit in 1975, which gave tax credits to intact families that earned beneath specified levels — tax credits and eligibility that were substantially increased in subsequent decades. The Congress enacted the Comprehensive Employment Training Act (CETA) in 1973 that was reminiscent of some work-relief programs of the New Deal. Federal assistance for low-income housing doubled in the 1970s.

Nixon and the Congress also enacted federal sharing of revenues with states and local governments through the Local Fiscal Assistance Act of 1972. He hoped to devolve many federal programs to state and local governments, but he was unable to persuade Congress to support most of his devolution proposals.

Some social service programs were adopted in the 1970s, including the Juvenile Justice and Delinquency Prevention Act of 1974, the Education for All Handicapped Children Act of 1975, and the Adoption Assistance and Child Welfare Act of 1980. The Occupational Safety and Health Act of 1970 was landmark legislation that propelled the federal government into oversight of the safety standards of American industry.

Traditional histories of the American welfare state failed to give sufficient recognition to the size and scope of reforms of the 1970s as compared to the Great Society and the New Deal. They were at least as significant as these two prior eras — and far more significant when measured by the size of fiscal commitments to them. Although many gaps existed in them, the reforms of the 1970s gave the United States for the first time a system of safety-net programs for persons who lacked resources, regardless of their age and gender. A single woman with preschool or school-aged children could receive, for example, AFDC, Food Stamps, Medicaid, and subsidized housing.

Devolution of Federal Programs to the States and to Individuals in the Presidencies of Ronald Reagan and George W. Bush

The notion that the states and local governments should be the primary building blocks of the American welfare state has an ancient history in the

United States. Because of political and constitutional barriers, the federal government only emerged with a substantial social welfare role in the New Deal—or more than 140 years after the Republic was founded.

Often chafing when liberals succeeded in developing a substantial federal role, conservatives often wanted to turn the clock back to times when states and local governments had been the predominant actors. They had three options: (1) downsize federal social programs by cutting their funding, (2) devolve federal social welfare programs back to state and local governments, or (3) privatize the welfare state. If President Ronald Reagan led the devolution and retrenchment efforts, President George W. Bush made privatization his major goal.

Some accounts of social policy from 1981 through the present understandably emphasize the fragility of the American welfare state. Yet the American welfare state proved to be remarkably resilient, leaving many conservatives frustrated by their failure to gut it.

President Reagan initiated fiscal and spending policies that placed extraordinary downward pressure on social spending. By getting huge tax cuts enacted and increasing military spending while not cutting entitlements except for ones that were means-tested like Medicaid and AFDC, Reagan created unprecedented peacetime deficits. He used these deficits to argue that the discretionary annual federal budget had to be severely cut, and he targeted an array of social programs that focused on poor persons for major cuts. He succeeded in cutting domestic discretionary spending by roughly 25 percent during his presidency (Jansson, 2001).

Determined to devolve many federal social welfare programs to the states, Reagan succeeded in getting Congress to eliminate 57 federal social programs (called "categorical programs" because the federal government dictated how they would be administered by the states) and to replace them with seven "block grants" in 1981. These block grants gave states broad latitude in how they used these grants in such areas as social services; community services; alcohol, drug abuse, and mental health services; maternal and child health services; community development services; primary health services; and preventive health services.

Reagan was unable, however, to devolve entitlements, failing to persuade Congress to devolve Food Stamps to the states. Nor were such Republicans as House Speaker Newt Gingrich—and subsequently President George W. Bush—able to convince Congress to devolve Medicaid to the states. Unless conservatives could get entitlements devolved, which constituted the vast bulk of federal spending on entitlements, their quest to devolve social programs would remain substantially unfulfilled.

Partly because he believed that President Reagan had achieved sufficient retrenchment and devolution of the American welfare state, Republican Congressman Newt Gingrich led a conservative movement to achieve these goals. Engineering a Republican takeover of both Houses of Congress in 1994, Gingrich sought to force President Bill Clinton to make drastic cuts in social spending and to devolve Medicaid to the states. He, too, was frustrated in these goals. Not only did President Clinton outmaneuver him, but Gingrich was deposed as Speaker of the House by his fellow Republicans when Democrats made surprising gains in the Congressional elections of 1998.

Conservatives were successful in obtaining the devolution and block-granting of AFDC when they persuaded President Bill Clinton to sign their version of the Personal Responsibility and Work Opportunities Act of 1996, which converted AFDC from an entitlement to the Temporary Assistance for Needy Families (TANF) block grant. While Clinton, too, had espoused "changing welfare as we know it" in his presidential campaign of 1992, Republicans convinced him to sign a far more conservative version of TANF than he had originally wanted.

The United States had long used the tax code to achieve social welfare aims. Immediately after the 16th Amendment to the Constitution was enacted in 1913 to allow the federal government to collect income taxes, the Congress voted so-called tax expenditures into existence. They allowed persons to deduct state and local taxes and mortgage interest payments from their gross income when calculating income subject to federal income taxes (Witte, 1985). Congress then enacted an array of deductions, exclusions, deferrals, and credits over the next 95 years. So huge were these tax expenditures that just from 1975 through 2004, tax expenditures cost the federal government $10.9 *trillion* in lost tax revenues from 1975 through 2004—or more than *half* of the total federal revenues from individuals' income taxes in 2004 (Jansson, 2001). Deductions of home-mortgage payments, which totaled $53 billion in lost federal income in 2004, are by far the nation's largest subsidized housing program, greatly exceeding federal subsidies for rent of low-income persons or for the construction of public housing.

If the politics of federal programs subsidized through general revenues and payroll taxes are relatively public and controversial, the politics of tax expenditures are usually "subterranean" (Hacker, 2002). When the federal government failed to enact national health insurance after World War II, for example, insurance companies, corporations, and health interest groups persuaded Congress to allow corporations to deduct their costs of purchasing health care for their employees from their corporate income. Banks and investment companies persuaded Congress to give citizens tax incentives to establish private retirement accounts, whether Individual Retirement Accounts (IRAs), where they pay no taxes on funds they place in IRAs until they withdraw them after retirement, or Roth Retirement Accounts, where they pay no income taxes on retirement funds until they retire.

The Earned Income Tax Credit (EITC) is possibly the largest anti-poverty program in the American welfare state. Enacted in 1975, it gives employed heads of low-income families a tax rebate. The federal government also subsidizes considerable numbers of low-income persons by not requiring them to pay federal income taxes if their incomes fall beneath specific levels.

When considered together—and with notable exceptions like the EITC—the American penchant for tax expenditures has proven to be highly inequitable (Jansson, 2001). Partly because they possess considerable taxable income as compared to less-affluent persons, affluent Americans benefit disproportionately from many tax expenditures. Renters do not benefit from home-mortgage deductions. Low-income employees who work for employers who do not fund their health insurance receive no benefit from employers' tax deductions for costs of funding employees' health insurance. Persons who lack resources to pay into a retirement plan do not benefit from IRA and Roth tax deferrals and deductions.

As compared to most European nations, moreover, American tax rates favor relatively affluent persons, who pay about 35 percent tax rates on that portion of their income that exceeds $250,000—as compared to rates that are often double this level in European nations. Taxes on capital gains are only taxed in the United States at a rate of 15 percent, even though they are primarily realized by affluent persons when they sell investments. The greater income inequality in the United States as compared to Europe, Canada, and Japan partly stems from the inequitable nature of American tax rates and tax expenditures.

Firmly believing that the creation of wealth benefits the entire society, President George W. Bush made tax cuts a centerpiece of his domestic policy. Immediately after taking office, he sought and obtained a $1.35 trillion tax cut—with roughly 40 percent of the tax cut's benefits going to the wealthiest 1 percent of the population. He achieved another $700 billion tax cut in 2003, which eliminated taxes on stock dividends, even though stocks are primarily owned by relatively affluent persons. He frequently argued in political speeches that citizens' income belonged to them rather than to government, implying that taxes should be cut even further.

If Presidents Nixon and Reagan had favored devolving many federal programs to the states, President Bush wanted to devolve some of them to individuals by promoting personal accounts with tax incentives. He wanted citizens to develop private retirement accounts (in place of Social Security) or health savings accounts (in place of Medicare and Medicaid) by not taxing funds that citizens placed in these accounts up to a specified annual amount.

Bush was unable to convince Congress that a radical restructuring of the American welfare state was meritorious. Although Congress enacted his proposed tax cuts, they did not adopt his proposal to devolve much of the American welfare state to individuals—or to convert Medicaid into a block grant. Their opposition to his policies partly stemmed from their inequitable nature. Those persons who pay no or low federal income taxes would receive no or low tax benefits from placing their personal funds into private accounts, even if they had sufficient resources to establish them in the first place. It would take most citizens years to build accounts of sufficient size to fund their retirements or major health costs, making it inequitable to end Social Security, Medicare, and Medicaid in the interim.

Strong Democratic gains in the Congressional elections of 2006 made it even less likely that President Bush's privatization policies would prevail. Yet both Presidents Reagan and George W. Bush had articulated devolution, retrenchment, and privatization alternatives to the American welfare state that would likely resurface in coming decades whenever conservatives controlled the presidency or the Congress.

If policy analysts often focus on retrenchment and devolution in the period from 1981 through 2006, they ought to give greater emphasis to the *resilience* of the American welfare state. Overall domestic spending *increased* in this period, even if at a slower rate than in some preceding eras. Conservatives were unable to obtain the roll-back in the American welfare state, and historians should analyze in more detail those defensive strategies that their opponents utilized to achieve this result.

Social Reform in a Polarized Context: Presidents Bill Clinton to Barack Obama

The presidency of Bill Clinton (1993–2001) followed Presidents Ronald Reagan (1981–1989) and George H. W. Bush (1989–1993) and preceded the presidency of George W. Bush (2001–2009). Clinton enacted some notable social reforms, but his presidency can also be viewed as a period of stalemate because conservatives wrested both Houses of Congress from the Democrats in 1994 Congressional elections led by Republican Congressman Newt Gingrich. Clinton was able to enact the Family and Medical Leave Act in 1993 and the Children's Health Insurance Plan (CHIP) in 1997, which respectively allowed parents to obtain leaves from their jobs when family members experienced illness or when spouses gave birth and which funded health insurance for children from low- and moderate-income families that possessed too much income to be eligible for Medicaid (Jansson, 2011).

Clinton was mostly bogged down, however, in battles with Republicans over annual budgets and other matters. He also enacted sweeping welfare reform to the chagrin of many liberals, which converted AFDC from an entitlement into a block-grant program known as the Personal Responsibility and Work Opportunities Act that contained the Temporary Assistance to Needy Families welfare program (TANF). Liberals disliked many of its provisions. States had license to cut welfare more easily because the program was not protected by entitlement status. States were required to place adult recipients in work or work-related activities after they had received two years of cumulative benefits. States were prohibited from giving welfare benefits to recipients for more than five years over their lifetimes with limited exceptions. It gave states remarkable latitude, such as allowing them to eliminate cash aid and replace it with any combination of cash and in-kind assistance; to deny assistance to teen parents or other kinds of recipients; and to establish even more severe time limits.

Liberals' hopes were dashed, moreover, when Al Gore, Clinton's Vice President, lost the presidential election of 2000 against George W. Bush—a bitterly contested election ultimately decided by the Supreme Court. Barack Obama, a relatively unknown African American U.S. Senator, threw his hat in the ring for the upcoming presidential election of 2008—and soon discovered that his principal opponent in the Democratic presidential primary was Hillary Clinton, wife of former president Bill Clinton. Most persons discounted Obama's political chances in the ensuing primary election, but Obama gathered strength rapidly to allow him to become the Democratic presidential nominee.

Obama faced off against John McCain, the Republican nominee, in Fall 2008 and won a landslide victory in November, where Democrats obtained a large majority in the House and a one-vote majority in the Senate. Obama encountered many obstacles. The worst recession since the Great Depression began in late 2007 and extended into 2009, but only modest recovery had taken place even well into 2012. This recession, experts agree, was triggered by American banks when they engaged in excessive speculation and enticed many Americans to purchase houses at the height of a housing bubble by offering them low interest rates that soon ballooned to much higher levels. Many home purchasers also lost their jobs in a recession where unemployment exceeded 12 percent of workers.

Obama had little success in enacting national health insurance, banking legislation, or other reforms during his first year in office because of extreme polarization between liberals and conservatives, although the House enacted a version of national health insurance and banking regulations. He oversaw the implementation of a huge Stimulus Plan to revive the economy. He was able to enact the Patient Protection and Affordable Care Act in 2010, which was the most ambitious health reform since the enactment of Medicare and Medicaid in 1965. It promised health coverage for 32 million of the 46 million uninsured Americans by 2014 through expansion of Medicaid's eligibility and provision of private health insurance to millions of Americans through so-called state exchanges. It promised, as well, to build several hundred primary health clinics in underserved areas, to require private insurance companies not to set lifetime limits on coverage, and to expand preventive services—among many other provisions.

He was also able to enact the Dodd-Frank Wall Street Reform and Consumer Protection Act of 2010, which placed restrictions on banks' speculation and allowed the federal government to examine their solvency every year and (if necessary) close down ones that were in precarious financial shape. It also established a federal credit agency to make credit-card issuers, as well as providers of home mortgages, be more transparent in their terms with consumers (Jansson, 2011).

Democrats were unnerved, however, by Republicans' huge gains in the Congressional elections of 2010, where they regained control of the House by a substantial margin, even though Democrats retained a narrow majority in the Senate. Ideological polarization between the two parties was accentuated, moreover, by the emergence of the so-called Tea Party in 2009—and the election of many of its members to local, state, and federal legislatures and governorships. Tea Party members hew to a conservative ideology that emphasizes considerable reductions in the roles of government, large cuts in government budgets, reductions in taxes, relatively harsh treatment of immigrants, privatization of Social Security, and removal of entitlement status from Medicare and Medicaid. They support strong national defense spending.

Political gridlock marked Obama's presidency from 2010 into 2012 as Republicans, infused by many elected members of the Tea Party, opposed increases in taxes and cuts in military spending even as the nation faced a huge national debt. In a pattern reminiscent of the Clinton presidency, Republicans and Democrats began to face off in annual budget battles beginning in spring 2010, but extending into 2011 and beyond. If Democrats wanted to keep entitlements intact, but to raise taxes and cut military spending as troop wind-downs took place in Iraq and Afghanistan, Republicans wanted to remove entitlements, privatize Social Security, and entertain some tax cuts.

Social service programs were threatened with huge budget cuts not only at the federal level, but in state and local jurisdictions from 2008 onward due to depletion of their revenues from the Great Recession. Facing huge budget deficits, state and local governments slashed the budgets of education, public health, and social programs.

It was unclear as the presidential elections of 2012 approached whether Democrats would regain lost ground or endure greater losses. If they lost control of both chambers of the Congress and the presidency, the renewal of relatively liberal policies initiated by President Obama would dissipate into a new round of conservative policies in a nation gridlocked by ideology. If they kept the presidency and regained control of the House, further enhancements of the liberal agenda, such as immigration reforms, might ensue.

Topics for Further Research

Further historical research is needed to better understand how the welfare state has grown over the past three centuries. For an extraordinarily long period—from 1789 through 1933—the American welfare state existed in a primitive state when measured by aggregate expenditures, including both direct allocations of funds and tax expenditures. Many traditional histories and some historians risk exaggerating the actual importance of specific reforms—or the size of the American welfare state—by not examining the actual resources devoted to them.

Our brief analysis of eight eras suggests that the American welfare state grew by a process of *accretion*. With the slate nearly wiped clean by 1800, Americans focused on residual institutions and welfare programs while focusing on land distribution and public education in the 19th century. During important periods of American history, massive social problems overwhelmed the nation's primitive welfare state, such as during and after the Civil War—and arguably in the Progressive era and New Deal, when urbanization and a catastrophic depression created social problems that the nation addressed inadequately. By a process of accretion, the American welfare state gradually took form through regulations (the

Progressive era); substantial but mostly temporary federal work-relief and relief programs, as well as permanent programs of the Social Security Act (the New Deal); social and medical services as well as civil rights (the Great Society); and resource and in-kind programs (the 1970s). Throughout the 20th century, Americans gradually constructed an elaborate set of tax expenditures that supplemented direct expenditures, leading to combined spending that was by the late 1970s quite substantial in size and even not that much lower than many European nations when measured as a percentage of GDP.

History suggests, as well, that the federal American welfare state grew through a series of spurts. The Progressive era, New Deal, Great Society, and the 1970s produced growth spurts in regulations, work-relief and entitlement programs, social service and personal rights, and cash and in-kind programs. Less dramatic reforms occurred between these spurts, such as incremental expansion of Social Security, addition of regulations, enactment of low-profile tax expenditures, enactment of small programs funded by the discretionary budget, and extension of civil rights to groups like the disabled. When considered in aggregate, these isolated reforms have considerable importance, even if they were less dramatic than reforms during spurts.

As the American welfare state grew within and between spurts at the federal level, a similar process took place in the states. Some state spurts were linked to federal spurts because the federal government required the states to commit considerable resources or administrative effort to federal initiatives. Many New Deal and Great Society reforms required, for example, not only state fiscal contributions but also the creation of many new state-level administrative entities. States had to create state-level welfare and work-relief agencies in the New Deal and agencies to administer Medicaid in the Great Society.

When the federal government devolved many programs during the presidency of Ronald Reagan, it catalyzed a rapid growth of states' administrative capabilities, because states now *had* to oversee 57 programs that had previously been overseen by the federal government. When the federal government allowed states to administer programs of the Occupational Safety and Health Administration (OSHA) in the early 1980s and when it converted AFDC into the TANF block grant in 1996, it similarly fostered a surge in the growth of state bureaucracies.

Social reforms also spurted when states had Governors or legislative leaders with expansive agendas. When Pat Brown, Sr. was Governor of California from 1959 to 1967, for example, he persuaded the state legislature to fund massive increases in California's education and mental health programs, as well as its infrastructure. By contrast, far fewer reforms occurred during the tenures of many Republican Governors, such as Ronald Reagan and George Deukmejian.

Policy spurts in states are limited in their size and number, however, by fiscal realities that confront states. When the federal government finally increased federal income tax to a substantial size during World

War II and expanded it even further in succeeding decades, it effectively placed limits on states' fiscal resources, since their citizens would have objected to substantial taxing of their incomes from *both* state and federal governments. States remained heavily dependent, then, on lesser sources of income, including property taxes and sales taxes, even if some states *did* tax incomes at far lower rates than the federal government. (Revenues of all states when aggregated totalled roughly one-half the size of federal revenues in 2000.) Elected officials in states were deterred from raising taxes too high, moreover, by the fear that many citizens and businesses would depart for states with lower taxes.

Those taxes that states and localities collected, moreover, were often reserved for social welfare programs traditionally funded by them, including education, general relief, police, fire, infrastructure, and corrections. Their resources were preempted, as well, by required matching fund contributions for some federal programs—often having to devote more than one-quarter of their entire state budgets to their matching contributions to the Medicaid program in 2007. States had to implement some unfunded (or partially funded) federal mandates, as well, such as mainstreaming developmentally and physically challenged children into the public schools as required by federal law.

Histories of the evolution of the American welfare state must account both for the tension between its *reluctance* and its *resilience*. I identified a relatively full list of factors that I hypothesize, singly and in tandem, promoted reluctance, including various cultural, economic, political, legal, institutional, and social factors, as well as the extraordinary power of American conservatives and the late development of the American welfare state (Jansson, 2005). Although many theorists implicate one or several factors, such as the weakness of class-based movements (Shalev, 1983); culture (Hartz, 1955); ideas of policy elites, organizational features of the U.S. state structure, and interest group pressures (Skocpol, 1995); manipulation of race by political elites (Edsall, 1991); or the role of corporate capitalists (Berkowitz & McQuaid, 1980), I hypothesized that multiple interacting factors have shaped the reluctance of the American welfare state.

The American welfare state has been reluctant as compared to some other welfare states in Europe, but it has displayed remarkable resilience in the past three decades. Just three of its programs (Social Security, Medicare, and Medicaid) grew from about 2 percent to 8 percent of GDP from 1960 to 2004, and they are slated to grow at phenomenal rates in the next three decades as the boomers (persons born between 1946 and 1964) age. The contemporary American welfare state is like a sprawling empire with legions of providers, complex relations with state and local governments, legislative and presidential allies and opponents, links with courts at all levels, and relations with governments and providers in foreign nations. When tax expenditures are included, Hacker (2002) contends that the American welfare state is not that different in its total size as a percentage of GDP than many European welfare states.

American scholars need to devote more research, then, to analyzing why the American welfare state has grown so rapidly in the last four decades—and which parts of it have grown most rapidly. If federal entitlements and tax expenditures have grown rapidly, for example, federal domestic discretionary spending has hardly grown as a percentage of GDP from 1978 to the present (Jansson, 2001).

Social Security, Medicare, and Medicaid have grown rapidly partly because Americans have viewed their recipients as deserving—and because so many Americans use them, including the friends and relatives of conservatives. The aging of the American population is certain to contribute to these programs' growth for pensions and health care—and for nursing home care, which is largely funded by Medicaid. Americans' emphasis on medical technology has also fueled the growth of Medicare and Medicaid. Unless the United States enacts national health insurance, Medicaid will continue to grow rapidly. As entitlements, moreover, these programs are automatically funded by the Congress to the level of claimed benefits each year, immunizing them from cuts in annual budget battles.

Tax expenditures are highly popular, as well, because they disproportionately assist relatively affluent persons with their health, pension, housing, and other costs. Legislators like them because they can be expanded behind closed doors as compared to the public and controversial politics that usually accompany legislation to establish or expand social programs. When wanting to cut federal spending, legislators typically focus on social programs rather than tax entitlements because they are more visible and more controversial.

The growth of the American welfare state has been facilitated by electoral policies and partisan politics. Legislators and presidents increase their popularity by claiming credit for social programs that have helped their constituents—even relatively conservative ones who might otherwise want to cut American social spending for ideological reasons. It is not surprising, then, that Social Security has been called the "third rail" of American politics—to be cut only at significant political risk. Democrats have been the initiators of the overwhelming majority of new social programs in the United States in the past four decades, even though Republican moderates and idiosyncratic Republican presidents like Richard Nixon have lent their weight to social reforms.

Americans have placed considerable emphasis on opportunity-creating programs from the colonial period onward. It is not surprising, then, that Americans have developed a relatively robust junior-college and college system, even as they have evolved relatively harsh programs that address the survival needs of low-income persons.

The links between interest groups and the financing of political campaigns means that large interest groups have more power in the United States than in many other nations. Mortgage-interest tax deductions and tax incentives that promote retirement accounts like IRAs have been strongly supported by real estate, banking, and mutual-fund industries. The Food Stamps program and the medical programs of the Veterans Administration have been strongly supported by agricultural interests and veterans groups such as the American Legion. Interest groups have the power not only to enact new programs but also to block ones that they dislike, as witnessed by the way that health insurance companies assumed a key role in defeating President Bill Clinton's proposal for national health insurance.

Americans have possessed considerable empathy for groups that are widely perceived to be deserving from the colonial period onward, resulting in welfare programs for mothers, blind and disabled persons, as well as retirees, temporarily unemployed persons, and victims of natural disasters.

Historians and policy analysts should also devote more attention to the tension between *retrenchment* and *resilience* in the American welfare state. Conservatives *did* fashion important cuts in the American welfare state from 1981 through 2006, yet overall social spending increased markedly in this period, suggesting the importance of policy momentum. Once enacted, social programs often foster their own growth as their beneficiaries—as well as specific interest groups that form to protect them—oppose major cuts or terminations even during intensively conservative periods (Pierson, 2000). Social Security expanded, for example, from a relatively small to a massive program as its benefits were successively extended to widows, dependent children, disabled persons, and children in college over many decades, just as Head Start expanded from serving low-income children to include children with developmental and physical challenges.

Policy momentum occurs, as well, in areas of group rights. Once women, Latinos, the disabled, and gay men observed the important civil rights gains of African Americans in the mid-1960s, for example, they demanded similar protections for themselves.

The sheer size of the American welfare state is relatively inconsequential, however, if it fails to achieve important social objectives—whether in aggregate or in its specific programs or regulations. To what extent does it reduce inequality? To what extent does it not grant important rights to specific vulnerable populations? What gaps or omissions exist in its extension of rights and services to the American population? Which of its programs are based on faulty premises, thus doomed to fail? Which programs are ineffective? Which programs produce outcomes that are not sufficiently cost effective—or mostly wasteful? Which policies are inequitable, such as many tax expenditures?

Where Next?

The aging of the American population will require extraordinary expansion of not only Social Security and Medicare, but also social services, home health, and nursing-home care of the elderly population. The costs of these programs and services, when coupled with the extraordinary growth of the

American national debt, will create a shortage of resources that can be met in three ways: (1) increasing economic growth by importing younger immigrant workers, (2) increasing taxes substantially, or (3) cutting many other social programs. Each of these options will be controversial, suggesting a volatile politics beginning sometime around 2016 when many persons born between 1946 and 1964 (the so-called boomers) reach age 65 and older.

The American welfare state will likely have to increase its international reach in coming decades by seeking minimum wage, work-safety, and anti-pollution requirements in treaties and trade policies. With many American workers earning only poverty-level wages, increasing efforts to level the playing field by requiring corporations in other nations to increase their wage scales is likely to occur—or a substantial American backlash against free trade will emerge.

Already spending roughly 15 percent of their GDP on health care in 2007, Americans will be hard-pressed to afford continuing escalation of medical costs in coming decades. None of the panaceas have worked, including managed care, competition between health plans, corporate provision of health care, reviews of physician practices, and advanced authorizations for services, and it is unlikely that computerizing of medical records will substantially cut medical costs. Many experts agree that the relatively unrestrained use of medical technology by providers and consumers lies at the heart of cost escalation, but no strategies for containing it have proved successful.

High levels of inequality in the United States, which show no signs of dissipating, could eventually bring considerable domestic discontent and exacerbate such social problems as crime, poor health, and poor educational performance. No panaceas have yet emerged to bridge this chasm, and it remains uncertain what effects it will have on the nation's social, economic, and political systems. The United States has funded entitlements relatively generously, but it has been excessively frugal in funding domestic discretionary spending that invests in low-income persons' education, health care, job training, and social services.

If the past is prologue, the American welfare state will again be put to the test as it addresses these coming issues. We can expect considerable controversy in coming decades between liberals and conservatives, red and blue states, and the two dominant political parties as contending factions put forward different approaches to coming challenges.

Key Terms

safety net	*sociological vulnerable*	*model vulnerable*
welfare state	*populations*	*populations*
economic vulnerable	*nonconformist*	
populations	*populations*	

Review Questions for Critical Thinking

1. Is the American welfare state on its deathbed?

2. The American welfare state is characterized as a complex intersection of different levels of government and funding streams. To what extent do these factors determine the kinds and quality of services that low-income persons receive?

3. Why was the United States so tardy in committing resources to the global AIDS epidemic even though the Central Intelligence Agency once called it the most serious threat to the national security of the United States?

4. To what extent does morality, so evident in the mid-to-late 19th-century social welfare programs, continue to influence program design in the 21st century?

5. The history of the American welfare state shows both a reluctance to create public programs and a resiliency to maintain a core or base of welfare programs. What do you think the American welfare state will look like in 2050? Will current programs, such as Social Security, SNAP, and EITC, still be available? Will welfare be reduced to a level that such programs will rely primarily on the private, nongovernmental sector?

Online Resources

Social Welfare History Group: www.historians.org/affiliates/social
_welfare_his_group.htm

Portrait of the USA, The Social Safety Net: http://usinfo.org/enus/
government/social/ch9.htm

Almanac of Policy Issues: www.policyalmanac.org/social_welfare/
index.shtml

U.S. Government Spending: www.usgovernmentspending.com/us
_welfare_spending_40.html

U.S. Government Printing Office, Green Book: www.gpo.gov/fdsys/
browse/committeecong.action?collection = CPRT&committee =
wmcommittee&chamber = house&congressplus = green/index&
ycord = 0

References

Appleby, J. (1992). *Liberalism and Republicanism in the historical imagination.* Cambridge, MA: Harvard University Press.

Axinn, J., & Levin, H. (1982). *Social welfare: A history of the American response to need.* New York, NY: Harper & Row.

Berkowitz, E., & McQuaid, K. (1980). *Creating the welfare state: The political economy of twentieth century reform.* New York, NY: Praeger.

Boyer, P. (1978). *Urban masses and moral order in America, 1820–1920.* Cambridge, MA: Harvard University Press.

Brody, D. (1980). *Workers in industrial America: Essays on the twentieth-century struggle.* New York, NY: Oxford University Press.

Davis, K. (2007). Lecture at the School of Social Work of the University of Southern California, Los Angeles, CA.

D'Emilio, J. (1983). *Sexual politics, sexual communities: The making of a homosexual minority in the United States, 1940–1970.* Chicago, IL: University of Chicago Press.

Dyer, T. (1980). Theodore Roosevelt and the idea of race. Baton Rouge, LA: Louisiana University Press.

Edsall, T. (1991). *Chain reaction: The impact of race, rights, and taxes on American politics.* New York, NY: Norton.

Friedman, L. (1982). *Gregarious saints: Self and community in American abolitionism.* Cambridge, UK: Cambridge University Press.

Gordon, L. (1994). *Pitied but not entitled.* New York, NY: Free Press.

Hacker, J. (2002). *The divided welfare state: The battle over public and private social benefits in the United States.* New York, NY: Cambridge University Press.

Halloran, P. (1989). *Boston's wayward children: 1830–1930.* London, England: Associated University Presses.

Harris, B. (1978). *Beyond her sphere: Women and the professions in America.* Westport, CT: Greenwood Press.

Hartz, L. (1955). *The liberal tradition in America.* New York, NY: Harcourt, Brace.

Jansson, B. (1988). *The reluctant welfare state: A history of American social welfare policies.* Belmont, CA: Wadsworth.

Jansson, B. (2001). *The sixteen-trillion-dollar mistake: How the U.S. bungled its national priorities from the New Deal to the present.* New York, NY: Columbia University Press.

Jansson, B. (2005). *The reluctant welfare state: American social welfare policies: Past, present, and future.* Belmont, CA: Brooks/Cole.

Jansson, B. (2011). *The reluctant welfare state: American social welfare: Engaging history to advance social work practice in contemporary society.* Belmont, CA: Brooks/Cole/Cengage Learning.

Kawachi, I., Daniels, N., & Robinson, D. (2005). Health disparities by race and class: Why both matter. *Health Affairs, 24*(2), 343–352.

Leff, M. (1984). *The limits of symbolic reform: The New Deal and taxation, 1933–1939.* Cambridge, UK: Cambridge University Press.

Leiby, J. (1978). *A history of social welfare and social work in the United States.* New York, NY: Columbia University Press.

McWilliams, C. (1968). *North from Mexico: The Spanish-speaking people of the United States.* New York, NY: Greenwood Press.

Mennel, R. (1973). *Thorns and thistles: Juvenile delinquents in the United States, 1825–1940.* Hanover, NH: University Press of New England.

Nash, G. (1976). Social change and the growth of pre-revolutionary urban radicalism. In A. Young (Ed.), *The American revolution: Explorations in the history of American radicalism* (pp. 11–30). De Kalb: Northern Illinois University Press.

Peterson, M. (1975). *Portable Thomas Jefferson.* New York, NY: Viking Press.

Pierson, P. (2000). The new politics of the welfare state. In R. Goodwin & D. Mitchell (Eds.), *Foundations of the welfare state* (pp. 421–465). Northampton, MA: Elgar.

Rohrbough, M. (1968). *The land office business: The settlement and administration of American public lands, 1789–1837.* New York, NY: Oxford University Press.

Sachs, J. (2005). *The end of poverty.* New York, NY: Penguin Books.

Sellers, C. (1991). *The market revolution: Jacksonian America, 1815–1846.* New York, NY: Oxford University Press.

Shalev, M. (1983). The social democratic model and beyond: Two generations of comparative research on the welfare state. *Comparative Social Research, 6,* 315–351.

Skocpol, T. (1995). *Social policy in the United States: Future possibilities in historical perspective.* Princeton, NJ: Princeton University Press.

Smith, R. (1993). *Patriarch: George Washington and the new American nation.* Boston, MA: Houghton Mifflin.

Snell, K. (1985). *Annals of the laboring poor: Social change and agrarian England, 1660–1900.* Cambridge, UK: Cambridge University Press.

Stiglitz, J. (2002). *Globalization and its discontents.* New York, NY: W. W. Norton.

Takaki, R. (1989). *Strangers from a different shore.* Boston, MA: Little, Brown.

Thelen, D. (1975). Not classes, but issues. In A. Mann (Ed.), *The Progressive Era: Major issues of interpretation.* Hindale, IL: Dryden Press.

Trattner, W. (1979). *From poor law to welfare state: A history of social welfare in America.* New York, NY: Free Press.

Tyrell, I. (1979). *Sobering up: From temperance to prohibition in antebellum America, 1800–1862.* Westport, CT: Greenwood Press.

U.S. Office of Management and Budget (2012). Historical Budget Tables. Washington, D.C.: U.S. Government Printing Office, p. 55.

Walch, T. (Ed.). (1993). *Immigrant America: European ethnicity in the United States.* New York, NY: Garland.

Weinstein, J. (1975). It's good for business. In A. Mann (Ed.), *The Progressive Era: Major issues of interpretation.* Hindale, IL: Dryden Press.

Witte, J. (1985). *The politics and development of the federal income tax.* Madison: University of Wisconsin.

Wood, G. (1992). *The radicalism of the American Revolution.* New York, NY: Alfred A. Knopf.

Chapter 3
Human Security and the Welfare of Societies

Jody Williams

Do you foresee a time when there will not be a need for armies and wars, but rather countries will embrace openness, fairness, and justice for all people? Will Human Security be the common belief that unites nations around the world? Or will nation-states' Homeland Security programs further drive a wedge between nations that results in mutual, ongoing tensions and hostilities and the possibilities of an all-out nuclear war?

Introduction

True peace cannot and will not ever be achieved without justice. No matter what peace treaty is signed, unless matters of social justice are completely reconciled, peace will never be reached. The 2011 so-called Arab Spring that erupted from the simmering frustrations of denied human rights, abuses, and atrocities changed governments and opened the door, even if only slightly, to human justice and equality. Western nations too felt the strains of protests that rallied against oppression and discrimination. Throughout 2011 and into 2012, the Occupy Movement led to protests throughout Europe, while in the United States, Occupy Wall Street is, in its own words, "fighting back against the corrosive power of major banks and multinational corporations over the democratic process, and the role of Wall Street in creating an economic collapse that has caused the greatest recession in generations" (source http://occupywallst.org/). As nations and people grapple with social justice, the idea of moving to a Human Security framework suggests that governments' concerns should be directed toward people. When people are treated justly throughout the world, so-called Homeland Security will not be necessary. The Arab Spring sent a clear message: People can be heard and want to reclaim their say in how their countries are governed. But even with the evidence of the Arab Spring and the Occupy Movements, will true change really occur and be lasting?

How do we define *security*? For at least four centuries, it has generally meant national security, with the focus on the security of the state. If a country is safe, it would naturally follow that the people who lived in it are also safe. In that construct, keeping the state secure requires military thinking and planning and armed forces and weapons systems to back that up. That, in turn, requires human and financial resources, sometimes on a massive scale, that cannot be used to ensure that competing needs of a society are met.

What if we were to look at security through a different lens? What if we were to think about it in terms of meeting the needs of the citizens of a country? A people-centered security instead of that of the nation-state. The world would look quite different, and how our resources were allocated would be very different. The focus would shift from national security to human security. Although there has been a lot of thinking about a human security framework over the past few decades, it is still a relatively obscure concept, but it deserves renewed emphasis in the 21st century.

Mahbub ul Haq, a late Pakistani economist, is credited with much important thinking behind the development of the concept of human security for the United Nations Development Program (UNDP). The use of the term is generally traced back to its 1994 Human Development Report, entitled *New Dimensions of Human Security*. In his own writing, Haq eloquently captured its essence when he wrote, "We need to fashion a new concept of human security that is reflected in the lives of our people, not the weapons of our country" (Haq, 2000).

As exemplified by the thinking of Haq and the UNDP, with the end of the Cold War—now more than three decades ago—different ideas of what constitutes security began to emerge. Many people hoped to see bold efforts to redefine global and national security in that new, unipolar world. With the diminished military threat after the collapse of the Soviet Union, there were expectations for reductions in standing armies and military budgets. Some even dared to believe that the number of nuclear weapons in silos, submarines, and airplanes around the world would be drawn down.

The dramatic fall of the Berlin Wall sparked guarded optimism in people around the world that perhaps war and militarization would no longer define the contours of our future. Such changes could even spur a dramatic decrease in the global arms race, and the resulting "peace dividend"—resources no longer spent on military budgets and weapons—could be used to resolve some of the intractable problems facing humankind. The welfare of individuals and societies—human security—could take precedence over the voracious appetites of militaries and defense budgets that have consumed precious resources for war—national security—since time immemorial. If such changes did occur, arguably the globe as a whole, and most of us in it, would be more secure.

At the same time, many who would also have preferred a world full of new and exciting possibilities did not expect to see that happen. Their more sober view recognized that crafting a new approach to a changed and changing world would require deliberate and concerted efforts by all sectors of society, including the military. Pessimists—some might call us realists of a different cloth—had little doubt that the sole remaining superpower would begin to seek new global enemies in part because real threats exist, but also in order to justify its continued militarism as the United States contemplated how to react to—and, more importantly, how to consolidate—its unique position as the military, economic, and technological behemoth in the immediate post–Cold War world.

Throughout the 1990s, the UNDP continued its work around creating a human security framework. Then-Secretary General of the U.N. Kofi Annan spoke out strongly in support of its core concepts of "freedom from want" and "freedom from fear." Significant impetus was breathed into the emerging human security paradigm with the wildly successful work of the International Campaign to Ban Landmines, which pushed small and medium-sized countries to come together and, independent of the lethargic negotiating process at the UN Convention in Geneva, create the 1997 Mine Ban Treaty.

Emboldened by the success of that process, Canada, Norway, and other countries that had led the charge on banning landmines formed in 1999 the Human Security Network. Having stood up to the intense pressure of the United States and other powerful countries to derail the landmine ban and succeeded, through the Network they planned to see what more they could accomplish together to bring tangible security to the lives of individuals around the world. They wanted to shift the emphasis of security from that of the nation-state to that of people.

The attacks of September 11, 2001, in New York and Washington, D.C., resulted in huge and negative impacts around the world. The post-9/11 world is very different from the one of earlier post–Cold War dreams and expectations. Instead of any so-called peace dividend, the concentration of resources on the military and intelligence agencies has skyrocketed—primarily, but not only, in the United States. Human security as an alternative to national security, barely standing up on weak legs anyway, was knocked to the mat.

The human and financial costs of the post-9/11 war on terror, including the full-scale invasions of Afghanistan and Iraq, are truly incalculable. Estimates of the expenditures for the debt-financed wars range from $1.29 trillion by the end of fiscal year 2011 by the Center for Defense Information to $3.2–4 trillion in a study released by Brown University in mid-2011 (Center for Defense Information, 2012; Brown University, 2011; Infoplease, 2012).

These mind-numbing figures, which will hobble the economy far into the future, coupled with the financial collapse beginning in 2007–2008, have had a huge impact on the social fabric of this country and around the globe. Now faced with the emergence of global economic powers such as China, India, and Brazil—nations requiring increased access to limited resources to fuel their growth—new tensions are arising, and the world is experiencing an ever-increasing divide between the global haves and have-nots; and the have-nots have not been silent in the face of the change.

The Occupy Wall Street movement has brought tens of thousands into the streets of New York City and other cities in protest of the rising economic disparities, and millions more have done the same in countries around the world. Millions poured into the streets across Europe from Spain to Greece. Economic issues, poverty, and other social ills and insecurities also helped fuel the uprisings of the Arab Spring.

No one can accurately predict how all of these variables will ultimately play out to shape the future of the country and the world. What is increasingly clear to many in the aftermath of 9/11 and the global economic collapse is that providing for the security of societies is much more complicated than simply thinking about the security of the nation-state. A fundamental question to be honestly confronted in this tremendously unstable world is how we as a global community will define what *security* means for the billions of us who live in our world today.

Will it continue to be defined in terms of national security, bigger weapons, and more militarization, or will it be understood through the lens of international law, human rights, and human security? Will democracy, justice, and human rights continue to be eroded around the world to protect us from terrorism and economic instability, or can we step back from the collective brink and make difficult and sober assessments of what framework will best ensure peace, socioeconomic justice, and security in an increasingly globalizing world?

The Need to Redefine Security for the 21st Century

Since the mid-1600s, power in the world has been defined almost exclusively through the military and economic might of individual, sovereign nation-states. The Peace of Westphalia, which ended the Thirty Years War in 1648, is taken to mark the beginning of the modern international system as a universe composed of sovereign states, each with exclusive authority within its own geographic boundaries (Krasner, 1995–1996, p. 115). In this Westphalian model, global stability—or "peace"—is maintained through a balance of power among these sovereign nations (O'Donnell). This framework continues to dominate thinking, reinforced by the extremely militarized response to 9/11, even as we are still coming to grips with the fact that in today's world, like it or not, many factors influence power among states and many of those factors are interconnected, transnational in character. Continuing to cling to the increasingly outmoded notion of security as defending the nation-state behind its borders is potentially dangerous and destabilizing in and of itself.

Before the 2007–2008 economic collapse, globalization brought to mind the seemingly effortless movement of capital and business around the world, with little apparent regard for sovereign borders. The proponents of this economic scenario have pushed it as a positive force that would inevitably lead to increasingly higher standards of living and the democratization of the planet. This, in turn, could only result in increased security.

Others questioned the relationship between democratization and corporate entities that, largely lacking in accountability, have little apparent regard for workers' rights, the environment, or their impact on the social fabric of any particular country. The 2008 collapse and its aftermath demonstrated the horrific impact on social welfare wreaked by corporate greed and irresponsibility. Some have argued that globalization itself brought down the global economy (Creamer, 2009).

Even with the economic uncertainties now, corporations and even some individuals continue to amass fortunes that can dwarf the budget of a nation—or even an entire region of the world. The rules of the game of the global marketplace, whatever those might be, are shifting, and the worldwide reach of business continues to call into question the very relationship between the nation-state and such corporate entities—even though for many of us, we think of these financial aspects when the term *globalization* comes to mind, and it is not confined to the economic sphere alone.

Other global linkages have also increased exponentially and will continue to do so far into the future. The mass movement of people, coupled with 24-hour access to information, has helped fuel a global marketplace of ideas and has begun to blur the lines between what traditionally have been seen as domestic or international issues. As people, ideas, and images move with lightning speed around the world, the challenges grow for individual states to try to predict and manage the outcomes of such interactions. What does that mean for Westphalian concepts of security?

Witness the protesters of the Arab Spring, who have used cell phones and the Internet for some of their organizing. Governments and militaries were caught flat-footed, and in many countries they lost power. Security threats can also have more serious global implications through this spread of knowledge and information.

Today it is much harder for a state to effectively isolate its population and focus their concerns on domestic issues while claiming sole purview over the international sphere. The domestic impact of foreign policy decisions has often become too glaring for citizens to ignore. The horrific example that immediately comes to mind is the September 11, 2001, terrorist attacks, which have roots in decades of U.S. foreign policy decisions toward the Middle East that were viewed as unfair by people in that region and that have fueled intense dislike and distrust of the United States.

People are faced not only with economic instability and growing disparities of wealth, and with war, terrorism, and armed violence around the world, but also with weapons proliferation, including weapons of mass destruction; global organized crime, including the trafficking of human beings, particularly women and children; perhaps irreversible destruction of our environment and the threats posed by global warming; widespread, pervasive poverty (this since time immemorial); and new and deadly diseases—to name but a few. Many factors influence both evolution of the problems themselves and also possible responses to them. In addition to global business, international and regional institutions as well as nongovernmental organizations (NGOs) and (transnational) civil society all have an impact in today's world.

This complex array of variables has made it increasingly difficult for countries to predict or confidently manage their place in the world. Old concepts of state-based security in our global political and economic environment no longer offer long-term answers to today's threats and challenges. Yet the resistance of governments to any open and meaningful analysis and discussion of what will bring us security—collectively and individually—is extremely strong and pervasive.

Such discussion is even more difficult to generate given that one of the most lucrative exports for U.S. companies are weapons, often justified as enhancing our own security. In 2010, the U.S. Department of Defense revealed to Congress its plans to sell approximately $103 billion worth of weapons outside of the United States. A Deutsche Bank analyst noted that this is a phenomenal increase over the $13 billion sold annually between 1995 and 2005 (Kimes, 2011). To counter pending cuts in the defense budget, given the economic situation and the massive U.S. budget deficit, U.S. weapons manufacturers are increasingly taking production outside of the country. The long-term implications of that strategy for global human security are frightening to contemplate.

Despite the resistance from many fronts, discussion about what kind of security people should seek must take place. Despite the knock that thinking about human security took after 9/11, with all of the dramatic changes taking place globally since the economic collapse, it is time for us to seriously approach a human security framework as the best answer for meeting the needs of individuals and the societies they live in.

Human Security: Its Fundamentals and Its Roots

As noted previously, during the 1990s, some bold new initiatives provided collective solutions to various problems of global scope and also affected security thinking. One of those initiatives was the movement to ban antipersonnel landmines. The landmine campaign is important not only because it led to an international treaty in 1997 that, for the first time in history, eliminated a long and almost universally used conventional weapon. It also provided a successful model of government–civil society–international institution partnership that offered a concrete example of how the global community could work together to resolve common problems.

Another such successful effort resulted in the creation of the International Criminal Court after 50 years of work to create an independent court to try war crimes and crimes against humanity. The Rome Statute, establishing the court, was adopted at a diplomatic conference that took place in Rome on July 17, 1998.

Partly inspired by these accomplishments, the nucleus of a movement beyond the UNDP began exploring ways to enhance global security not by increasing national security but by addressing human security needs as the fundamental linchpin upon which all security rests. Any number of governments, international institutions, and civil society alike began exploring the framework as a distinctive concept for addressing global insecurities.

One effort grew out of discussions between Canada and Norway, expressly resulting from their work in the landmine ban movement. The Human Security Network was founded by a group of like-minded countries at a ministerial meeting in Norway on May 20, 1999. It sought to apply a human security perspective to political processes aimed at the prevention or resolution of conflict as well as promoting peace and development. Ministers of the member countries continued to meet after the Norway meeting to maintain a "dialogue on questions pertaining to human security," but the response to 9/11 left the Network somewhat frayed. Canada, in particular, has done an about-face.

Lloyd Axworthy, the Canadian Foreign Minister of the Liberal Government of that period, had taken the lead on the government side in banning landmines. He also played a significant role in human security thinking within both the Canadian government and the Human Security Network. When the Liberals lost power in 2003, the new Conservative government began moving away from ideas and actions that had defined the Liberals. Finally, when Prime Minister Stephen Harper took power in February 2006, the Conservative government fully reverted to a much more state-centered concept of security with a correspondingly muscular foreign policy. By mid-2009, the government had gone so far as to systematically expunge the term *human security* from its governmental and diplomatic lexicon (Davis, 2009). The UN has most systematically carried forward the banner of human security.

Following on the earlier work of Haq and the UNDP, an independent Commission on Human Security was launched in 2000 at the UN Millennium Summit. The Summit focused on two key pillars of human security: freedom from want and freedom from fear. The Commission, an initiative of the Japanese government, began its work in January 2001.

During its two-year life, the Commission considered the human security agenda to formulate its report, entitled *Human Security Now: Protecting and Empowering People*, which it presented to the Secretary General on May 1, 2003. The Commission's press release of that date said,

> *The report proposes a new security framework that centers directly and specifically on people. Human security focuses on shielding people from critical and pervasive threats and empowering them to take charge of their lives. It demands creating genuine opportunities for people to live in safety and dignity and earn their livelihood. At a time when the consensus on the meaning of security is eroding, there is growing fear that existing institutions and policies are not able to cope with weakening multilateralism and global responsibilities. Nevertheless, the opportunities for working toward removing insecurities facing people are greater than ever.*

> *(Commission on Human Security Press Release, 2003)*

Thus, at the core, human security policies seek to enhance both individual and societal security by promoting freedom from want and freedom from fear. This concept was also underscored by observations of UN Secretary General Kofi Annan around that time that security, development, and human rights are interlinking elements of real security and that if all of those elements are not advanced simultaneously, ultimately none will prevail.

Subsequent to the Commission, and to follow up on its proposals, the UN created the Human Security Unit in May 2004, housed in the UN Office for the Coordination of Humanitarian Affairs (OCHA). The primary functions of the Unit are to mainstream human security concepts and action throughout UN activities as well as to administer the UN Trust Fund for Human Security (UNTFHS), established by Japan and the UN in March 1999 (United Nations Office for the Coordination of Humanitarian Affairs). Until its transfer to the Unit in OCHA, the Trust Fund for Human Security was managed through the Office of the UN Controller.

As described on the Trust Fund's webpage, the

> *objective of the UNTFHS is to finance activities carried out by UN organization(s) and/or designated non-UN organization(s), which translate the human security concept into practical actions, in particular those at the field level, to demonstrate its added-value in view of promoting and disseminating the concept.*
>
> (UN Trust Fund for Human Security)

It has supported projects ranging from enhancing food security in Cambodia to preventing the trafficking of women and children in Cambodia and Vietnam to rebuilding communities in post-conflict Liberia.

Although definitions of *human security* vary, in essence a human security framework recognizes that in a globalized world, many actors can have an impact on outcomes, so the means to address issues must be as broadly multilateral as possible. Dialogue, cross-cultural understanding, and conflict resolution enhance human security. Globalized relations, interaction, and communication enhance human security. The use of force is not scorned, under certain circumstances, but it is recognized as the absolute last resort, employed only if all other methods to resolve conflict have failed.

Part of the logic behind this thinking is that if the basic needs of the majority of the people of the world are met, providing them with a stake in and hope for their own future, the root causes of conflict are diminished. When a small minority has access to the majority of goods, services, and resources of the planet, those who have nothing have nothing to lose in giving up their lives on a suicide mission. Considering even a few of the commonly used statistics on poverty is numbing, and many of them are from the period ending just as much of the global economy was falling apart.

In 2008, the World Bank determined the international poverty line to be $1.25 per day (at 2005 purchasing power parity); previously it had been considered to be $1.00 per day. It estimated that 1.4 billion people were living below $1.25 per day and another 2.6 billion were living below $2 per day (Haub and Sharma, 2010).[1]

All the weapons in the world will not save us from angry and desperate people who are willing to fly airplanes into buildings to take the lives of thousands and sow the seeds of terror. The human security framework would help sow seeds of hope by providing for socioeconomic justice and more equitable distribution of the world's resources.

As even George W. Bush—the world's strongest champion of a muscular, national security–based approach in his war on terror—opined in a speech at the United Nations on September 14, 2005, we share a "moral duty" not only to fight terrorism, but also the poverty, oppression, and hopelessness that give rise to it (Baker, 2005).

"Real" Security and Attacks on the Human Security Framework

Mr. Bush's words were one thing; the actions taken by a state are what really matter. And the national security realists throughout U.S. administrations, and particularly during that of the Bush administration, have a very dim view of any meaningful debate about human security. It has been regularly painted as a wishy-washy concept conceived by "lesser powers" (read: irrelevant) who do not have the military might or the "spine" to deal with real security issues.

"Real" security is the purview of the individual, sovereign state based on nation-to-nation interaction. It then follows that if the nation is secure, by rights its people are secure. Human security is dismissed as utopian, unrealistic, and idealistic and therefore not worthy of real discussion.

The human security framework is also criticized as being too vague and a catch-all attempt to try to resolve all problems facing humanity rather than confine itself narrowly—therefore, effectively—to real security issues. Critics of human security also imply that those who do support the framework see it as an either/or situation—either you are for human security or you are for national security, but apparently they cannot coexist. And how could such a vague security framework possibly replace the centuries-old system of nation-states interacting through a delicate balance—or not—of a global chess match of power?

In this chess match, states with the most access to resources tend to dominate global politics and back that dominance with military might. Security, then, is the ability of the state to advance and maintain its interests, generally at a cost to other states. Because security is state to state, realists also argue that national security is generally far too complex for the average citizen to understand, let alone have a voice in. They would also

---

[1] This is measured in 1993 purchasing power parity (PPP), which the Bank defines as "a method of measuring the relative purchasing power of different countries' currencies over the same types of goods and services. Because goods and services may cost more in one country than in another, PPP allows us to make more accurate comparisons of standards of living across countries."

argue that even if some people had been able to delude themselves in the immediate period after the fall of the Berlin Wall that the world was changing, the 9/11 attacks and ensuing war on terror should have dispelled all those fuzzyheaded notions.

Others argue that human security rhetoric is not matched with "concrete policy that makes a difference to the safety of people whose security is threatened" (Hataley & Nossal, 2004). This argument seems to imply that the critical measure of a human security agenda is whether or not a state engages in humanitarian intervention to "ensure the safety of ordinary people in other places" (Hataley & Nossal, 2004). Humanitarian intervention is a hotly debated issue in and of itself and is not—and should not—be the sole or even primary measure of a human security approach to global security.

For some—particularly U.S. neo-conservatives—discussion of a human security framework is not just an attempt at an objective assessment of what would really make the world as a whole more secure. They argue that it must be seen for what it really is: an attack on American values.

As one article states:

> This is a dramatic and fundamental distortion of the right to be secure. The effort to "broaden our view of what is meant by peace and security" obscures and runs counter to the long-standing right of nation-states to secure their own territories and populations from external threats—a principle upon which international legal traditions and treaty organizations such as the U.N. are based. The human security agenda has the potential to undermine not only the nation-state model on which the U.N. was founded, but also the principles of sovereignty, accountability, and national security that the United States holds as fundamental.
>
> (Carafano & Smith, 2006)

The human security framework is not an attack on the "values" of any nation. It is an attempt to respond to security needs in the dramatically different world of the 21st century. However, it is not primarily concerned with the security of the nation-state in isolation from the security of people inside and outside the confines of national boundaries. Terrorism, crime, and war are all examples of violence that destabilize the security of people. But their security is also affected by deprivation—whether it is the result of poverty or unemployment or environmental pollution or disease or malnutrition or illiteracy or all of them combined.

If we stop for a moment to consider just the consequences of the economic collapse in the United States alone, what do we see? For many in this country, their security has been directly affected. More people have been plunged into poverty, including more than 2.8 million children whose family income is $2 or less per individual per day (National Poverty Center, 2012). Unemployment climbed and job security fell. Millions lost their homes, and schools across the country closed. Despite the United States spending $2.6 trillion on health care in 2010, which is more than the entire economy of England or France, Kaiser Health reported in September of that year that 50.7 million people, 16.7 percent, in the United States were uninsured (Cohen, 2012; Galewitz & Villegas, 2010). Millions of Americans are not free from want, nor could they be considered particularly secure.

Piecemeal and scattershot responses to individual problems and crises will not address the root causes of violence and conflict or enhance global security. Because the human security framework looks at the myriad of problems that affect security, effectively enhancing security means attempting to take an integrated approach to addressing the problems.

Those who advocate that a human security agenda enhances the security of us all generally do not necessarily see human security and national security as mutually exclusive. The two, instead, can be complementary parts of a whole. But to meaningfully carry out a human security agenda would require, for example, significant reallocation of the billions and billions of dollars spent around the world annually on war, on defense and preparations for war, and on the equipment of war.

All of the aspects as described in the previous section must be pursued coherently in order for such a human security agenda to make sense and to change lives. Security, development and empowerment, and human rights are mutually reinforcing; if all do not advance together, no one aspect will prevail ultimately.

To make human security really work requires a major shift of policies, institutions, and choices about global resource allocation to address the basic needs of people everywhere rather than providing for the security of the relative few who make those policies and control those resources. This obviously is a huge challenge in today's world.

Is There a Future for a Human Security Framework?

Even if one accepts human security as a viable approach to global security, why hasn't it had more traction? Considering the launch of the Human Security Network, it can convincingly be argued that the same governments that promoted and sang the praises of the landmine ban movement and the civil society–government partnership that is its hallmark wanted to limit the reach of such partnerships. Although not likely wanting to return to status quo ante, when governments did meet in Oslo, Norway, to discuss and launch the Network, NGO involvement even in the discussions about the concept was minimal at best.

The situation appears much the same in the work on human security at the UN. Neither the UN's Commission on Human Security nor the subsequent Advisory Board on Human Security have either NGO–civil society involvement or even informal mechanisms for ongoing dialogue with them regarding this people-centered framework. For example, the report of a February 2006 workshop on human security organized by the government of Mexico in cooperation with the government of Japan seems to underscore this disconnect.

In the section of the report entitled "Civil Society and Human Security," it states that the role of civil society in "making the concept of human security operative consists mainly in assuming the challenges of building human capacity through education and the promotion of renewed perceptions, as well as in pursuing new strategies to safeguard the security of people." The "strategies" put forward essentially refer to documenting abuses and promoting human rights and public security in the post-9/11 world (Report of the Workshop on Human Security).

Human rights are an area of intense work by civil society and NGOs, but it is not the only issue of the broad human security agenda that NGOs address. If, as the report of the workshop says, the "concept of human security is a response to the needs of civil society throughout the world," then surely civil society and NGOs have a much larger role to play than just in dealing with various aspects of human rights (Report of the Workshop on Human Security).

The Role of NGOs and Transnational Civil Society

Both NGOs and civil society in general have done little to connect the dots on human security and promote it. Even though the words *human security* appear more frequently, the concept does not yet really resonate for many NGOs, let alone for the general public. NGOs must actively promote the concept of human security as the appropriate framework for global security in a globalized world. People must be educated to understand that by advancing human security, the security of the globe is advanced.

To raise awareness and advocate for this change, NGOs must identify their individual work as part of a larger human security agenda when reaching out to the broader public. Everyone must understand that protecting and promoting human rights is work that enhances human security. Efforts to advance sustainable development enhance human security. Every time the flow of weapons of war is limited—or weapons are banned outright—human security is advanced. Involving women meaningfully in all aspects of conflict prevention and peace building and in decision making in general is enhancing human security. Addressing poverty through debt repudiation, fair trade, and better aid—coupled with promoting good governance and tackling corruption—is enhancing human security.

Yet too often, opportunities are lost to make those connections. Too often NGOs limit their own work and a broader-ranging effectiveness by choosing to not make those connections. Every time those issues are delinked, NGOs undercut collective efforts to promote a broader understanding and acceptance of a human security agenda as the framework to better prevent violent conflict. To effectively campaign and lobby, NGOs must find and use every opportunity to make the general public understand that our common security is increased by working together to meet the most basic needs of the majority of the planet—by working collectively to free women, men, and children from fear and want. By providing that majority with a stake in and hope for their own future, the root causes of conflict can be diminished. The opportunities to move away from reacting to violent conflict and toward its prevention are increased and, along with them, a sustainable peace can be developed.

Conclusion

All of the changes in the world since 9/11 require open and public discussion about how we as a global community define security. Will it continue to be defined in terms of bigger weapons and more militarization or will it be defined in terms of international law and human security? Will democracy, justice, and human rights continue to be eroded around the world to protect us from terrorism, or can we step back from the collective brink and make difficult and sober assessments of what framework will best ensure peace and justice and security in an increasingly globalizing world?

To really begin to move the world away from a national-security-only view of global security, governments, international institutions, and NGOs alike must work consistently and collectively to change the global mindset about what constitutes real global security and about what peace building really is, particularly in this post-9/11 world. But a fundamental element of effective campaigning and advocacy to change that mindset is setting the agenda. So far, it appears that neither governments nor NGOs have come anywhere close to setting an effective agenda to advance a clearly articulated human security framework and how it should be applied in today's world. Broad and deep and bold involvement by governments and NGOs and transnational civil society is also key to bringing about such change.

In his 2003 book, *War Is a Force That Gives Us Meaning*, Chris Hedges, a nonpacifist war correspondent for about 20 years, captures some of the difficulties inherent in changing the collective mindset about violent conflict—and therefore how best to counter it. He writes:

> The effectiveness of the myths peddled in war is powerful. We often come to doubt our own perceptions. We hide these doubts, like troubled believers, sure that no one else feels them. . . . The myths have determined not only how we should speak but how we should think. The doubts we carry, the scenes we see that do not conform to the myth are hazy, difficult to express, unsettling. . . . [W]e struggle uncomfortably with the jargon and clichés. But we have trouble expressing our discomfort because the collective shout has made it hard for us to give words to our thoughts. This self-doubt is aided by the monstrosity of war.

> (Hedges, 2003)

As Hedges notes, the myths peddled in war are powerful, but perhaps the myths peddled about war might be even more so. Moving beyond the collective shout that insists that if you want peace you must prepare for war is a huge challenge. Moving beyond the collective myth that creating a peaceful world is the fuzzy dream of human security idealists is a huge challenge. Governments and NGOs must work together to meet those challenges and raise our collective awareness about the rights and the responsibilities of civil society in working to move beyond reacting to violence and toward actively setting the agenda to prevent it.

Finally, thinking about violence must be demystified. People can no longer hide behind the dismissal of violence with the commonly heard explanation that it is simply human nature to be violent. Violence is a choice—whether it is the choice of a man to beat the woman he supposedly loves or the choice of one nation to invade another in the name of freedom or any other name, or the choice of terrorists of any stripe to attack civilian targets anywhere in the world to make their political point. Violence is a choice. The human security framework promotes the making of nonviolent choices to resolve conflicts. It is a viable alternative to militarism and violence and war that can actively move the world beyond the collective myth that building peace is a fuzzy dream of utopian idealists.

A world increasingly dominated by the few, who give the perception of not caring much for the needs of the many, can only become increasingly insecure as the desperate and disenfranchised try to equalize the playing field. There is something wrong in a world that spends close to a trillion dollars on weapons and defense while spending a few billion on education globally. There is something profoundly unjust in a global economic system where a handful of billionaires have more income than entire regions of the world.

Until the global community works together to address the common threats to human security posed by gross political, social, and economic inequalities, we will not live in a secure world. But hope for a more secure world is not enough. Neither governments nor NGOs can abdicate our individual and collective responsibilities to participate in developing new strategies and policies to ensure our collective security. No one government, no one institution, can possibly provide for the needs of us all. New coalitions must seek new solutions to seemingly intractable problems. Change will not happen overnight, but that can never be an excuse to not seek it.

Key Terms

justice	*global security*	*peace*
NGO	*human security*	

Review Questions for Critical Thinking

1. What are the differences between Human Security and Homeland Security? Will Human Security lead to Homeland Security, and will Homeland Security result in Human Security?

2. Social workers are employed throughout the world in NGOs. To what extent should NGOs be engaged with human security and social justice issues?

3. To what extent is the concept Human Security utopian, unrealistic, and idealistic? And if it is, should governments and international associations spend time discussing its implications?

4. How, if at all, is the Occupy Wall Street movement similar to the Arab Spring?

5. Is violence human nature, or is it a choice?

Online Resources

Embassy Magazine, Canada's Foreign Policy Newspaper: www.embassymag.ca/

United Nations: www.un.org/en/

Population Reference Bureau: www.prb.org

Globalization: http://globalization.icaap.org/

Eurozone: www.eurozine.com/

References

Baker, P. (September 15, 2005). Bush, at U.N., links anti-poverty agenda to war on terrorism, *Washington Post*, A8.

Brown University, 'Costs of war' project press release. (June 29, 2011). Estimated cost of post-9/11 wars: 225,000 lives, up to $4 trillion. Retrieved on March 20, 2012, from http://news.brown.edu/pressreleases/2011/06/warcosts

Carafano, J. J., & Smith, J. A. (September 1, 2006). The muddled notion of 'human security' at the U.N.: A guide for US policymakers, The Heritage Foundation, Backgrounder #1966. March 20, 2012, from www.heritage.org/Research/WorldwideFreedom/bg1966.cfm/

Center for Defense Information. (2012). Estimated war-related costs, Iraq and Afghanistan. Retrieved on March 20, 2012, from www.infoplease.com/ipa/A0933935.html

Cohen, Nicole. (March 19, 2012). One nation, two health care extremes, *NPR Health Blog*. Retrieved on March 20, 2012, from www.npr.org/blogs/health/2012/03/19/148920950/one-nation-two-health-care-extremes

Commission on Human Security Press Release. (May 1, 2003). Retrieved on March 16, 2012, from http://ochaonline.un.org/humansecurity/CHS/finalreport/pressrelease.html

Creamer, R. (January 8, 2009). How globalization set the stage for the 2008 economic collapse. Retrieved on March 3, 2012, from *The Huffington Post*, www.huffingtonpost.com/robert-creamer/how-globalization-set-the_b_156172.html

Davis, J. (July 1, 2009). Liberal-era diplomatic language killed off: Key phrases like "good governance" and "public diplomacy" are being discreetly purged from Canadian foreign policy. Retrieved on March 19, 2012, from *Embassy Magazine*, http://embassymag.ca/page/view/diplomatic_language-7-1-2009

Galewitz, P., & Villegas, A. (September 16, 2010). Uninsured rate soars, 50+ million Americans without coverage. Retrieved on March 20, 2012, from *Kaiser Health News*, www.kaiserhealthnews.org/Stories/2010/September/16/census-uninsured-rate-soars.aspx

Haq, M. (2000). Cited in K. Bajpal, *Human Security: Concept and Measurement*, School of International Studies, Jawaharlal Nehru University.

Hataley, T. S., & Nossal, K. R. (2004). The limits of the human security agenda: The case of Canada's response to the Timor crisis. *Global Change, Peace & Security*, *16*, 1.

Haub, C., & Sharma, O. P. (January 2010). What is poverty, really? The case of India. Retrieved on March 3, 2010, from The Population Reference Bureau, www.prb.org/Articles/2010/ indiapoverty.aspx

Hedges, C. (2003). *War is a force that gives us meaning*. New York, NY: Simon & Schuster.

Infoplease. Estimated war-related costs, Iraq and Afghanistan. Retrieved on March 20, 2012, from www.infoplease.com/ipa/A0933935.html

Kimes, M. (February 24, 2011). America's hottest export: Arms. Retrieved on March 3, 2012, from *CNNMoney*, money.cnn.com/2011/02/10/news/international/ america_exports_weapons_full.fortune/index.htm

Krasner, S. D. (Winter, 1995–1996). Compromising Wesphalia. *International Security*, *20* (3), 115–151.

National Poverty Center. (2012). Extreme poverty in the United States, 1996–2011, Policy Brief #28, February 2012., Retrieved March 20, 2011, from www.npc .umich.edu/publications/policy-briefs/brief28/policybrief28.pdf

O'Donnell, P. S., 2004. Sovereignty past and present. Retrieved on October 24, 2006 from http://globalization.icaap.org/content/v4.1/odonnell.html

Report of the Workshop on Human Security organized by the Government of Mexico, in cooperation with the Government of Japan, Mexico City, February 9–10, 2006. Retrieved on March 20, 2012, from http://ochaonline.un.org/webpage .asp?Site = hsu

United Nations Office for the Coordination of Humanitarian Affairs, Human Security webpage. Retrieved on March 20, 2012, from http://ochaonline.un.org/ webpage.asp?MenuID = 9671&Page = 1494

UN Trust Fund for Human Security webpage. Retrieved on March 20, 2012, from http://ochaonline.un.org/TrustFund/TheUnitedNationsTrustFundforHuman Security/tabid/2108/language/en-US/Default.aspx

Chapter 4
Social Policy From a Global Perspective

Robin Sakina Mama

Social workers speak to the right of self-determination, embracing difference and acceptance of others. As you read this chapter, consider if this is truly possible to uphold, or do we only subscribe to such positions of openness, acceptance, and tolerance when they benefit our status?

Introduction

The environmentalist slogan "Think globally, act locally" is becoming a central refrain in the social work community. Throughout most regions of the country, the demographic patterns are significantly shifting and creating growing, diverse communities. The inscription on the Statue of Liberty, "Give me your tired, your poor, Your huddled masses yearning to breathe free," provides hope and portends that a country with openness and acceptance based on justice and fairness awaits all people. Yet, we have seen that is not necessarily the case following the horrific terrorist attacks of 9/11. Now, more than any other time in American history, we must have a broad understanding of the many cultures, their norms, values, mores, and folkways, and how these are translated in public policy. The United Nations provides a forum for the world's nation-states to meet and grapple with global matters. The UN Declaration of Human Rights and many other similar declarations provide worldwide statements on how we treat others. But is this right? Who is to say that one country's beliefs or those of a group of nation-states are more correct than another's?

Social workers are challenged every day to consider the global and international aspects of their practice. Many social workers now work with immigrants, refugees, and survivors of torture and trauma from other parts of the globe. A client's residence status can help or hinder his or her treatment or access to service. Families are often dealing with adjustments to living in the United States, while their relatives are struggling in another country. Detention centers that house new asylees or refugees have become a permanent part of our urban landscape.

International social work is not a new idea or a new field of practice. Many social work professionals have been interested in understanding the international dimensions of social work practice since social work gained professional status (Findlay & McCormack, 2005). Social workers' involvement in international collaboration began after World War I, as evidenced by the establishment of several international organizations, such as the International Federation of Social Work and the International Association of Schools of Social Work (Healy, 2001). This involvement increased after World War II, as social workers became involved with rebuilding efforts after the War and with the United Nations. This involvement waxed and waned over the years, but it is now moving to the forefront as social workers realize that the idea that we work only within the boundaries of our own nation-states is no longer true. Influences beyond our borders are increasingly acknowledged as having a direct influence on local and national issues. The process underlying these changes is globalization (Findlay & McCormack, 2005).

Globalization

It is not possible to discuss global social policy without first discussing globalization. Globalization has a complex definition, which social scientists have been researching for several years (Guillén, 2001). Most agree that globalization is a process (or set of processes) (Hay, 2006) that encompass economic, political, and sociocultural (Guttal, 2007) dimensions. Other social scientists have defined globalization in a more detailed way so that it might be quantified empirically. For example, "'globalization is a process (or set of processes) that embodies a transformation in the spatial organisation of social relations and transactions, generating transcontinental or inter-regional flows and networks of activity, interaction and power'" (Held, as quoted in Hay, 2006, p. 3). The forces that drive globalization include human migration, international trade, foreign policy, and the integration of financial markets.

Economic Dimensions of Globalization

Economically, globalization has been characterized by trade liberalization, increased international competition, and investment, all driven by an increase in technological change. This increase and dependence on technology should not be easily dismissed. Developments in technology, both in computing and telecommunications, are changing the marketplace and the workforce. "Global E-commerce surged from 130.2 billion in 1999 to nearly 1.640 billion in 2003" (Technology: Industrial Structure and Jobs, www.globalization101.org, para 5). This surge in technology has created a knowledge economy, where access to information and the ability to use it create productivity and prosperity. Mobile phone usage, for example, has dramatically increased, with 302.9 million Americans subscribing to cell phone plans in 2010. In many developing countries, people use cell phones more than they use landline phones (www.globalization101.org).

The decline in the price to purchase a computer is a factor in spurring the growth of computers in the developing world.

Computer and technological access varies widely from country to country, however, with less-developed countries lagging severely behind. These gaps in access are called *digital divides*, and they are beginning to reinforce national and international gaps in living standards. Digital divides occur in almost every country. The United States has made some progress in closing its digital divides. From 1997 to 2005, U.S. adults with Internet access increased from 24 to 79 percent. Broadband usage in the United States has also increased, but rural households still lag behind urban and suburban households by 14 to 16 percent (Digital Divides and Privacy and Security Concerns, www.globalization101.org).

When these numbers are compared to international access to IT, the number of people in the world who have Internet access is much lower, and is very unequal around the world. One way to examine access is to look at how much Internet access costs within one's earned income. In many developing countries, the cost of Internet access is a much larger proportion of income than it is in developed countries. For example, in the United States, Internet access is less than 1 percent of average monthly income, whereas in Nepal monthly Internet charges account for 270 percent of average monthly income (Information Technology, www.globalization101.org).

The implications of this digital divide are significant, and a great deal of work at the United Nations has gone into narrowing this divide globally. The World Summit on the Information Society, held in Geneva in 2003 and Tunis in 2005, delineated several concrete steps toward closing the digital divide gap. First of these recommendations was on meeting basic needs, in terms of health care, clean water, food, sanitation, and the like. Access to information technology does little when one does not have food or clean water (Fors, 2003). A second important recommendation is for infrastructure and the need to be creative when developing IT infrastructure. Wireless technology is seen as one of the key ways to begin to provide access and infrastructure in developing countries (Fors, 2003; Sehrt, 2003).

Political Dimensions of Globalization

Politically, globalization has been characterized by American power and the influence of global institutions, such as the International Monetary Fund (IMF). Many consider that the recent rise in the influence of globalization has been brought about by the creation of new international organizations, such as the World Bank (WB), the International Monetary Fund (IMF), and the World Trade Organization (WTO) (Mama, 2004). These organizations seem to have had a homogenizing effect on the social and welfare policies of many countries, and have created a "'globalization of approaches', whereby a particular social, economic or political approach, judged beneficial by one of the cross-national organizations, is seen as appropriate for many countries regardless of cultural differences" (Findlay & McCormack, 2005, p. 233). The processes that these international organizations require countries to follow in order to qualify for aid are seen as undermining the capacity of countries to act autonomously, although there may be some facilitation of democratic procedures (Walby, 2000). Politically, globalization is not a uniform process; resources are often pitted against each other in order to satisfy international markets. For example, there can be calls for the state's protection of human rights at the same time that the country's welfare state erodes (Walby, 2000).

Cultural Dimensions of Globalization

Culturally, globalization has been seen as resulting in dissemination of global ideas and values (McClelland & St. John, 2006). Some authors have suggested that the globalization of cultures and values has tended toward homogeneity, with a process of McDonaldization of society occurring, along with the processes of

> *Ikea-isation, CNN-isation, Nike-isation and Survivor-isation. The same brand of clothing, the same home furniture, the same culinary taste, the same movies and shows, and the same news, debates and images of reality are found all across the globe.... In a short space of time we are now being nourished and nurtured by the same sources of mediating symbols.*
>
> *(Ahmadi, 2003, p. 16)*

Ahmadi further suggests that this globalization of consciousness has the consequence of the globalization of social problems, with an intensification of individualism as its direct component (2003). The emphasis on individualism is a frightening aspect of globalization to those cultures that traditionally have focused on community and clan.

Cultural diversity and its role in globalization, especially of market products, is coming under scrutiny. How are cultural products different from other goods and services? The definitions of *culture* have evolved over time, initially being referred to only as "arts and literature" (Chan-Tibergian, 2006). After the World Conference on Cultural Policies in Mexico City in 1982, culture was "regarded as the set of distinctive spiritual, material, intellectual and emotional features of a society or social group, and . . . encompasses, in addition to art and literature, lifestyles, ways of living together, value systems, traditions and beliefs" (UNESCO, 2002, p. 18). These are significant changes, as the Permanent Form on Indigenous Peoples takes these meanings to new levels in their fight for patents for cultural products or indigenous products.

Globalization as Process

Globalization is not a new phenomenon. Several processes of globalization have been operating simultaneously for many years—the globalization of economics, politics, knowledge, and culture (Ahmadi, 2003). This phenomenon, however, has challenged traditional social, political, and economic structures. Globalization has been brought about by cost reduction in transportation and communication, in addition to the dissolution of artificial barriers to trade, services, capital, and knowledge across borders (Mama, 2004). Advancements in applied sciences, technology, and communications are also factors that have made globalization possible. (Guttal, 2007).

Many people would argue the benefits of globalization: open markets, positive competition, increased use of technology, and the potential to enrich many people, especially the poor. Globalization has reduced the sense of isolation felt by many in the developing world (but only those with the access to technology). The expansion and increased use of technology has provided access to knowledge and information that before was limited to only the wealthiest countries. Globalization has also increased the amount of interaction among people of varied cultures. People from all over the world meet together to a much greater extent than they had in the past, and consequently begin to influence and understand each other. This global culture has led to the creation of new identities and new forms of literature, music, and art. There is now a very large global market for these "creative industries," which figure to be around US $800 billion per year (Chan-Tibergian, 2006, p. 92).

There are just as many critics of globalization, however, as there are proponents. Globalization has not succeeded in reducing poverty as was promised; in fact, the gap between the haves and the have-nots in developing countries is widening. The Center for Economic and Policy Research published in 2003 a score card on globalization from 1980 to 2000. Several facts from this comparison with the time period 1960 to 1980 are disturbing:

1. Life expectancy was reduced for four out of the five groups of countries examined, which cannot be explained by the AIDS pandemic.
2. Reduction of infant mortality was slower.
3. Progress in education slowed. (Weisbrot, Baker, Kraev, & Chen, 2003)

Globalization has also not provided for stability in undeveloped countries. Latin America and Asia are two good examples of how financial crises affect the entire global economy. In addition, globalization has had ill effects on the environment, with many poor countries using precious environmental resources in the name of development. The sustainable development movement is an attempt to preserve the environment while still providing for development opportunities (Mama, 2004).

Globalization as It Relates to Policy

One often-used example of how globalization relates to social policy is to examine the welfare state (Adelantado & Calderón, 2006; Brady, Beckgield, & Seeleib-Kaiser, 2005; Genschel, 2004; Wilson, 2006). David Brady and his colleagues suggest that four theories of the relationship between globalization and the welfare state have emerged:

1. Globalization may cause an expansion of the welfare state.
2. Globalization may generate a crisis and retrenchment of the welfare state.
3. Globalization may have curvilinear effects and contribute to welfare state convergence.
4. Globalization may not affect the welfare state. (Brady et al., 2005, p. 922)

Taking each point separately, in the first theory, globalization causes an expansion of the welfare state because globalization triggers political dynamics that result in generous welfare programs and corporatist labor market institutions. Some studies that support this theory have shown that trade openness significantly increases social welfare expenditures. This supposedly comes about because social welfare expenditures must increase with trade openness (Brady et al., 2005).

In the second theory, a crisis and retrenchment of the welfare state occurs as states undergo neoliberal restructuring to foster flexibility and competitiveness. The welfare state is reduced because of a need to be internationally competitive with a flexible labor force and austere fiscal policy (Brady et al., 2005). For example, the United States, Great Britain, New Zealand, Canada, and Australia have all adopted neoliberal approaches to social policy, which have had a direct effect on welfare spending. The neoliberal approach usually follows certain characteristics: tightened conditions of eligibility, extension of means testing, transferring financial responsibility to individuals, families, or employers, and a move away from simple provision of benefits for the unemployed (Findlay & McCormack, 2005, p. 233). In this case, globalization forces reductions in the welfare state because of the need for a flexible labor force to remain internationally competitive (Brady et al., 2005).

The third theory, globalization as convergence, contends that "globalization originally triggers an expansion of the welfare state with economic development. But at higher levels, globalization causes contractions in mature, generous, already developed welfare states" (Brady et al., 2005, p. 924). The curvilinear effects suggest that globalization forces a mean level of welfare effort by both high and low spenders.

Finally, some scholars believe that globalization has an insignificant effect, if any, on the welfare state. According to Brady, these skeptics can also be classified into four categories: those who believe (1) that globalization has a contingent effect in certain circumstances, (2) that welfare states reflect the "status quo" in affluent democracies, (3) that "politics as usual" will drive the welfare state, and (4) that deindustrialization drives welfare state expansion, not globalization (Brady et al., 2005).

Philipp Genschel (2004) offers one additional theory on globalization and policy: that globalization is a consequence of the problems with the welfare state, but then can also be part of the welfare state's solution. This revisionist theory holds that the problems of the welfare state are self-inflicted, mostly a result of high taxes and deductions, which drain the economy. The pace of economic growth is slowed. The interesting question in this argument is "How does globalization help save the welfare state?" Genschel (2004) suggests that revisionists believe that the intensity of the feeling of crisis that comes from globalization will help sustain the welfare state. Globalization forces policy makers to reevaluate and then change policy. Revisionists also believe that as market integration deepens with globalization, countries will specialize in sectors in which they are competitive so that economic structures diverge across countries and become more homogenous within countries.

The other question that arises is to consider whether there is global social policy. Deacon (2005) argues that global social policy comprises global social transfer (funds for various diseases, drug pricing, etc.), global social regulation (labor standards, food quality regulation, etc.), and global social rights (the UN agenda and its advancement, for example). Global governance has a great deal of competition from several agencies, all seeking to imprint their vision of global policy. The result is often a fragmented approach to global policy (Deacon, 2005).

These theories and arguments indicate that significant concern exists as to how the forces of globalization affect social policy. These concerns raise another important issue concerning globalization and social policy—the ethics of globalization.

Globalization and Ethics

The ethics of globalization ultimately centers around two questions: Who is globalization good for? Who is it bad for? For those whose interests lie in the health and environmental movement, ethical principles such as autonomy, beneficence, nonmalfeasance, justice, utility, and stewardship are important to the discussion. For others, global ethics must support social equity and cultural diversity, as well as developing common global goals.

Global ethics are difficult to discuss without giving some thought to the role of morality. But this further complicates the discussion, because one has to ask "which morality?". Is it the morality of the Western democratic societies? Many people are looking to the religious communities of the world to provide some answer to this question. In a publication entitled "Our Creative Diversity," published by the World Commission on Culture and Development, the UN, and UNESCO, the Commission lists several elements of a global civic culture that could provide the framework for a global ethical code, including human rights and responsibilities, the peaceful resolution of conflicts, democracy and civic governance, the protection of minorities, fairness of negotiation, and intergenerational equity (Pérez de Cuéllar, 1997).

Many are now calling for global ethics that emerge from a process of discussion and debate from global grassroots movements. These organizations proved to be quite powerful when they worked together to protest the WTO meetings in Seattle, Washington, and the campaign against the WB and the IMF. Their ability to join together across continents allowed for an understanding of shared values and objectives. The production of common statements of protest and organized actions begins to set the stage for discussion on global ethics. The question now is who will facilitate this process and take responsibility for the ensuing debate (Mama, 2004).

Globalization, Policy, and Social Work Practice

Social workers see the concerns of globalization played out in their professional work. Exploitation of a low-wage-accepting workforce in one country affects the employment policies and labor market of another country. Sex tourism and exploitation of women and children in some parts of the world become a legal and public health concern in other places. Immigration, whether legal or illegal, has consequences for health and welfare systems, school systems, and legal systems, as they attempt to help or hinder these immigrants from residing in any one permanent place.

The first challenge for social work is to continue to raise the consciousness of the profession to these global linkages with social policy. Irving, Yeates, & Young (2005) propose beginning this consciousness-raising by developing curriculum that integrates a global perspective into social policy courses. They suggest that a global perspective on social policy promotes understanding of:

- Attempts to formulate new forms of collective action to address social needs
- Institutions and political processes that lie outside the control of a single government
- Health and welfare arrangements and policy issues in countries at different levels of socio-economic development
- The external social policies of governments as implemented bilaterally, plurilaterally, or multilaterally
- The social welfare dimensions and implications of foreign policy in relation to trade, aid, finance, and economic development (Irving et al., 2005, p. 478)

Policy courses that integrate global perspectives encourage students to learn to better identify the actions and policies of their own country vis-à-vis the consequences of these choices in other parts of the world.

Social workers need to be engaged at all levels of government in thinking about solutions and approaches to social problems that are different from past ideas. New welfare policies and new social work practices need to be created, especially those that aim to integrate the world's cultures in a productive and culturally sensitive way.

Globalization, even though it has the ability to exploit, can create opportunities for social justice:

> *International social work can, via its extensive contacts and cooperation on core issues of social policy and social work, and by providing examples of alternative forms for organizing social welfare and for a fairer distribution of income among different groups, and furthermore, by disseminating the belief in the international conventions on human rights and the rights of specific groups, enhance the idea of democracy and human rights.*

> *(Ahmadi, 2003, p. 18)*

Social work is also well prepared to work on policy that leads to solidarity and peace building among nations, which will have a direct impact on global social policy. The profession has the ability to take on global issues of poverty, women's rights, children's rights, and indigenous peoples' rights, and can contribute to a global effort toward human values and ethics.

Key Terms

global ethics   *globalization*   *social work*
social policy   *economics*

Review Questions for Critical Thinking

1. How does an understanding of global issues and interconnectedness impact the daily work of a social worker in the United States?

2. How has technology influenced globalization?

3. How do you see technology impacting the social work profession's role in an ever-increasing globalized world?

4. Should there be global policies that apply to all people and all nations in the world?

5. For whom and in what countries is globalization good and bad?

Online Resources

Globalization101: www.globalization101.org/

Global Agenda on Social Work and Social Development: www.globalsocialagenda.org/

International Social Work Associations

International Association of Schools of Social Work: www.iassw-aiets
.org

International Federation of Social Workers: http://ifsw.org/

International Council on Social Welfare: www.icsw.org

References

Adelantado, J., & Calderón, E. (2006). Globalization and the welfare state: The same strategies for similar problems? *Journal of European Social Policy, 16* (4), 374–386.

Ahmadi, N. (2003). Globalisation of consciousness and new challenges for international social work. *International Journal of Social Welfare, 12,* 14–23.

Brady, D., Beckgield, J., & Seeleib-Kaiser, M. (2005). Economic globalization and the welfare state in affluent democracies, 1975–2001. *American Sociological Review, 70* (6), 921–948.

Chan-Tibergian, J. (2006). Cultural diversity as resistance to neoliberal globalization: The emergence of a global movement and convention. *Review of Education, 52,* 89–105.

Deacon, B. (2005). The governance and politics of global social policy. *Social Policy & Society, 4* (4), 437–445.

Digital Divides and Privacy and Security Concerns. Retrieved on February 11, 2007, from www.gloablization101.org/index

Findlay, M., & McCormack, J. (2005). Globalisation and social work: A snapshot of Australian practitioners' views. *Australian Social Work, 58* (3), 231–243.

Fors, M. (2003). What the United Nations can do to close the digital divide. Retrieved on February 13, 2007, from the UN Chronicle Online Edition, http://www.un.org/wcm/content/site/chronicle/

Genschel, P. (2004). Globalization and the welfare state: A retrospective. *Journal of European Public Policy, 11* (4), 613–636.

Guillén, M. F. (2001). Is globalization civilizing, destructive, or feeble? A critique of five key debates in the social science literature. *Annual Review of Sociology, 27,* 235–260.

Guttal, S. (2007). Globalization. *Development in Practice, 17* (4–5), 523–531.

Hay, C. (2006). What's globalization got to do with it? Economic interdependence and the future of European welfare states. *Government and Opposition, 41* (1), 1–22.

Healy, L. M. (2001). *International social work: Professional action in an interdependent world*. Oxford, UK: Oxford University Press.

Information Technology. Retrieved on March 13, 2011, from www.globalization101 .org/category/issues-in-depth/technology

Irving, Z., Yeates, N., & Young, P. (2005). What can global perspectives contribute to curriculum development in social policy? *Social Policy & Society, 4* (4), 475–484.

Mama, R. (2004). *Ethics of globalization* (rev. ed.). Pasadena, CA: Salem Press.

McClelland, A., & St. John, S. (2006). Social policy responses to globalization in Australia and New Zealand, 1980–2005. *Australian Journal of Political Science, 41* (2), 177–191.

Pérez de Cuéllar, J. (1997). *Our creative diversity: Report to the World Commission on Culture and Diversity*. Paris, France: UNESCO.

Sehrt, M. (2003). E-learning in the developing countries: Digital divide into digital opportunities. Retrieved on Feburary 13, 2007, from the UN Chronicle Online Edition, www.un.org/Pubs/chronicle/2003/issue4/0403p31.asp

Technology: Industrial structure and jobs. Retrieved on February 11, 2007, from www.globalization101.org

UNESCO. (2002). *Universal declaration on cultural diversity, Cultural Diversity Series No. 1*. Document for the World Summit on Sustainable Development in Johannesburg. Paris, France: UNESCO.

Walby, S. (2000). Gender, globalization, and democracy. *Gender and Development, 8*(1), 20–28.

Weisbrot, M., Baker, D., Kraev, E., & Chen, C. (2003). *The scorecard on globalization 1980–2000: Twenty years of diminished progress*. Washington, DC: Center for Economic and Policy Research.

Wilson, G. (2006). Local culture, globalization and policy outcomes: An example from long-term care. *Global Social Policy, 6*(3), 288–303.

Chapter 5
Social Justice for Marginalized and Disadvantaged Groups: Issues and Challenges for Social Policies in Asia

Joseph Kwok

> Does a government do its citizens any good by creating short-term, low-paying work, knowing that the program's future sustainability is minimal at best? Would it be better to redirect public and private resources to other programs that have a broader and much more lasting impact (e.g., public education)? In other words, can a government do everything for all people, even if it is able to receive assistance form the private sector?

Introduction

There are only two givens in life—death and taxes. We might add a third notion: No single model of social justice cuts across all cultures in the north, south, east, and west. Some pieces may thread their way around the world, but clearly the idea of a universal approach is nonexistent. Many countries have an overwhelming desire to provide marginalized population groups with additional supports so they can contribute to the larger society and move to a level of self-dependence and independence. This paper explores how pathways and opportunities for persons with disabilities are created in order that they can develop a sense of self while contributing to the greater good. To do so, however, requires strong commitments to social and economic change that are realized through very different social policies. The resulting programs engage both the private and public sectors to create these new opportunities. As is seen, however, the fragility of such models is a result of an erratic and weak economic structure to purchase goods while governments are not able to sustain or grow the infusion of fiscal supports into new businesses. Thus, the issue of sustainability raises its head: Should a program be supported if it is not able to sustain itself after a period of time? Such a question takes on even more significance during periods of severe economic difficulties, such as the current global recession.

The world has become wealthier over the past decades, as evidenced by more people owning more cars and electronic appliances and living in highrise buildings, particularly in urban areas, in both developed and developing economies. However, the wealth continues to be spread unevenly. The World Bank reports that 1.4 billion people worldwide live on less than $1.25 per day, down from 1.9 billion persons in 1981 (World Bank, 2008). Even with this decline, in some parts of the world, the number of people living in extreme poverty is increasing (UNDP, 2003).

In recent years, the global community seems to be reshaping itself in political, economic, and social terms. No matter where one lives, change has been and remains inevitable. There have been unimaginable large-scale disasters, both human-made and natural, affecting millions of people, including tsunamis, earthquakes, oil spills, and nuclear disasters. Add to these the constant threats of terrorism and actual bombings that have killed unsuspecting citizens; the growing unrests with governments evidenced by the Arab Spring; and the global Occupy Movements cross many geographic borders around the world as well.

Such developments create situations where one country's problem can easily become one for its neighbors, if not for the region and the world. Many of the issues today, as evidenced by the fragile Euro economy, show that local challenges require international solutions.

Asia is one of the fastest-developing regions in the world. Asia is particularly active in supporting disability-concerned policies and measures. It is the first region that promoted, through intergovernmental platforms hosted by the United Nations Economic and Social Commission (UNESCO), a comprehensive policy mandate, the Asian and Pacific Decade of Disabled Persons 1993–2002, and subsequently extended this to the Biwako Millennium Framework 2003–2012.

Given the developments in Asia, social policy and social justice are better studied with a broad, multisectorial perspective, both global and local, as well as treated as evolving concepts. They will also be studied with an inclusive and rights-based approach, as promoted by the United Nations and its special systems. Disability-concerned measures at national and regional levels will be used to illustrate how issues and challenges are being tackled by different policies in Asia.

Social policy and social justice often appear as twin concepts, although these two concepts are often interpreted and applied differently in various situations and countries, each with their own unique, diverse culture. Social policy and social justice practice results in varying interpretations and sometimes even opposing views, depending on the position of those affected, whether on the giving end or the receiving end of the policy. For example, a common and recurring question faced by many nations is "How much is too much and how much is too little in the means-tested cash benefit provided to people in need?" This question becomes more pragmatic and politicized when a government is facing economic hardship, such as the global recession of 2008, in finding new resources to meet its commitments and obligations.

This chapter explores the two concepts of social policy and social justice, drawing references from ancient Asian philosophy and modern rights-based approaches. Furthermore, the chapter examines selected Asian experiences in formulating social policy frameworks that guide regional and local actions commonly faced by human services professionals.

Social Justice: An Asian Perspective

Social justice is a relatively modern concept. One school refers social justice to *distributive justice*, which is defined by Roemer as "how a society or group should allocate its scarce resources or product among individuals with competing needs or claims" (1996, p. 1). The United Nations (2006) approaches social justice from a human rights perspective and provides pivotal mandates for practices in the international and national levels, as evidenced by the United Nations Declaration of Human Rights and other such conventions.

Simply stated, social justice is about human well-being and is found throughout world history. For example, in Chinese civilization, debates about social policy and social justice are found in the classical teachings of the ancient philosophers whose works are still included in Chinese schools and classes today. Mencius (372–289 BCE) was the outstanding Confucian sage of the Warring States period in China (475–221 BCE) who developed Confucius's doctrines on benevolence as applied to governance of an empire. Mencius's most famous and often-quoted teaching to a ruling king was

> Do reverence to the elders in your own family and extend it to those in other families; show loving care to the young in your own family and extend it to those in other families—do this and you would find it as easy to rule the world as to roll something on the palm of your hand.

> (Mencius, 1999, p. 19)

This ancient teaching from more than two millennia ago illustrates that social policies should educate the powerful and the rich while shaping the relationship between the governing and the governed. It is also about changing people's attitude and behavior and about sharing of resources. Mencius also asked, "Why should Your Majesty have mentioned the word 'profit'? What counts is benevolence and righteousness.... If those above and those below snatch profit one from the other, the state will be endangered" (Mencius, 1999, p. 3). Mencius was clear that social justice concerns more than material benefits and extends to the complex relationship among different sectors of a society.

Some connections may be found between the doctrine of benevolence of Confucius and Mencius with the modern-day rights-based approaches promoted by the United Nations for humankind and people with special needs.

The application of justice to humankind is grounded solidly in the United Nations' 1948 Universal Declaration of Human Rights Charter, which promulgated that human rights are based on respect for the dignity and worth of all human beings and seek to ensure freedom from fear and want. The Universal Declaration is further elaborated by several important international conventions, in particular the eight core UN international rights treaties,[1] including the *International Covenant on Civil and Political Rights* (ICCPR); *International Covenant on Economic, Social and Cultural Rights* (ICESCR); *International Convention on the Elimination of All Forms of Racial Discrimination* (CERD); *Convention on the Elimination of All Forms of Discrimination Against Women* (CEDAW); *Convention against Torture and Other Cruel, Inhuman or Degrading Treatment or Punishment* (CAT); *Convention on the Rights of the Child* (CRC); *International Convention on the Protection of the Rights of All Migrant Workers and Members of Their Families* (MWC); and *International Convention on the Rights of Persons with Disabilities*.

Although all human rights promulgated by the UN are equally valid and important, the obligations placed on stakeholders, in particular member states of the UN, have different requirements. Some obligations are immediate, whereas others are progressive in kind.[2] Immediate state obligations in protecting human rights are sanctioned by domestic and international law courts. Progressive state obligations are realized through social policies that either facilitate other stakeholders and/or directly meet those obligations. These are the domains where social justice shares a great deal of commonalities with those human rights permitting progressive obligations from governments and other stakeholders. This also requires a close interface between social policy and social justice through a human rights–based framework.

Social Justice and Social Harmony

Fulfilling obligations to protect human rights is one of many goals in achieving social justice. All governments are challenged by conflicting demands and interests from different sectors of a society. Providing social justice to one sector does not necessarily benefit other sectors in a society. Therefore, seeking social justice must include goals that are prosperous,

---

[1] See United Nations Treaties Database, Retrieved on October 22, 2006, from http://untreaty .un.org/English/access.asp

[2] See UN Committee on Economic, Social and Cultural Rights. (2006). General comment no. 3. Retrieved on October 22, 2006, from www.ohchr.org/English/bodies/cescr/comments .htm

harmonious, and inclusive for all people, not just one group of a population. China again offers some interesting examples.

One of the guiding principles for China's 11th Five Year Plan (2006–2011)[3] is to strengthen the construction of a harmonious society, which is people based; a group's felt needs and practical problems are resolved and emphasize coordinated economic and social development that (1) creates employment opportunities; (2) encourages the development of social services that promote the whole person; and (3) strengthen the emphasis on social equality, which allows all people to enjoy the fruits of reformed development. Social equity is essentially China's official way of saying social justice is the distribution of economic and social advancement for all people.

Worth noting are five of the 11th Five Year Plan's targets: (a) coverage of rural cooperative medical scheme from 23.5 percent to more than 80 percent; (b) old age insurance coverage in towns and cities from 174 million to 223 million; (c) new employment opportunities that add 4.5 million jobs every year; (d) increase the mean disposable income of urban people from RMB10,493 to RMB13.390; and (e) increase the mean income of rural people from RMB3,255 to RMB4,110. According to The Plan, the first two targets are mandatory, while the remaining three are indicative targets.

Hong Kong, a city known for blending the cultures of the West and East, illustrates the application of social justice in its criminal justice system, particularly with the police department. The Chief Executive of the Government of Hong Kong Special Administrative Region gave social justice a special heading in his 2005 annual policy address. Tsang (2005) writes that upholding social justice is a foundation of a harmonious society, in addition to the rule of law upheld by an independent judiciary, the free flow of information, a clean government, and a level playing field for business. Tsang included anti-discrimination legislative measures (e.g., Sex Discrimination Ordinance and Disability Discrimination Ordinance), the promotion of cultural diversity, equity in governance and a collaboration with nongovernmental organizations (NGOs) to secure equal opportunities for all in society, preemployment measures including workplace attachment training allowance to encourage and equip young people to find work, and capacity-building programs to support women.

Mainland China's conception of social equity or social justice focuses on the distribution of economic and social advancement for all people, whereas Hong Kong's version promotes anti-discrimination legislative measures, equity in governance, and equal opportunities for all people. Such differences should not be surprising given the unique history and relationship of and between Hong Kong and Mainland China. This does open up

---

[3] See The Central People's Government of People's Republic of China. (March 16, 2006). The National Economic and Social Development 11th Five Year Plan (2006–2011). Retrieved on October 8, 2006, http://big5.gov.cn/gate/big5/www.gov.cn/ztzl/2006-03/16/content_228841 _2.htm

the more complex question of how social policies could be developed to make a society conducive to social justice for all.

Social Policy

Policy may be viewed in a narrow or broad framework. A narrow perspective is restrictive and suggests that programs and services are targeted to a specific group of people, generally those in need. Famed British theorist Richard Titmuss (1974) employed a narrow approach to the assessment of policy. Titmuss (1976, p. 20) asserted that,

> *We are concerned with the study of a range of social needs and the functioning, in conditions of scarcity, of human organization, traditionally called social services or social welfare systems, to meet those needs. This complex area of social life lies outside or on the fringes of the so-called free market, the mechanisms of price and tests of profitability.*

Since the 1980s, a broader, more inclusive view of social policy gained prominence in the global community. The World Summit for Social Development 1995 (United Nations, 1995), for example, proposed a wide-ranging, multisectorial, interdisciplinary approach to achieving the Summit's actionable development goals. The 1995 World Summit stressed that policies and programs designed to achieve poverty eradication should include specific measures to foster social integration, including by providing marginalized socioeconomic sectors and groups with equal access to opportunities.

Social policies dealing with social justice are not primarily about tangible services and redistribution of resources. They are also concerned with educating those in power, the powerless, the haves, and the have-nots. A well-argued and justified social policy may be poorly received and ineffective if concerned stakeholders do not own the policy, do not wish to follow its spirit and direction, and do not wish to contribute to its implementation, but rather try all means to get maximum profits from the policy and from not contributing to the goals of the policy.

The purpose of a social policy addresses a variety of situations, such as the following:

- Improving quality-of-life situations
- Eliminating social inequalities through the redistribution of resources
- Strengthening measures that result in the equal treatment of individuals
- Providing resources to those who cannot help themselves to meet their needs

- Creating opportunities for persons and groups to become self-sufficient

Social policy may embrace and spell out short- and/or long-term targets. Short-term targets often deal with critical situations that should require immediate remedial action, such as massive unemployment of out-of-school youth. Conversely, long-term targets are often concerned with coordinated and sustainable developments of a nation.

Actors of social policy may be governmental organizations, statutory organizations that have a governmental role in enforcing concerned legislation, such as anti-discrimination legislation and in delivering public services, NGOs, and the private sector. These actors may act on their own or as collaborators.

The target systems of a social policy may be referred to as social welfare in a narrow approach or to include a wide array of social systems, such as health, education, housing, transport, information communication, and so on. For target beneficiaries, social policy may target the wider society or a minority sector with special needs. For procedures and measures, social policy may be governmental action agenda concerning fiscal policies, affirmative policies, legislative measures, and regulations.

In most societies, governmental social policies with clear purposes to address social justice often target critical issues of national concern. These issues are often driven by major events such as armed confrontation within a nation or between nations, civil unrest as a result of protests against government corruption, racial confrontations, and uneven impacts of globalization. In other words, social disharmony, social exclusion, social unrest, people movements, and terrorist activities, all of which are common phenomena throughout the world, all have a root in the lacking of achieving adequate social justice through governmental policies.

An Asian Context on Social Policy and Social Justice

The Regional Financial Crisis

The regional turmoil started in May 1997 when currency speculators began their attack on the Thailand financial currency, the Thai Baht. The Baht fell on May 2, 1997, and the turmoil spread fast to the Philippines Peso, Malaysian Ringgit, Indonesian Rupiah, and South Korean Won. Within a short time these Asian currencies fell sharply from around 30 percent to 50 percent. Asian stock markets followed a similar pattern of freefall. The vicious cycle carried on as currency and stock market crashes hurt the confidence of domestic and foreign investors, who started further rounds of capital withdrawal. A few countries were able to rehabilitate themselves faster and graduated from loans and stringent measures from development agencies such as the IMF, which offered help at times of crisis. All peoples have suffered from the financial crisis to varying degrees.

Hong Kong in Turmoil

Hong Kong provides an example with far-reaching implications for social policy studies. At the start of the financial turmoil, Hong Kong was fully engaged with the handover of sovereignty on July 1, 1997. Before curtains were drawn on the handover fanfares and ceremonies, the Hong Kong financial markets were under siege from speculators. In order to defend the linked exchange rate (US$1:HK$7.8) of the Hong Kong dollar, the interest rates were once raised to beyond 200 percent. Finally, the government went into the currency, stocks, and futures markets with US$15.1 billion (HK$118 billion). The speculators were beaten off.

An unexpected happy surprise was that by June 1999 the government had made a paper profit of about US$11.5 billion (HK$90 billion) from the financial incursion. Two years after the currency speculation battle, there was a drastic downturn of the Hong Kong economy, as shown by the sharp fall of the GDP from 5.3 in 1997, −5.3 percent in 1998, to −4.1 percent for the quarter January to March 1999 (Tsang, 1999). Rising unemployment became a major problem. The unemployment rate for the period March to May 1999 was 6.3 percent, and the underemployment rate was 2.9 percent. For the period March to May 1999, the size of the total labor force was provisionally estimated at 3,462,000 persons, while the number of unemployed persons and underemployed persons was provisionally estimated at 216,000 and 103,000, respectively (Wong, 1999). Unemployment hit hardest for the younger and older members of the workforce and those with lower education and skill levels. This was not the previous experience for a community that was used to an unemployment rate of between 2.5 and 3 percent for most of the previous two decades. At the same time, wages were frozen or reduced, and property prices for residential units and offices fell by up to 50 percent. Undoubtedly, ordinary people were going through a very painful adjustment.

The Hong Kong government was forced to undertake major reforms in its public policies in the direction of "small government and big market" covering all sectors, involving a trimming of spending and new modes of providing public services, involvement of the private sector, and a changed role for the government. Social policies enacted after the crises have been subject to severe criticism and protests from the grassroots and middle-class people who were hardest hit by such policies.

Turmoil and Emerging Social Issues in Other Asian Countries

Other Asian countries faced challenges similar to those of Hong Kong and Thailand. Asia experienced major natural disasters, including the Kyoto earthquake in 1995, the September 21, 2000 earthquake in Taiwan, the frequent massive flooding in China and Bangladesh, the unprecedented tsunami in December 2004, and the more recent 2011 earthquake in Japan that led to a nuclear disaster. These and other natural disasters resulted in an untold number of human casualties and incalculable economic losses whose real impact will not be known for years to come.

Asia, like regions around the world, experiences racial, ethnic, and religious bigotry and confrontations. In 1998, Indonesia targeted ethnic Chinese over frequent racial and religious conflicts, and armed confrontations in several countries, including Malaysia, Thailand, Timor Leste, terrorist insurgents in Philippines, and broader confrontations.

Political upheavals are also commonplace throughout Asia. The people's movements in the Philippines toppled two presidents, while a similar movement in Nepal in 2006 resulted in a new constitution and a new government. Massive demonstrations against government corruption in Thailand and Taiwan in 2006 resulted in a military coup in Thailand that ended in military rule after 19 years of constitutional democracy.

Tensions continue to reverberate throughout Asia after the 9/11 terrorist attacks in the United States, while heightening the alert surrounding similar terrorist insurgents throughout Asia. Compounding these tensions were the nuclear tests conducted by North Korea in 2006 and the continued threats as recently as 2012 following the death of long-term President Kim Jong-Il and the so-called test missile firings.

Asian countries have since become more proactive in combating causes that resulted in extreme and confrontational ideologies and seeking closer collaborations in tackling terrorism worldwide. A wide array of short-term measures have been installed, including those focused on national security policies and measures. As expected, a substantial portion of public revenue has been diverted to anti-terrorism policies, though, not surprisingly, at the expense of social policy provisions.

An Asian Perspective on Social Policy Development

Social policy is influenced by complex factors such as those previously discussed. Other significant matters include the role of state governance as it confronts poverty and consideration of globalization with economic and social impacts. For example, agreements made by the World Trade Organization are strongly influencing national social policies, especially those concerning migrant workers, cross-border marriages, sex trading, drug trafficking, free-trade agreements on domestic employment, and employment of selected sectors of a society.

Asia's challenges in recent decades have strongly supported the thesis that no single government can rely solely on its own policies and resources to handle domestic issues. No single national social policy can steer and manage a society to achieve its intended goals because of the interconnectedness of the nation-states.

Social policies at the national level have to respond to national situations, while regional initiatives have shown to be effective in guiding national practices toward common goals of social justice. This is an opportunity for the United Nations, and its programs have been most effective in dealing with a range of critical issues.

Social Policy and Social Justice for People With Disabilities: Asian Experiences

People with disabilities in Asia face critical and severe situations. Based on the modest estimate of 1 in 10 adopted by the World Health Organization, the number of disabled people in Asia is larger than the entire American population. The size of the population is one matter, but where these people are located creates another set of unique issues, as 80 percent of Asian people with disabilities live in rural or remote areas. Although comprehensive figures are difficult to come by, estimates suggest there may be between 250 million and 300 million people with disabilities, with 200 million having severe or moderate disabilities that require special services or assistance. Furthermore, 238 million people with disabilities in the region are of working age (Perry, 2002; Statistics Division, UN, 2004).

Persons with disabilities are grossly underrepresented in the workforce. If employed, they tend to be underemployed or may work in informal settings where they lack protection with regard to security, safety, and decent wages. At the same time, people with disabilities often lack access to the services that could lead to successful participation in the economic mainstream. As a result, one should not be surprised to learn that the unemployment rate of people with disabilities in most Asian countries ranges between 40 and 80 percent.

Processes in Developing a Regional Policy Framework

Asia comprises about 60 percent of the world's population, including some of the oldest civilizations and religions in history. At the same time, Asia includes countries with some of the most advanced and the poorest economies in the world. Governments are as diverse as the countries, reflecting the various cultures and beliefs that are imbued in the nations. When it comes to disability concerns, there is a surprisingly strong sense of brotherhood and sisterhood, as well as examples of deep collaboration among governments and peoples in Asia.

Immediately following the close of the United Nations Decade of Disabled Persons 1983–1992, the United Nations Economic and Social Commission for Asia and the Pacific (ESCAP), with the unanimous approval of all its member governments, proclaimed the Asian and Pacific Decade of Disabled Persons 1993–2002, the first-ever UN regional mandate of its kind, and a demonstration of a rather exceptional Asian solidarity and strong political will. In 2002, ESCAP, again with unanimous approval of its members, proclaimed the extension of the Decade to 2003–2012, and the proclamation of the Biwako Millennium Framework (BMF) for compliance of its member governments. The *Biwako Millennium Framework:*

Towards an Inclusive, Barrier-free and Rights-based Society for Persons with Disabilities in Asia and the Pacific, which was adopted at the high-level intergovernmental meeting in Japan in 2002, identifies seven priority areas including training and employment of people with disabilities:

> *Recognizing the lack of formal job opportunities in many countries, Governments, international agencies, donors, NGOs and others in civil society must ensure that persons with disabilities and organizations of and for persons with disabilities have equitable access and are included in programmes related to business development, entrepreneurship and credit distribution.*[4]

The NGO sector has been working very closely together in promoting the Asian and Pacific Decade. A Regional NGO Network for the Promotion of the Asian and Pacific Decade was founded in 1993, and reorganized in 2002 as the Asia Pacific Disability Forum, and comprises all major NGOs and international NGOs. One of its major activities is the annual campaigns for the Decade, which are held in rotation among its member countries. The involvement of major stakeholders of both governmental and nongovernmental sectors in the development and monitoring of the regional framework has proven to be useful in sensitizing and supporting interventions at national and local levels.

Asian initiatives have been supportive of the global disability movement. In March 2000, the first International NGO World Summit was held in Beijing, and unanimously committed to urge the United Nations to adopt an international convention on the rights of disabled persons. Several member states followed with their own initiatives in working with United Nations systems to bring the Convention idea to reality. Finally, after six years of an intensive drafting process, the International Convention on the Rights of Persons with Disabilities was adopted in August 2006 by the drafting UN Ad Hoc Committee and a target for endorsement by the UN General Assembly in December 2006.[5]

Asian stakeholders are among the most active players in the drafting process, including both governmental and nongovernmental representatives, and organizations of persons with disabilities. The UN drafting process had been open and inclusive, permitting active interventions from all interested and concerned NGOs. The Asian sector met regularly during the drafting period, involving stakeholder representatives, UN regional experts, and subject matter experts, and produced important documents for

---

[4]See ESCAP Biwako Millennium Framework: Towards an inclusive, barrier-free and rights-based society for persons with disabilities in Asia and the Pacific. Retrieved on October 22, 2006, from www.unescap.org/sps/disability.htm
[5]See Ad Hoc Committee on a Comprehensive and Integral International Convention on the Protection and Promotion of the Rights and Dignity of Persons with Disabilities Eighth session, New York, August 14–25, 2006. Draft Convention on the Rights of Persons With Disabilities and Draft Optional Protocol. Advanced unedited version. Retrieved from www.un.org/esa/socdev/enable/rights/ahc8adart.htm

the reference of the UN Ad Hoc Committee, including the often-referenced Bangkok Recommendations 2003 (ESCAP, 2003).

The Convention proclaimed its protected target population, the framework of rights items, the international monitoring and remedies system, and interstate meetings and conferences to promote the Convention at national and local levels. It should be noted that the framework includes rights from various existing UN conventions plus additional items specific to disability situations, such as sign language, access, and barrier-free items.

The Convention drafting process is itself a significant awareness-raising and capacity-building process for all stakeholders. The follow-up processes of involving member states to be signatory countries to the Convention enhances further awareness-raising and commitments from high-level governmental bodies.

As far as Asia is concerned, the adoption of the International Convention is a major step forward. The region will now be working on a twin track approach in involving all stakeholders in monitoring the implementation of the BMF and the Convention at regional, national, and local levels (Takamine, 2003).

Specific Measures in Promoting Employment of People with Disabilities

The first quota system in Asia was set up by Japan as early as 1966. Generally speaking, the quota system is regulated by legislation, with some countries applying a financial levy or penalty for noncompliance (e.g., China, Japan, Korea, Mongolia, Thailand, Vietnam); other nations limit fines for noncompliance to the government (e.g., Bangladesh, Sri Lanka, Pakistan, India, and Philippines); and Indonesia limits its penalties to the private sector (Perry, 2004). The levy is usually calculated on the market medium or minimum salary. The funds generated from the fines are used in support of training for people with disabilities and loans for self-employment.

The success of the quota system is dependent on the effectiveness and efficiency of the implementation agency. In Japan, the quota and levy system has been extended from people with physical challenges to include people with intellectual challenges and psychiatric difficulties.[6] However, the overall quota has seldom been fully filled because of the inadequate supply of people with disabilities who possess the required job skills (Matsui, 1998). As a result, the funds generated from the fines have grown and remain largely unspent. This is perhaps one of the reasons why the implementing agency was given an expanded portfolio to cover the employment of seniors beginning in 2003.

---

[6]See Japan Organization for the Employment of the Elderly and Persons with Disabilities. (2006). Employment measures for persons with disabilities. Retrieved on October 22, 2006, from www.jeed.or.jp/english/supporting.html

In China, the local branches of the China Disabled Persons' Federation (CDPF) are given the authority to monitor the implementation of the quota and levy system. The implementation is left to the provincial and city governments in accordance with the laws promulgated by the Central Government.[7] Some CDPF branches have reported success in creating job opportunities for people with disabilities, through their close liaison with business concerns. Based on these successes, the CDPF is setting a target 85 percent employment rate for some urban localities.

In the case of the Philippines, although the Magna Carta[8] provides for a quota system, the business sector's awareness and application of the law is low. A similar situation is also reported in Vietnam, where a quota levy system is provided for in Article 125 of the Labour Code, but the enforcement is uncertain and the fund is not operational.

Affirmative Policies Concerning Work Facilities for People with Disabilities

Several Asian countries have given workshops that hire a relatively large proportion of people with disabilities the exclusive rights or priorities in obtaining a limited range of public contracts (e.g., Philippines,[9] India[10]) or regulate such practices (e.g., South Korea[11]) by law. These facilities are commonly called sheltered workshops, social work centers, community workshops, welfare factories, supported employment, and disability-concerned enterprises. These facilities provide income-generating work to people with severe physical and mental challenges. In some countries, sheltered workshops are generally considered as welfare facilities, and people working there are treated more like trainees or welfare recipients and, as a result, are not considered to be workers under the normal legal definition. Welfare factories are commonplace in China and Vietnam, are owned and managed by the Government, and receive substantial tax exemptions and government supports. In the 1970s and 1980s, sheltered workshops in developed economies, such as Hong Kong, received substantial government funding support, handling mainly labor-intensive, low-skilled work. The workers were low-skilled and received very little salary for labor-intensive work, while also receiving daycare services.

---

[7]See Law of the People's Republic of China on the Protection of Disabled Persons, effective 1991.

[8]Magna Carta for Disabled Persons (RA 7277), An Act Providing for the Rehabilitation, Self-Development and Self-Reliance of Disabled Persons and Their Integration Into the Mainstream of Society and for Other Purposes.

[9]See Foundation for International Training. (2002). Identifying disability issues related to poverty reduction: Philippines Country Study, prepared for Asian Development Bank. Retrieved from www.adb.org/Documents/Conference/Disability_Development/phi.pdf

[10]Law of India: The Persons with Disabilities (Equal Opportunities, Protection of Rights and Full Participation) Act, 1995 (No. 1 of 1996).

[11]See Republic of Korea: Act Relating to Employment Promotion, etc. of the Handicapped Law No. 4219, Jan. 13, 1990.

In the 1990s, the mission and characteristics of these facilities were drastically changed. First, there was a drop in government funding. Second, as low-skilled jobs in developed economies were shifting to China, sheltered workshops began to change and reflect the shifting market conditions.

Overall, the number of sheltered workshops for disabled people in developed economies has increased because of the lack of employment opportunities for people with severe disabilities. In Japan, more than 23,000 sheltered workshops with more than 25,000 staff members serve 84,000 disabled people (Maruyama, 2003). The objective of these sheltered workshops is to help their clients obtain employment in the open labor market, but their annual placement rate in business and industry, not surprisingly, remains low at 2 percent. In the meantime, the workers' length of stay at sheltered workshops is increasing, with the majority staying for more than five years (Matsui, 1998).

It is worthwhile to note that sheltered workshops in Japan are now given a new name: social work centers. Japan also incorporates a national network of small-scale community workshops for disabled people, the Japan Association of Community Workshops (JACW). These workshops are mainly grassroots initiatives and are not supported by the central government. The national network includes approximately 5,000 community workshops serving more than 75,000 disabled people (Tateoka, 2003). JACW is a very active member of Workability International and serves as its regional secretariat.

A Missing Link Between Social Policy and Social Justice: Social Capital Investment in Support of Persons with Disabilities

A human rights approach to social policy requires a multisectorial and multidisciplinary approach, which emphasizes both processes and outcomes, that attends to the interfacing of interventions at international, regional, and national levels. Accordingly, a multistakeholder involvement and participation in the process is necessary.

The lack of social capital among all stakeholders is a critical factor that results in an unsuccessful policy outcome. In economic development projects, development assistance for less-developed economies has shown mixed outcomes. The World Bank (2006) refers to *social capital* as relationships and norms that shape the quality and quantity of a society's social interactions. The World Bank considers social capital to be a major factor affecting the sustainability of its world poverty eradication programs. It is commonplace for projects to have failed in bringing sustainable social and economic improvements to disadvantaged sectors of a society because of the lack of social capital. Indeed, social capital in social policy has received increasing attention from leading global development agencies beyond the World Bank. For example, the Organisation for Economic Co-operation and Development (OECD, 2001) extended its interests from human capital to include social capital and its impact on sustainable social development; the Asian Development Bank (2004) incorporated social capital as a critical factor in its poverty alleviation programs, and urges that

When poverty is pronounced, social cohesion is often weak, and communities suffer from conflict, marginalization, and exclusion. In such cases, strong, proactive policies are required to reverse perceptions of social and psychological inferiority, to foster a sense of empowerment, and to create genuinely participatory institutions. Social capital and a more inclusive society can be promoted through antidiscrimination legislation, land reform, legal recognition of user groups, and accessible systems of justice. Specific measures may be required to provide suitable social services and equitable access to economic opportunity for ethnic minorities.

Social Enterprise and Social Capital

Social enterprise refers to income-generating organizations that are operated like private businesses but that also serve a primary social purpose of supporting the rights and welfare of disadvantaged groups. Social enterprise may be operated by a government, an NGO, or a private business; the enterprise is primarily mission driven, self-sufficient, and market driven. Social enterprise is different from a private enterprise, which is profit driven and values corporate accountability.

Kwok, Chan, and Chan's[12] (2002) study of two social enterprise organizations, one in the Philippines and the other in Taiwan, offers some useful information in understanding the impacts on people with disabilities from a proactive social policy involving social enterprises and social capital investment.

Philippine Case Study

In the Philippines, the government allocates 10 percent of its purchasing budget to cooperatives of persons with disabilities. Cooperatives that meet the disability-related criteria and have the manufacturing capacity bid for these government contracts. These cooperatives are formally registered under the related cooperative ordinances. The National Federation of Cooperatives of Persons with Disabilities provides support to the local cooperatives in capacity building, technical training, and funding support. The national body essentially nurtures and helps develop local cooperatives in all administrative areas of the Philippines.

The National Federation negotiates with governmental departments and works with local cooperatives to build their capacity to engage in the manufacturing work, in building manufacturing workshops, and in recruitment and training of disabled people to engage in business and manufacturing operations. The National Federation has a twofold challenge: (1) the government contract does not guarantee profitable business; and (2) a significant hurdle is securing credit lines to support the operation, as

---

[12]These discussions are based on preliminary findings of a study conducted by the author as principal investigator and supported by a research grant from the City University of Hong Kong, project number 7001571–640.

government payment of such contracts is usually some months behind after delivery of goods.

The national body and local branches have invested significant time and effort in building positive networks with political leaders, with central government departments, with development agencies and funding bodies that offer loans to businesses for development concerns, with potential customers such as private colleges and schools, and with other organizations of and for people with disabilities. The social networks developed by the selected organization cut across many sectors.

One successful local cooperative that has the capacity to engage in large-scale manufacturing contracts has demonstrated dedicated, committed leadership with the required business expertise. Their social networks with the government, the business community, and the civil society are highly functional, with their leaders recognized in several local and nationwide award presentations. Their social enterprise has received affirmative policy support from local government, at least in providing low-cost workshop venues; their products have received high recommendations from their customers; and their leaders, being alumni of local schools and colleges, also have the informal networks in support of their business marketing.

Despite the high quality of social capital, which supports the social enterprise, the national and local bodies face significant challenges with the business operation's outlook very questionable. First, the restricted tender portion of government contracts is unstable and short term, which cannot support long-term job provision of the employees of the organization. Second, the credit lines may not always be adequate and, for those available, still carry an interest rate that requires very efficient business operation. Third, the trend of decentralization of government operation to regional levels has prevented the national body from engaging in contract tendering for its local branches, many of which do not have the required financial and technical capacity to engage in such manufacturing businesses.

To overcome the challenges and to pave the way for future development, the National Federation is lobbying the government to recognize the Federation's central role in bidding the government's restricted tender. The National Federation is also considering a major campaign to set up a trust fund that will provide the financial credit support to its manufacturing arm.

Experiences of the Selected Organization from Taipei, Taiwan

In Taiwan, there is a mandatory employment quota system with a levy. Funds raised from the levy provide subsidies to other organizations that exceed the quota. There are additional income subsidies to disadvantaged groups in their initial job placement up to around 36 months, renewable annually, although subject to project performance appraisal. The government also allocates a small percentage of its purchase budget for products of sheltered workshops, including those for people with disabilities.

The Taiwanese organization was founded by a highly respected leader with a disability in the early 1980s. What began as a small group of disabled people engaged in advocacy became one of the largest organizations of and for people with disabilities throughout Taiwan, with more than 2,500 employees. A large portion of its services are government contracts. The organization has set up a social enterprise department to engage in a range of income-generating activities, which also provide job training and work to disabled employees. The range of activities includes special transport services, bottled waters and stationery bearing the organization's name, a sheltered workshop enterprise, a cafeteria, insurance, and a call center.

One of the largest business operations of the organization is its sheltered workshop business. The workshop operates in partnership with private companies in the manufacturing of wheelchairs and assistive devices. The workshop was built in the area that was most devastated by the September 2000 earthquake. Disaster relief funds were used to build and equip the workshop; funds came from both the government and private donations, with the primary purpose to support the livelihood of disaster victims.

The leaders of the workshop, through their relationships with political leaders, central and local governments, and the private sector, have nurtured a functional partnership with all parties to support the operation of the workshop. Its major job, building wheelchairs, has seen orders come from charity sales, private companies, and fundraising campaigns. The wheelchair project acquired quality accreditation from international bodies and has grown into the private market as a major competitor.

The Taipei NGO also engages in business partnership with interested private companies in marketing products that bear the brand name of the private partners. The organization is functioning as a service operator receiving commissions to support the salaries of the employees, many of whom are disabled, and the business operation. The private partners are primarily interested in the moral value of the NGO in support of disadvantaged and minority groups, and not so much concerned with monetary profits. The private partners view the moral value of the organization and the involvement of disabled employees as an important match that supports the company's mission and the healthy lifestyle pursued by its employees, business partners, and customers. In this regard, the NGO benefits from government affirmative policies in support of disabled employees through the levy funds of the employment quota scheme and the special, time-limited grants that support employment of disadvantaged social groups. The NGO also benefits from the business networks and expertise in support of the operation. The private partners also provide a good source of volunteer support and charity fundraising pools of people.

The realization of all these social enterprises is the result of the vast social networks of the leaders and organizers of the NGO, who invested in the building of social capital across all sectors, including governmental, private, and religious sectors. The leaders, both paid and volunteers, are appointed to influential committees of national and local governments, have been recognized publicly for their contributions, and have received national awards in recognition of their work.

Like other businesses, the NGO faces a range of challenges to develop the sustainability of the social enterprises. The organization-driven wheelchair workshop, because of its space requirements, is facing high workshop rentals. Similar private businesses moved their manufacturing sites to Mainland China, where land and labor are much less costly. The organization's wheelchair workshop also faces high operating costs. As a result, there is a price disadvantage to compete in the private market. An additional confounding factor is the unstable nature of contracts from charity and restricted government; basically, the NGO does not have long-term, constant contracts, which would allow for organizational stability and growth.

The business-driven partnership projects, while enjoying high brand-name status and high product and service quality, are facing labor efficiency factors, as the operations have to employ more employees to match the performance output requirement. The profit margins of all these operations remain low and often have to seek donations to ensure that all expenses are covered.

Implications for Government Policy in Support of People With Disabilities

The Philippine and Taiwanese cases illustrate the dynamic interaction among government affirmative policy, development agencies, NGO funding bodies, and the private sector, in bridging and linking the interested and concerned sectors to develop and nurture social enterprises in support of organizations of people with disabilities. The impacts in creating capacity-building and income-generating opportunities by the two NGOs rely on their active social networks and long-term relationships built across all sectors. The two cases share a common theme that without continued government funding, their continued and sustainable development will end. They both share a common objective of nurturing a sustainable social enterprise that in turn supports the sustainable development of the mother bodies.

Social enterprises are primarily businesses in nature, although they subscribe to a high moral value; however, such values do not guarantee the running of a successful and sustainable business. This moral value may in some situations render social enterprises less competitive in a market economy that is subject to heavy competition. Furthermore, the NGOs may not have the capacity, such as the high-level physical, financial, and human capital, needed to respond proactively to rapidly changing market conditions.

Social capital investment, therefore, becomes critical and strategic for organizations of persons with disabilities. With a strong social capital, these organizations may be able to survive through stormy market conditions, but there needs to be an investment before they can generate positive social capital to support their social enterprises. The investment has to come from both within these organizations and the stakeholders at the local, national, and regional levels.

Developing a Comprehensive and Proactive Social Policy to Support Social Capital Development for People With Disabilities

Local and National Responsibilities

At the national level, government affirmative policies in areas of mandatory employment quota and levy, restricted tendering, and earmarked purchase budgets are necessary practices. Such affirmative action will enhance disability awareness in the private sector and development agencies while stimulating their interests in seeking or responding to invitations of social enterprise partnership. Further affirmative policy in providing continued and sustainable capacity-building support to organizations of and for people with disabilities through government or government-directed public funding should be encouraged.

At the Regional Level

At the midpoint review of the Biwako Millennium Framework in 2007, it is timely to consider developing comprehensive and coordinated regional initiatives in building social capital that might contribute to successful social enterprises of NGOs. The regional initiative would be in the form of a tripartite platform for development, involving UN agencies, the governments, the private sector, and the civil society, with a primary purpose to support NGOs' involvement in social enterprises.

The World Bank and the Asian Development Bank committed to a proactive social capital strategy for poverty alleviation in the context of achieving the UN Millennium Development Goals. The BMF recognized social development as part of its overall agenda for action and brought in organizations of persons with disabilities as one of its policy targets. The International Labour Organization (ILO) and Food and Agriculture Organization of the United States (FAO) are among the leading UN agencies that already have proven experience in developing disability-based tripartite business councils for development, and in income-generating projects. From the private business sector, many multinational corporations have already demonstrated a sound understanding of the principles and practice of diversity in its human resources management, and have formed networks to promote diversity (e.g., the Global Diversity Network[13]).

---

[13]Global Diversity Network. (n.d.). Home page. Retrieved on September 11, 2006, from www .globaldiversitynetwork.com/

Conclusion

The world is facing rapid changes. Governments and peoples are facing uncertainties caused by unpredictable political and economic forces. New issues emerge while old issues are becoming even more critical in the modern era. Professionals seeking social justice for disadvantaged sectors will have to equip themselves with enhanced capacity, flexibility, creativity, and innovation in order to be a major stakeholder in multisectorial, interdisciplinary social policy development in dealing with such evolving, complex situations.

The social work profession has a strategic role in working with people at all socioeconomic levels. It is relevant to ask if and how well the social work profession is prepared to take a proactive role in the social policy-making process of the new era. In order to do so, social work professionals will need to adopt a new paradigm to equip themselves with broad helping perspectives and multi-dimensional skills in order to avail themselves as partners of all sectors in the society and engage in comprehensive policy-making processes in dealing with the challenges of modern times.

There are, however, clear indications that the social work profession is becoming marginalized by various mainstream sectors, as it fails to get involved in new and alternative solutions to deal with the challenges of welfare and economic transformation. Globally, the social work profession began its mission in arguing that social welfare was not a charity and adopted an empowerment model that stresses the well-being of individuals, groups, and communities. Social work is grounded in social justice and guided by perspectives that emphasize the developing strength of people and human diversity.

In the evolving technological world, however, social workers function in many nontraditional sectors of the society. They have multi-dimensional skills and take on posts in a wide range of settings. They may be employed in formal caring systems, but their intervention extends into the private market and informal caring systems. They have a broader role to ensure a seamless interface among sectors to build a total caring system in the society.

Apparently, a change of paradigm for the social work profession is needed, so that it will work in partnership with all sectors and all systems in society in order to deal with all challenges, current and future, at the micro, mezzo, or macro levels.

Social workers must continue to pursue social policies grounded in a human rights perspective, developed with the full participation of relevant stakeholders in the society, nurturing ownership and mutual support among all sectors, embracing multisectorial dimensions, and adopting interdisciplinary approaches. This is a formidable challenge. As mentioned at the beginning of this chapter, ancient philosophers believed in, preached about, and practiced educating kings with absolute powers over their subjects to share and care. Today, people are more educated, our social systems and institutions are well equipped, and the international and regional platforms are becoming more sensitized to human rights principles and values. With vision and perseverance — and a shift of paradigm in developing social policies in support of disadvantaged sectors — human services professionals would make their due contribution to the building of a society that is inclusive, barrier free, and rights based.

This study of persons with disabilities shows that positive change can dramatically redirect individuals' and communities' lives. This type of change directly promotes human justice. Such change requires a productive partnership between NGOs and governments, but what underlies such change is the belief in social justice, not as a concept but as a reality.

Key Terms

distributive justice   *social harmony*   *social capital*
human rights   *social enterprise*

Review Questions for Critical Thinking

1. To what extent does culture influence the interpretation of social justice?

2. Which is a stronger approach to engaging persons with disabilities, a distributive model of justice or a human rights based model of social justice?

3. What differences, if any, can you find with a government's response to natural disasters versus humanmade disasters?

4. What role should the United Nations play in promoting social justice for persons with disabilities?

5. What three key pieces can Western nations learn from the experiences of Asian countries on how to engage and integrate people into the workforce and society?

Online Resources

World Trade Organization: www.wto.org

Global Summit Against Discrimination and Persecution: www.ngosummit.org

UN Economic and Social Commission for Asia and Pacific: www.unescap.org

China Disabled Persons federation: www.cdpf.org/cn/english

Workability International: www.workability-international.com

References

Asian Development Bank. (2004). *Enhancing the fight against poverty in Asia and the Pacific: The poverty reduction strategy of the Asian Development Bank*. Retrieved on September 7, 2006, from www.adb.org/Documents/Policies/ Poverty_Reduction/2004/foreword.asp

ESCAP. (2003). Expert group meeting and seminar on an International Convention to Protect and Promote the Rights and Dignity of Persons with Disabilities, Bangkok, Thailand, June 2–4, 2003. Retrieved on October 24, 2006, from www.worldenable.net/bangkok2003/default.htm

International Council on Social Welfare. (2003). Mission Statement. Retrieved on October 20, 2006, from www.icsw.org/

Kwok, J. K. F., Chan, R. K. H., & Chan, W. T. (2002). *Self-help organizations of people with disabilities in Asia*. Westport, CT: Auburn House.

Maruyama, I. (2003). Promoting social employment of people with disabilities in Japan. *Proceedings of International Conference on Sheltered Workplace, Industry and Environmental Improvement for People with Disabilities 2003*, Taipei, Taiwan, September 1–3, 2003, pp. 67–71. Taipei, Taiwan: Eden Social Welfare Foundation.

Matsui, R. (1998). An overview of the impact of employment quota system in Japan, *Asia Pacific Disability Rehabilitation Journal*, *9*(1).

Mencius. (1999). Book 1. Translated by Zhao et al. in *Library of Chinese Classics*: *Mencius*. China: Hunan People's Publishing House (pp. 1–25).

Organisation for Economic Co-operation and Development. (2001). *The well-being of nations: The role of human and social capital*. Paris, France: OECD.

Perry, D. A. (2002). Situation of people with disabilities in the region: Disability issues in employment and social protection. Paper presented at the Regional Workshop on Disability and Development, Asian Development Bank, ADB Headquarters, Manila, Philippines, October 2–4, 2002. Retrieved from www .adb.org/Documents/Events/2002/Disability_Development/perry_paper.pdf

Perry, D. A. (2004). *Disability issues in the employment and social protection*. Bangkok, Thailand: International Labour Office.

Roemer, J. E. (1996). *Theories of distributive justice*. London, England: Harvard University Press.

Statistics Division, United Nations. (2004). Indicators on unemployment. Retrieved from http://unstats.un.org/unsd/demographic/products/socind/unempl.htm

Takamine, Y. (2003). Disability issues in East Asia: Review and ways forward. Retrieved on October 22, 2006, from http://siteresources.worldbank.org/ DISABILITY/Resources/Regions/East-Asia-Pacific/Disability_Issues_in_East _Asia_Takamine.pdf

Tateoka, A. (2003). Japan Association of community workshops for disabled persons, in *Proceedings of International Conference on Sheltered Workplace, Industry and Environmental Improvement for People with Disabilities 2003*, Taipei, Taiwan, September 1–3, 2003, pp. 59–62. Taipei, Taiwan: Eden Social Welfare Foundation.

Tsang, D. (1999). Speech of the Financial Secretary, Mr. Donald Tsang, moving the second reading of the Appropriation Bill 1999: "1999–2000 Budget: Onward with new strengths," March 3, 1999.

Tsang, D. (October 2005). 2005–2006 Policy Address by Chief Executive of HKSAR. Retrieved on October 8, 2006, from www.info.gov.hk/gia/general/200510/12/ P200510120112.htm

Titmuss, R. M. (1974). *Social policy*. London, England: Allen and Unwin.

Titmuss, R. M. (1976). *Commitment to welfare* (2nd ed.). London, England: Allen and Unwin.

UNDP. (2003). *Human Development Report 2003*. New York, NY: Oxford University Press.

United Nations. (1995). Report of the World Summit for Social Development, Copenhagen, Denmark, March 6–12, 1995. United Nations publication, Sales No. E.96.IV.8.

United Nations. (2006). *Social justice in an open world: The role of the United Nations*. New York, NY: United Nations.

Wong, W. P. (1999). Press release of W. P. Wong, Secretary for Education and Manpower, June 15, 1999.

World Bank. (2006). Social capital. Retrieved on September 10, 2006, from http://web .worldbank.org/WBSITE/EXTERNAL/TOPICS/EXTSOCIALDEVELOPMENT/ EXTTSOCIALCAPITAL/0,,menuPK:401021~pagePK:149018~piPK:149093~the SitePK:401015,00.html

World Bank. (August 2008). New data shows 1.4 billion live on less than US$1.25 a day, but progress against poverty remains strong. Retrieved on April 12, 2012, from www.worldbank.org

Chapter 6
Welfare Reform: The Need for Social Empathy

Elizabeth A. Segal

> Does the current welfare program, as exemplified by Temporary Assistance for Needy Families, reflect the profession's social justice model? If so, how? If not, what would such a welfare program include?

Introduction

The public has had an uneasy, often hostile relationship with welfare in the United States and during the colonial period of the 16th through 18th centuries. The prevailing belief was that those in need (e.g., the poor) were somehow inferior to those who worked and were able to care for themselves and their families. This all changed in the Great Depression of the 1930s, when nearly one in four people were unemployed, and virtually everyone knew people who had lost their jobs through no fault of their own. The federal government stepped in, and the modern-day welfare state was born. Public welfare and the government's role expanded throughout the remainder of the 20th century, although the calls for welfare reform took on a greater and broader chorus of critics. At one time considered an entitlement, the late-20th-century welfare reform effort radically redesigned the American welfare system. As you read this chapter, consider the many challenges the public welfare system faces while reflecting on what is meant by social justice from the social work profession's perspective.

The history of welfare in America parallels public opinion and reflects values and beliefs that are deeply held. As a public policy, welfare today is typically regarded as the cash assistance program of Temporary Assistance for Needy Families (TANF), which evolved from the 1935 Aid to Dependent Children (ADC) provisions of the Social Security Act. However, TANF is actually a very small part of the social welfare programs and services provided through government. Federal, state, and local efforts to provide for social well-being are vastly greater than TANF. In the context of our entire social well-being, government involvement in programs such as Social Security and Medicare far outweigh the contributions to TANF.

Consider that in 2011 the federal financial effort for Social Security and Medicare was $1.2 trillion, or 35 percent of the entire U.S. budget, while expenditures for TANF were $26 billion (which included temporary emergency funds), or .7 percent of the budget (Congressional Budget Office, 2012). Despite its very small size, TANF and its predecessors ADC and later Aid to Families with Dependent Children (AFDC) have been the focus of welfare reform. We can conclude that this emphasis defines welfare in America as cash assistance to the poor, not government interventions for social well-being. Thus, the policy discussions and changes regarding cash assistance for the poor are the focus of this discussion on welfare reform.

The original design of the ADC program was temporary, intended as an emergency response to the needs of poor widows and their children in the wake of the Great Depression. It was thought that once the major part of the program—the social insurance provisions that have come to be known as Social Security—had time to take hold, there would no longer be a need for cash assistance to poor women and children. The view at the time was that these needy families were deserving of help, and "by devoting themselves to mothering, the female recipients were performing what God, nature, and society intended women to do and doing so, moreover, under difficult circumstances" (Gordon, 2001, p. 17). So what happened over the next 60 years? Why, by 1996, were politicians and the public calling for welfare reform to "end the dependence of needy parents on government benefits by promoting job preparation, work and marriage . . . to enable them to leave the program and become self-sufficient"? (U.S. Department of Health and Human Services, 1996)

How did the nation move from wanting to care for poor families by using government support to keep women in the home to insisting that these mothers go to work and stop receiving government support? The years from 1935 to 1996, and the more than 15 years since the latest experiment in welfare reform, reveal a journey in societal policies and programs that reflects shifting values and beliefs and calls for a new approach that is truly kinder and gentler, one that reflects social empathy (Segal, 2011).

Social empathy is based on interpersonal empathy, the ability of a person to understand what life is like for another person, coupled with deep contextual understanding. It is nonjudgmental and unsentimental, as is sympathy. Sympathy feels bad for someone, and may even evoke thoughts of irresponsible behavior on the part of the person for whom we feel bad. Empathy is imagining yourself in another person's situation and imagining what that would feel like and what you would wish to be done. It does not deny personal responsibility, but it is not the focus. Social empathy in regard to poverty places empathy in the larger societal context and asks those who are in power and with resources to imagine what life would be like if they did not have those resources. It requires an ability to view others' life circumstances as if they were your own. The evolution of welfare from 1935 to the present reflects a great deal of sympathy and blame but little social empathy.

A Brief History of Welfare Reform

The Great Depression was the catalyst for federal policy involvement in personal well-being, a course that continues today. Social Security has become an institutionalized social welfare program that has widespread support and is considered the right of every working man and woman in America. Its counterpart, welfare, does not enjoy such support. In 1935, President Roosevelt did not want the federal government to become entrenched in providing relief, and he knew that direct relief was not enough to correct the economic problems brought on by the Depression:

> The Federal Government must and shall quit this business of relief. . . . I am not willing that the vitality of our people be further sapped. . . . We must preserve not only the bodies of the unemployed from destitution but also their self-respect, their self-reliance and courage and determination.

> (President Franklin D. Roosevelt, Annual Message to Congress, January 4, 1935)

The Depression disproved the concept that poverty was caused by personal laziness and unworthiness. The evidence was that millions of hardworking, responsible, and previously economically stable workers were unemployed and could not find work. The overall failure of economic institutions lessened the resistance toward adopting a national welfare policy (Trattner, 1999). Those in power could see the impact of the Great Depression in ways that were understandable, on people they could relate to, who were hard working and part of the economic system. Although the Social Security Act of 1935 contained both the long-term social insurance provisions of Social Security and the short-term cash assistance provisions of welfare, the two parts were anything but equal. Even the early founders were not invested in both programs:

> The Bureau of Public Assistance was in charge of a despised program, which, at least in theory, the Social Security Boards intended should wither away, whereas the Bureau of Old Age and Survivors Insurance was in charge of a preferred program that was expected to grow until, again in theory, it virtually supplanted the first.

> (Derthick, 1979, p. 160)

Thus, the two parts of public economic support — social insurance and public assistance — evolved in very different directions. Although the original ADC program seemed to embrace poor families, this has not been the typical policy response. Welfare historically faced reform when the need for cheap labor arose, when patriarchal arrangements were challenged, or when public perception held that welfare interfered with social expectations (Abramovitz, 2000; Axinn & Hirsch, 1993; Piven & Cloward, 1971).

The original Aid to Dependent Children (ADC) program was passed as Title IV of the Social Security Act in 1935. Although originally anticipated as a temporary response to poverty that would, in time, be unnecessary because of the expansion of Social Security, ADC instead expanded. In 1935, only needy, dependent children were covered. The federal program did not cover a parent or relative in the household. However, in 1950 the federal program began to include the coverage of a caretaker relative. The program was expanded again in 1961 to include unemployed parents, and in 1962 the coverage of a second parent was included, and the program was changed to Aid to Families with Dependent Children (AFDC; U.S. Department of Health and Human Services, 1998).

Temporary Assistance for Needy Families

Public cash assistance, or welfare as we commonly refer to it, was the target of 1996 welfare reform. Those reform efforts created the Temporary Assistance for Needy Families (TANF) program out of the Aid to Families with Dependent Children (AFDC) program. This reform shifted the emphasis of the program from an income support program to a welfare-to-work program. The ostensible goal of the program was to emphasize economic self-sufficiency and decrease the number of people receiving assistance by emphasizing employment. Specifically, one of the primary goals outlined within the law states that the purpose of creating TANF was to "end the dependence of needy families on government benefits by promoting job preparation, work, and marriage" [Sec. 401 (a)(2)]. The expected outcome was that fewer people would receive welfare, they would become employed and self-sufficient, and less federal money would be spent on welfare assistance.

Today, TANF is a time-limited, no-guarantee program. It provides temporary cash assistance, up to two years of assistance consecutively with a total lifetime maximum of five years, and requires work efforts for all participants. TANF recipients must participate in at least 30 hours per week of unsubsidized or subsidized employment, on-the-job training, community service, vocational training, or childcare for other parents involved in community service. In addition, states must achieve a 50 percent rate of work participation for families with an adult. This approach greatly deviated from the 60 years of AFDC. The substitution of TANF for AFDC changed the way public assistance had been provided to poor families. No longer was there unlimited enrollment as long as a family qualified, nor could mothers stay at home; rather, work was the ultimate goal.

The welfare reform of 1996 has stood, with only minor changes. Revisions came in 2005 as part of the Deficit Reduction Act (P.L. 109–171). With the program set to expire in 2002, Congress debated the legislation but could not reach consensus on reauthorization. For three years, stop-gap extensions were passed until reauthorization was agreed to in 2005. The new legislation reauthorized TANF through fiscal year 2010 at the same level of $16.5 billion per year; funded marriage promotion grants; increased childcare funding; and extended transitional medical assistance for one year. There efforts were intended to increase the work participation rate, but they proved to be unsuccessful. However, the new legislation mandated regulations that clearly defined what constitutes work activities and set standards for verifying work participation (Falk, Gish, & Solomon-Fears, 2006). The end result of these tighter work standards was to increase the work participation rate. These efforts were reinforcement of the goals of the 1996 reform by maintaining emphasis on work and marriage, and decreasing the role of government in supporting poor families.

Although TANF was slated for reauthorization in 2010, Congress has sidestepped that provision by passing annual extensions. Every year's extension has simply continued the program as is, making no substantial changes nor increasing funding. The fact that the recession greatly increased need was only addressed with temporary emergency funds, but no changes were made to the program.

Since its inception in 1996, TANF has been successful in decreasing the number of recipients. By 2004, TANF rolls dropped from more than 12 million participants, of whom 8.5 million were children, to less than 5 million, of whom 3.6 million were children (Social Security Administration, 2006). Even following the recession, a time when it would be expected to see an increase in TANF recipients, there were fewer recipients. In 2011, there were 4.4 million TANF recipients, of whom 3.3 million, or 75 percent, were children (Administration for Children & Families, 2012). While the goal of reducing the number of public cash assistance recipients was achieved by welfare reform, how successful have TANF and the welfare reforms of 1996 been in promoting work and marriage? And more important to social welfare advocates, how well has TANF done in alleviating poverty and improving life outcomes for poor children? Finally, in terms of reducing social welfare expenditures, how successful has welfare reform been in capping federal expenditures?

The Success of Welfare Reform

Research findings on the impact of TANF are mixed. Although more women left TANF for employment, they do not seem to be better off financially. They have full-time jobs that pay $7 to $8 per hour, and even though they may have transitional support, they eventually lose healthcare coverage from Medicaid (Acs & Loprest, 2004). Other researchers found similar results, that "welfare recipients tend to have unstable, short-term jobs, with few benefits and low wages" (King & Mueser, 2005, p. 2).

Data reveal that while the numbers of families on TANF have declined, more families today qualify but do not receive support. In 1995, 84 percent of families that met the eligibility requirements of the AFDC program participated, whereas by 2002, only 48 percent of eligible families were enrolled in TANF. The drop for poor children was even more severe. The share of children living in poverty who received AFDC/TANF dropped from a high of 62 percent in 1995 to a low of 31 percent in 2003 (Parrott & Sherman, 2006). This trend occurred despite growth in the numbers of poor children. There were almost 1.3 million additional children living in poverty from 2000 to 2003 (DeNavas-Walt, Proctor, & Lee, 2006). By 2010, almost 16 million children lived in families with incomes below the poverty threshold, yet only 3.3 million children received TANF benefits (DeNavas-Walt, Proctor, & Smith, 2011; Administration for Children & Families, 2012).

This means that today many eligible families are not receiving support, and fewer poor children are covered by the program. Thus, the success in decreasing the caseloads of public cash assistance programs seems to be a result of factors that do not include reducing poverty or decreasing need for the program. The decline in coverage of eligible families leaves millions of children living in poor households with a jobless adult and no income assistance from TANF. Even before the current data revealed the decline in TANF coverage, welfare advocates were alarmed by the impact of the 1996 welfare reform:

> As currently implemented, the welfare-to-work solution is a match made in hell. It joins together poor mothers with few resources whose family responsibilities require employment flexibility with jobs in the low-wage labor market that often are the most inflexible, have the least family-necessary benefits (vacation time, health care, sick days), and provide levels of pay that often are insufficient to support a single person, let alone a family.

> (Albelda, 2001, p. 68)

Poverty among children in the United States is still prevalent, especially following the years of economic downturn and recession. Concurrent with this trend is the decline in TANF, the primary anti-poverty program for poor households. With declines in low-income families' earnings accompanied by declines in public programs, the persistence of poverty among children worsens. Deeper poverty means diminished opportunities for positive development and life outcomes.

Who Receives Welfare?

When policy makers focus on welfare reform, who are they really targeting? To the public it sounds like major overhauls of our social welfare system. However, welfare reforms, particularly the changes of 1996, have historically been focused on public assistance recipients of the AFDC/TANF programs. As discussed previously, this represents a very small part of the national budget. Three-fourths of the recipients of TANF are children, most of whom are under the age of 12. The one-fourth of the program recipients who are adults are primarily single women, most of whom are lacking sufficient formal education or work experience. They are the poorest families in this country.

According to the Administration for Children & Families (2012), the typical TANF household consisted of one parent with one or two young children; 51 percent of TANF families had only one child, and 27 percent had two children, with 73 percent of all TANF children under 12 years of age.

Only 5 percent of the adult recipients had an education level beyond high school completion. Almost 70 percent are families of color, with 33 percent African American, 29 percent Hispanic, 2 percent Asian, and 1 percent Native American; 58 percent of the adult recipients were under the age of 30. The average family monthly benefit in 2009 was $389. These demographics reveal that TANF consists of very young families of color with single, never-married mothers who have minimal formal education. These families represent those who are on the edge of our social system in terms of economics, family composition, race, age, and education.

Why Welfare Reform Has Failed

How do we determine if welfare reform has been successful? That depends on our perceptions and expectations of the program. If the goal was to reduce the number of people receiving TANF, then welfare reform has been very successful, reducing the numbers by more than 63 percent. If the goal was economic self-sufficiency, then the changes have failed. What welfare reform did not change, and actually never addressed, was poverty. In fact, in Congressional discussions preceding the vote on the 1996 welfare reform, poverty was not addressed as a social issue, only as a personal responsibility (Segal & Kilty, 2003). So it is not surprising that the Personal Responsibility and Work Opportunity Reconciliation Act (PRWORA) barely addresses barriers to economic success. Other than childcare, no other resources to support self-sufficiency, such as healthcare, transportation, job availability, or education, are addressed. The only social programs that are included are promotion of marriage and discouragement of out-of-wedlock births.

No one wants to deal with the structural problems that face our nation: the budget deficit, a market economy that does not support full employment, a substandard minimum wage, the lack of universal healthcare, unequal access to quality education, and disregard for the future well-being of all children. Focusing on the poor person and his or her behavior rather than the systemic causes of poverty is not new, and this approach has been reflected throughout our modern history (Katz, 1989; Patterson, 2000; Wilson, 1987).

As has been done with other difficult public policy issues, deconstructing services has great appeal. Welfare has not worked, there are still poor people, so momentum arises to dismantle the system. For advocates of programs for the poor, the result of this dismantling, or "dewelfarization," would be millions of families, most of whom included young children, receiving less government support. Their analyses foretold that:

> The bill would make deep, often indiscriminate, cuts in basic support without including strategies for improving employability or making work pay. Increases in poverty, homelessness, and hunger for millions of children would almost certainly result, and states would likely end up paying a greater share of the costs of programs for the poor.

(Bloom, Parrott, Shapiro, & Super, 1994, p. xxi)

Research points to this outcome. According to an Associated Press analysis in 2007,

> *The welfare state is bigger than ever despite a decade of policies designed to wean poor people from public aid. The number . . . receiving cash benefits from welfare has plummeted since the government imposed time limits on the payments a decade ago. But other programs for the poor . . . are bursting with new enrollees.*

(New York Times)

While cash assistance spending dropped, expenditures on noncash assistance grew significantly. Table 6.1 outlines the changes in a nine-state sample conducted by the U.S. General Accounting Office (2006). Welfare-related healthcare costs grew the most, only marginally offset by reductions in cash assistance. In the nine-state sample, while the states cut back $8.4 billion in cash assistance, they spent an additional $25 billion in healthcare and $17.4 billion in noncash assistance programs, all in constant dollars controlling for inflation. Thus, while people were leaving the welfare rolls and no longer receiving a monthly cash assistance check, they were accessing other social support programs targeted for low-income families. The question this raises is: Did the loss of cash assistance create more hardships so that families needed support? And/or, does trying to assist poor adults in gaining employment and self-sufficiency cost more than providing monthly cash assistance payments?

What we do seem to know is that the efforts at welfare reform did not address poverty and true economic self-sufficiency for families receiving public assistance, especially following years of economic decline. Instead, we witnessed the frustration and anger of a society struggling with structural changes that are not easily addressed. Single-parent families are a reality at all economic levels, but the impact is especially felt for low-income families.

Table 6.1 Changes in Welfare-Related Expenditures, 1995–2004

Categories of Change in Real Spending	Median (%)	Total Dollars (in Billions)
Noncash assistance (employment services and training, work, other supports, and aid for at-risk families)	+45	+17.4
Welfare-related healthcare	+61	+24.9
Cash assistance	−62	−8.4

Note: Nine-state sample—CA, CO, LA, MD, MI, NY, OR, TX, WI

Author calculations based on data in U.S. General Accounting Office, 2006, *Welfare Reform: Better Information Needed to Understand Trends in States' Uses of the TANF Block Grant*. GAO-06-414. Washington, DC: Author.

Inherent Contradictions in Welfare Reform

TANF was designed to end welfare as we knew it. It was enacted to promote economic self-sufficiency and promote the nuclear two-parent family. It does this by limiting the amount of time a family can receive assistance and by mandating work efforts. It created rewards for marriage and penalized a woman for the birth of an additional child out of wedlock. These efforts, while touted as reform, raise several contradictions.

If the best people to raise a child are his or her parents, then support of the parents to be *with* their child would be imperative—hence the legislative incentives for marriage, pushing father involvement through child support enforcement, and deterring out-of-wedlock births. However, if those parental roles are not met, then the one parent who *is* willing and able to be with the child is mandated to *leave* her child during the day with someone else, and is not supported to stay at home to care for her child. This position deviated from the original intent of the program, which was to keep a mother at home to raise her children in the event that the father was gone. The effort at welfare reform reinforces the contradiction that although a child's own parent is the best caretaker, if that parent does not conform to the model of two-parent/male and female/married, then public support will not be provided.

The outcome is not at all focused on the well-being of the child or on the support of the caretaking parent, but only on perpetuating one and only one option of family structure, a structure that has declined in the overall society anyway. From 1960 to 2008, the rate of divorce in the United States increased 59 percent, and the rate of marriages declined by almost 20 percent (U.S. Census Bureau, 2011). It is difficult to mandate family constellations for those who are not dependent on government programs, but we do so for those who are.

Values Conflicts

Poverty is related to both individual behaviors and structural conditions. However, the continued existence of poverty in the United States goes beyond these two reasons. Why do Americans accept poverty as a perpetual part of the economy and social fabric? Why are we not distressed that in the wealthiest nation in the world there are millions of people who are living without enough food, clothing, and adequate shelter?

People are not opposed to the principle of government support for the needy, but instead there is a very strong perception that most people who receive welfare are undeserving. Gilens (1999), in a comprehensive study of public attitudes toward welfare, concluded that a major reason why higher-income people oppose welfare is because they lack personal experience with welfare and thus have different perceptions of how it impacts the lives of people who are poor. The reason for our disconnect between social well-being and poverty is our inability to relate to, and in turn understand, what it is to live in poverty and why people seem to be stuck there. In researching attitudes toward public assistance, Gilens (1999) found that:

> *Well-off Americans are more likely to want welfare spending cut, but this desire is not motivated by self-interest; rather, it reflects the different experiences with and perceptions of welfare that characterize Americans of different social classes.* (p. 31)

We are a conflicted nation when it comes to need and responsibility. Nearly two-thirds of the public believe that "The government should guarantee every citizen enough to eat and a place to sleep," yet 78 percent believe that "People should take responsibility for their own lives and economic well-being and not expect other people to help" (Bostrom, 2001). Several conflicting values reflect the split between believing in government support and expecting individuals to be personally responsible for their well-being (Segal, 2007). The following key areas where people's values and beliefs split compound the difficulties we face in trying to create social policies that address poverty and in turn welfare reform.

Undeserving vs. Deserving

The concept of who deserves to be helped and who does not officially dates back to colonial times and the adoption of the Elizabethan Poor Laws. Although public awareness grew that some people simply need help, the standard was that they should be deserving of that help. *Deserving* was translated into need through no fault of one's own. Thus, widows, orphans, people with physical disabilities, and the elderly fit into legitimate categories of need. Able-bodied adults who were not working were seen as undeserving. These differentiations continue today. However, what about a young man who might want to work, but who dropped out of school at 16? Do we hold that young man responsible for the rest of his life for the decision to leave school, or do we try and intervene to assist him? And if we do intervene, do we do it with a monthly cash assistance check, do we enroll him in a work program, or do we send him back to school? We tend to make that decision based on the next set of conflicting values.

Self-Sufficiency vs. Social Support

How much is each individual responsible for having enough to eat, a safe place to live, and an education? To what extent is it our collective social responsibility to ensure these things? If we view poverty as the result of a person's unwillingness to work hard enough or of mistakes the person has made in his or her life, then we are most likely going to focus on individual responsibility. If we view poverty as a consequence of social conditions, then we are most likely going to call for public policies and programs that address poverty through government and societal efforts. For some of us, the value of social responsibility is so strong that it may not matter who is at fault for poverty—the individual or society. Rather, our responsibility to others is greater than our focus on individualism. Thus, we believe it is important to take care of all people, regardless of the cause of their need. Even when we are willing to provide support, there is a values conflict over how to provide that support.

Entitlement vs. Handout

Being entitled implies an earned right to something. The sense is that for previous efforts one has given, he or she is now rewarded. The Social Security program falls under this model. A handout implies that a person is getting something yet doing nothing in return. In the early years of ADC, women heads of households were seen as doing a social good: They were raising their children despite having lost their husbands. Over time that perception changed as the type of women receiving assistance changed. No longer widows but divorced or never-married mothers, the perception became that of people getting something for doing nothing. By 1996 this belief was so strong that it was a major impetus behind welfare reform.

Sympathy vs. Empathy

Despite what may have seemed to be callousness in welfare reform policy, there was a great deal of talk about helping and caring. A few years later, the phrase "compassionate conservative" was coined and used by George W. Bush in his presidential bid and captured the sentiment behind welfare reform. Many welfare advocates were confused by this concept, viewing the changes as anything but compassionate. The confusion lies in the distinction between sympathy and empathy. Both call for examining what others have experienced, but the concepts differ in application. Sympathy, like compassion, involves feeling bad for people and hoping to help them. Empathy requires understanding the situation and circumstances around another person's situation and imagining what it would be like to be in those same circumstances. It tends to consider the environment and outside factors, whereas sympathy typically focuses on the individual's role and responsibility. Advocates for welfare reform displayed a great deal of sympathy, but very little empathy.

The Gap in Experiencing and Understanding Poverty

Contributing to welfare reform failure is the gap between those who experience poverty and those who decide what to do about it. Policy makers today are educated people of substantial economic means who live far removed from poor people for whom they create social programs. Table 6.2 outlines the differences between the recipients of public assistance through the

Table 6.2   Comparison of Temporary Assistance for Needy Families Adult Recipients and Members of Congress

	TANF Adults	Members of Congress
Average Age	31 years	55 years
Female	90%	14.4%
White	31.6%	87.1%
Black	38.3%	6.9%
Hispanic	24.9%	4.5%
More than a high school education	3.3%	92.7%
Employment rate	25.3%	100%
Millionaires	0	29.2%

From E. A. Segal, 2006, "Welfare as We *Should* Know It: Social Empathy and Welfare Reform" (p. 271), in K. M. Kilty and E. A. Segal, *The Promise of Welfare Reform: Political Rhetoric and the Reality of Poverty in the Twenty-first Century*, Binghamton, NY: Haworth Press. Adapted with permission.

TANF program and the policy makers who enacted welfare reform legislation that created the TANF program (Segal, 2006). The members of Congress who crafted and enacted welfare reform were predominantly older, married, white men with high levels of income and education. They were developing a program for unmarried young women, a majority of whom were women of color, with low levels of education and no income. The divide between the rich and the poor is not just about lifestyles; it is also about who makes decisions about and for people who are vastly different from themselves.

Although we are not often privy to the personal experiences or beliefs of policy makers and their families, the President's mother revealed the distance between herself and those who are poor, while doing so with great sympathy. In the fall of 2005 following Hurricane Katrina, former First Lady Barbara Bush toured hurricane relief centers in Houston, Texas. After her visit, she stated that "so many of the people here were underprivileged anyway. This is working very well for them" (Editor & Publisher, 2005). This was her response to the conditions for people who had lost their homes and all of their possessions, and who were likely to have been poor before the hurricane. Barbara Bush is not a mean person, but she lives far removed from the average person's life and even farther removed from someone living in poverty. She did not lack sympathy or compassion, but she did lack empathy.

Social Empathy

What Is Social Empathy?

Social empathy describes the insights one has about other people's lives that allow one to understand the circumstances and realities of other people's living situations (Segal, 2007, 2011). Why is empathy important?

Empathy for individuals is key to personal growth (Watson, 2002). Research suggests that people with empathy are more likely to be civic-minded and become responsible citizens (Loeb, 1999). In 1994, Daniel Goleman wrote about emotional intelligence and its importance for personal and social development. He outlined five key domains of emotional intelligence. Empathy serves as one of the key components (Goleman, 1994). Without empathy, people tend to behave in ways that are less socially productive. A lack of empathy is strongly correlated with destructive tendencies (Hoffman, 1984), the worst of which may be sociopathic behaviors (Stout, 2005). For the most part, research has focused on empathy and individual behaviors, but what is the impact on society when empathy is used in policy making, or the converse, when it is not?

Empathetic individuals, if they are in decision-making positions, can use their empathy to guide their course of action. But relying on empathetic policy makers can be hit or miss, and more miss today as the experiences of those at the top are so distant from those at the bottom. Although we can hope for empathetic individuals to come forward and serve in policy-making positions, we can also work to create a culture of empathy that focuses on social issues. That is the goal of social empathy: To use insights about the circumstances of peoples' lives to develop public policies and programs that are appropriate and responsive to those in need.

The Benefits of Social Empathy

When we have social empathy, we are more likely to develop practices, services, programs, and policies that promote social justice. Social empathy provides a framework for addressing the key social inequality of poverty. This perspective has been absent from welfare reform policy making in recent years. What difference might it make if we had a deep understanding of what it is like to be a young single mother, with perhaps only a high school education, living each day full of uncertainties such as where to sleep, if there is enough to eat, where to go to get medical care, how to get clothing, where to leave your young child while you go out and look for a job, and what to do if all of these basic needs are unmet? What difference would it make if we really understood the social and economic context of this mother's life? The difference it makes is that if we truly understand, if we can imagine ourselves in her situation, then we can better respond to those needs.

The foundation of TANF was the Great Depression. It is interesting to note that the piece of social legislation in the United States that gave rise to the ADC program, the Social Security Act of 1935, was sponsored by two members of Congress who intimately understood the limitations of poverty and social inequality:

> On January 17, 1935, President Roosevelt asked Congress for social security legislation. That same day, the administration's bill was introduced in both houses of Congress by men who had felt keenly the meaning of social insecurity.

Robert Wagner, who steered the social security measure through the Senate, was the son of a janitor; as an immigrant boy, he had sold papers on the streets of New York. Maryland's David Lewis, who guided the bill through the House, had gone to work at nine in a coal mine. Illiterate at sixteen, he had taught himself to read not only English but French and German; he had learned French to verify a translation of Tocqueville. The aged, Davy Lewis declared, were "America's untouchables... Even under slavery, the owner did not deny his obligation to feed and clothe and doctor the slaves, no matter what might happen to crops or to markets."

(Congressional Record, 74th Congress, 1st session, p. 5687, cited in Leuchtenburg, 1963, p. 131)

These members of Congress drew from their personal experiences with poverty. They supported legislation that addressed structural poverty, rather than solely focused on individual failures. Today, very few policy makers grew up impoverished. How can we expect today's privileged politicians to understand poverty firsthand? Because policy makers and those in positions of economic and social power are so far removed from the day-to-day experiences of people who are poor, it is necessary to help them to understand what it means to live in poverty. Developing social empathy is the key to creating social policies and programs that go much deeper in ameliorating the contributing factors to poverty.

Where Do We Go From Here? The Future of Welfare in America

Despite ongoing efforts to eradicate public welfare, dating back to even before passage of the Social Security Act in 1935, the program is still here. The reauthorization of TANF in 2005 and annual extensions demonstrate that while paring back the program, it appears to be entrenched in the social welfare landscape of America. The social value of regarding the program from the perspective of individual responsibility also seems to be entrenched. However, this perspective misses what may be the most important aspect of the TANF program, yet it is rarely addressed. What about the children? Three-fourths of TANF recipients are children. Demanding a change in their family structure ignores the day-to-day living situation of these children. To not promote healthy development of the children, regardless of what choices their parents made, is shortsighted. Research by a panel of national poverty experts highlights how shortsighted our social welfare policies are in terms of childhood poverty:

Our results suggest that the costs to the U.S. associated with childhood poverty total about $500B per year, or the equivalent of nearly 4 percent of GDP. More specifically, we estimate that childhood poverty each year:

- *Reduces productivity and economic output by about 1.3 percent of GDP*
- *Raises the costs of crime by 1.3 percent of GDP*
- *Raises health expenditures and reduces the value of health by 1.2 percent of GDP*

(Holzer, Schanzenbach, Duncan, & Ludwig, 2007)

Children are not capable of finding jobs that pay decent wages or securing adequate housing or healthcare or education. If we think those are necessities for poor children, then we need to reexamine welfare reform. And we need to do so from the perspective of what it means to be in that situation, using social empathy to construct effective public programs.

Key Terms

welfare and
   welfare
   reform

Aid to Families
   with Dependent
   Children

social empathy
public assistance
entitlement

Review Questions for Critical Thinking

1. Though there are exceptions, the maximum number of years a family is eligible for TANF assistance is five years. Explain how this is or is not a fair standard.

2. To what extent does TANF reflect the concept of social empathy?

3. Should welfare reform efforts emphasize education and training or focus on increased funding to families?

4. Is welfare the responsibility of the federal, state, and local governments? If so, identify statements from governing documents (e.g., Bill of Rights, your state's constitution, and your town or city's charter) that specify this responsibility.

5. How should programs such as TANF respond during periods of severe economic recession, such as the most recent global economic crisis that began in late 2008? Should benefits be expanded; should the time limit be waived; should there be aggressive program recruitment to ensure that all eligible people receive services?

Online Resources

The Brookings Institution: www.brookings.edu

The Urban Institute: www.urban.org

The Cato Institute: www.cato.org

U.S. Government Accountability Office: www.gao.gov

Administration for Children & Families: www.acf.hhs.gov

References

Abramovitz, M. (2000). *Under attack, fighting back: Women and welfare in the United States*. New York, NY: Monthly Review Press.

Acs, G., & Loprest, P. (2004). *Leaving welfare: Employment and well-being of families that left welfare in the post-entitlement era*. Kalamazoo, MI: W. E. Upjohn Institute for Employment Research.

Administration for Children & Families. (2012). TANF caseload data 2011. Available at www.act.hhs.gov/programs/ofa/data-reports/caseload

Albelda, R. (2001). Fallacies of welfare-to-work policies. *Annals of the American Academy of Political and Social Science*, *577*, 66–78.

Axinn, J. M., & Hirsch, A. E. (1993). Welfare and the "reform" of women. *Families in Society*, *74*(9), 563–572.

Bloom, D., Parrott, S., Shapiro, I., & Super, D. (1994). *The Personal Responsibility Act: An analysis*. Washington, DC: Center on Budget and Policy Priorities.

Bostrom, M. (2001). *Achieving the American dream: A meta-analysis of public opinion concerning poverty, upward mobility, and related issues*. New York, NY: Ford Foundation.

Congressional Budget Office. (2012). *The budget and economic outlook: Fiscal years 2012–2022*. Washington, DC: Government Printing Office.

DeNavas-Walt, C., Proctor, B. D., & Lee, C. H. (2006). *Income, poverty, and health insurance coverage in the United States: 2005*. Current Population Reports, P60-231. Washington, DC: U.S. Census Bureau.

DeNavas-Walt, C., Proctor, B. D., & Smith, J. C. (2011). *Income, poverty, and health insurance coverage in the United States: 2010*. Current Population Reports, P60-239. Washington, DC: U.S. Census Bureau.

Derthick, M. (1979). *Policymaking for Social Security*. Washington, D.C.: Brookings Institution.

Editor & Publisher (2005, September 5). Barbara Bush: Things working out "very well" for poor evacuees from New Orleans. Retrieved on March 20, 2012 from www.editorandpublisher.com/eandp/news/article/

Falk, G., Gish, M., & Solomon-Fears, C. (2006). *Welfare reauthorization: An overview of the issues*. Washington, DC: Congressional Research Service, Library of Congress.

Gilens, M. (1999). *Why Americans hate welfare*. Chicago, IL: University of Chicago Press.

Goleman, D. (1994). *Emotional intelligence*. New York, NY: Bantam.

Gordon, L. (2001). Who deserves help? Who must provide? *Annals of the American Academy of Political and Social Science*, *577*, 12–25.

Hoffman, M. L. (1984). Empathy, social cognition, and moral action. In W. Kurtines & J. Gerwitz (Eds.), *Moral behavior and development: Advances in theory*. New York, NY: John Wiley & Sons.

Holzer, H. J., Schanzenbach, D. W., Duncan, G. J., & Ludwig, J. (2007). *The economic costs of poverty in the United States: Subsequent effects of children growing up poor*. Washington, DC: Center for American Progress.

Katz, M. B. (1989). *The undeserving poor: From the War on Poverty to the war on welfare*. New York, NY: Pantheon Books.

King, C. T., & Mueser, P. R. (2005). Urban welfare and work experiences: Implications for welfare reform. *Employment Research*, *12*(3), 1–4.

Leuchtenburg, W. E. (1963). *Franklin D. Roosevelt and the New Deal*. New York, NY: Harper & Row.

Loeb, P. R. (1999). *Soul of a citizen: Living with conviction in a cynical time*. New York, NY: St. Martin's Press.

New York Times. (February 26, 2007). Welfare state growing despite overhauls. Available at: www.nytimes.com/aponline/us/AP-Welfare-State.html

Parrott, S., & Sherman, A. (2006). *TANF at 10: Program results are more mixed than often understood*. Washington, DC: Center on Budget and Policy Priorities.

Patterson, J. T. (2000). *America's struggle against poverty in the twentieth century*. Cambridge, MA: Harvard University Press.

Piven, F. F., & Cloward, R. A. (1971). *Regulating the poor: The functions of public welfare*. New York, NY: Random House.

Segal, E. A. (2006). Welfare as we *should* know it: Social empathy and welfare reform. In K. M. Kilty & E. A. Segal, *The promise of welfare reform: Political rhetoric and the reality of poverty in the twenty-first century* (pp. 265–274). Binghamton, NY: Haworth Press.

Segal, E. A. (2007). *Social welfare policy and social programs: A values perspective*. Belmont, CA: Thomson/Brooks Cole.

Segal, E. A. (2011). Social empathy: A model built on empathy, contextual understanding, and social responsibility that promotes social justice. *Journal of Social Service Research*, *37*, 266–277.

Segal, E. A., & Kilty, K. M. (2003). Political promises for welfare reform. *Journal of Poverty*, *7*(1/2), 51–67.

Social Security Administration. (2006). *Annual statistical supplement, 2005*. Washington, DC: Author.

Stout, M. (2005). *The sociopath next door*. New York, NY: Broadway Books.

Trattner, W. I. (1999). From poor law to welfare state: A history of social welfare in America (6th ed.). New York, NY: Free Press.

U.S. Census Bureau. (2011). *Statistical abstract of the United States* (131st ed.). Washington, DC: Government Printing Office.

U.S. Department of Health and Human Services. (1996). Personal Responsibility and Work Opportunity Reconciliation Act of 1996 (Sections 401 and 402). Retrieved on July 10, 2012, from www.acf.hhs.gov/programs/cb/laws-policies/cblaws/public_law/pl104_193/pl104_193/pl104_193.htm

U.S. Department of Health and Human Services. (1998). *Aid to Families with Dependent Children: The baseline*. Washington, DC: Office of Human Services Policy.

U.S. General Accounting Office. (2006). *Welfare reform: Better information needed to understand trends in states' uses of the TANF block grant*. GAO-06-414. Washington, DC: Author.

Watson, J. C. (2002). Re-visioning empathy. In D. J. Cain & J. Seeman (Eds.), *Humanistic psychotherapies: Handbook of research and practice* (pp. 445–471). Washington, DC: American Psychological Association.

Wilson, W. J. (1987). *The truly disadvantaged: The inner city, the underclass, and public policy*. Chicago, IL: University of Chicago Press.

Chapter 7

Not by the Numbers Alone: The Effects of Economic and Demographic Changes on Social Policy

Michael Reisch[1]

Is it possible to create effective social policies that do not pit one group against another (e.g., children vs. seniors, healthy vs. unhealthy, African Americans vs. Hispanics, Muslims vs. Christians)? Has globalization opened the door to intense discrimination and prejudice?

Introduction

The United States is experiencing dramatic human changes as a result of global economic and demographic transformations. As the world moves closer to the year 2025, the number of so-called super powers continues to grow. No longer do the Western nations reign supreme in the world; globalization is leveling the economic playing field while broadening the number of nations that now influence world politics and relations. To think that as the global situation changes that U.S. policy would not is far from accurate and certainly naive. Even as the offshoots of globalization continue to manifest themselves in all spheres of life, there is a growing resistance by U.S. elected officials and public employees to respond aggressively. There is a growing political fervor fueled by the so-called Tea Party to reduce and eliminate federal and state government core services, such as healthcare/health insurance and public education. Simply stated, some groups believe that the government has become too big, unwieldy, and intrusive, and is driving the United States into an economic oblivion.

[1] The author would like to thank his research assistant, Katie Januario, for her help in updating this chapter.

Since the 19th century, social policies in the United States have been shaped by rapid economic growth and sociodemographic transformation, particularly from the effects of industrialization, urbanization, immigration, and internal migration. These changes, which have altered the racial, ethnic, and religious makeup of U.S. society, have been compounded recently by the aging of the population, evolving gender roles, different conceptions of adolescence, and new cultural attitudes regarding marriage, parenting, the family, and sexual orientation. Some of these developments result from what Titmuss (1963) called the "diswelfares" of modern society, such as unemployment or underemployment, industrial accidents, and occupation-related illness. Others are the environmental byproducts of unrestrained economic growth or the emergence of new cultural norms in an increasingly complex, multicultural society.

In response to these changes, the United States has developed a form of welfare capitalism, which consists of a patchwork of state and federal policies designed to create a floor on aggregate consumption, while reinforcing longstanding cultural values about work through the stigmatization of dependency (Blau with Abramovitz, 2010; Jansson, 2005; McDonald & Reisch, 2008; Stern & Axinn, 2012). Government funding for social policies has been limited; the locus of policy making has often been decentralized; and the private, nonprofit sector has played an important role in the provision of what remains a fragmented network of services. Social policies have been rationalized by certain underlying assumptions about the relationship of government to the market, the motivations for individual and collective behavior, and the goals of the social welfare system. Among these assumptions is that economic, demographic, social, and cultural issues arise from distinct sources and can, therefore, be addressed separately in the policy arena. Over the past several decades, however, such assumptions have been challenged or undermined by dramatic shifts in the global economy and an unprecedented transformation of the nation's population (Reisch, 2012).

A major change has occurred, for example, in the scope of those issues that concern contemporary policy makers. It is now widely acknowledged that problems such as economic inequality, immigration, epidemic disease, and environmental degradation must be addressed in a cross-national context (Xu, 2007). Yet, our policy-making and policy implementation apparatus remains locked in anachronistic patterns (Ferrera, 2005). In addition, the devolution of policy making and implementation over the past quarter century has exacerbated the nation's inability to respond to such problems effectively and efficiently. If we cannot even formulate local or regional approaches to social and economic problems, how can we possibly begin to address them on a global scale? (Lorenz, 2006).

Economic Globalization

The most significant economic development during the past several decades has been economic globalization. Since the early 1970s, the global economic system has undergone revolutionary changes, which distinguish the world economy of today from the internationalization of commerce that has existed for millennia. The key features of this new global economy are the rapid mobility and liquidity of capital, the short-term nature of investments, the interlocking connections of national currency systems, the speed and growing importance of information transfer, the increased power of multi-national corporations, the specialization of knowledge and production, and the declining influence of countervailing political forces to direct or control these processes. As a consequence of globalization, manufacturing and service industries are outsourced overseas, fewer workers with higher skills are needed to maintain corporate productivity rates, gender distinctions in the workplace have been blurred, and a seemingly intractable and widening gap in income, wealth, education, skills, and status has emerged between classes and races both globally and in the United States (Center on Budget and Policy Priorities, 2011; Mourre, 2009; Rehbein, 2011; World Bank, 2010).

These trends have multiple implications for social policy development, some of them direct and explicit (such as the need to improve the nation's education system) and others more subtle and implied. For example, the domestic market has become a less significant source of corporate growth as a consequence of globalization (Bureau of Labor Statistics, 2011a; National Employment Law Project, 2010). This diminishes the importance of social policies, such as income transfer programs and wage/hour regulations, which over the past 75 years have been designed to maintain levels of consumption among Americans.

In a globalized economy, the efficiency of the corporate sector is increasingly predicated upon lowering the costs of production, especially labor, and shifting the social costs of the market (such as pollution and healthcare) onto the public sector (Kapp, 1972). In this context, the attraction of overseas markets, the lure of cheap, unorganized labor, and the opportunity to exploit less restrictive or nonexistent occupational safety and environmental policies encourage and facilitate the transfer of corporate production and service delivery to sites abroad. Under the guise of promoting free trade and economic growth, the U.S. government has abetted such steps through its tax policies and the passage of treaties like the North American Free Trade Agreement (NAFTA). Thus, while corrective measures to ameliorate the social impact costs of globalization are now considered an indispensable aspect of the international economic system, it is widely recognized that these costs cannot be eliminated or significantly reduced without a major revision of the system. Ironically, the short-term goals of the global market system, expressed most powerfully in the United States, preclude the implementation of such corrective steps (Bergman & Lundberg, 2006; Klein, 2007; Reisch, 2011).

These developments have also changed the nature of labor-management and corporate-community relationships, with consequences for those social policies that have traditionally provided workers and community residents with economic and social support. Recent labor-management conflicts in both the public and private sectors now focus increasingly on issues of givebacks, productivity demands, job security, and collective bargaining rights, rather than wage or benefit levels. Similarly, corporate-community relationships have been transformed by heightened interstate and intrastate competition for jobs. In an era of policy devolution and persistent state fiscal crisis, this has had devastating effects on the level of social provision that states and localities can afford (Johnson, Oliff, & Williams, 2011).

At a more fundamental level, the nature of property, property relations, and work itself have been changed by economic globalization. In other words, our assumptions about these fundamental building blocks of economic and social policies since the Industrial Revolution are far less valid today than they were even a few decades ago. For example, property is being transformed from cash, land, and other tangible commodities into credits. National and international economic and social policies now focus primarily on the protection of investors' property rights, rather than on the rights of the producers or consumers of wealth. Radical changes have also occurred in the nature of many occupations, the social basis of work, and the stability of employment (Bureau of Labor Statistics, 2011b; Burtless & Looney, 2012; Censky, 2011).

Economic globalization has been buttressed by an accompanying ideological rationale: that capitalist goals, values, and behaviors pervade the world economy and shape all major institutions and market mechanisms (Klein, 2007; Krugman & Wells, 2011). These changes appear in the language that guides policy discourse, in the distribution of power (both within the public domain and between the public and private sectors), and in views of politics itself (i.e., the process of determining and legitimating societal priorities). Although wide variation still exists in national economies, in most of the industrialized world, policy making reflects the logic of maintaining a system of global capitalism. Its proponents assert that the transfer of national resources from production for domestic use to production for export is required to promote consistent economic development and to maintain a competitive edge in the global market (Reisch, 2012).

Critics counter that an emphasis on foreign trade destabilizes longstanding institutions and community relationships, particularly in regions of the developing world with established, subsistence-model economies. Such effects are felt even in advanced economies like the United States. Since the mid-to-late 1970s, transnational corporations have destroyed local enterprises, precious natural resources have been privatized, social spending has been drastically reduced, taxation systems have become increasingly regressive, and both public and private debt burdens have soared.

Then, in 2007, the collapse of a speculative housing bubble, the rapacious behavior of financiers, and the timidity of policy makers nearly brought down the global financial system and wreaked havoc on the lives of tens of millions of people. The current obsession with debt, deficits, and austerity continues to threaten human well-being in both industrialized and developing nations (Palley, 2012). The social impact of these developments has also been dramatic, most notably in statistics that reflect negative social indicators, such as violent crime and neighborhood deterioration (Hulme, 2010; Kim, 2009; Lightman, Mitchell, & Herd, 2008).

Economic globalization has also revealed many of the anachronistic features of our policy-making system and the declining importance of political boundaries and allegiances. Simply put, national governments (to say nothing of state or local governments) lack the scope, speed of action, and institutional capacity to respond to economic, demographic, and social problems emanating from forces outside of their span of control. The 20th-century welfare state was founded on the belief that national governments could regulate the effects of national economies. Now that economies are transnational in scope, governments lack the authority and power (some suggest the will, as well) to change their social policies in response (Klein, 2007; Reisch, 2012).

In addition, globalization has diminished the role of organized labor in struggles to maintain or expand the share of the social wage received by working people. Particularly in industrialized nations such as the United States, real wages have decreased since the mid-1970s, and employment has become increasingly insecure (Economic Policy Institute, 2010; Mishel & Shierholz, 2011; U.S. Bureau of the Census, 2010). So-called "lean production" techniques, whose purpose is to enhance productivity and reduce labor costs, have led to such methods as on-time production, the substitution of unskilled for skilled workers, and outsourcing. These effects are now visible in the service sector as well, including health and mental health settings, universities, and child welfare agencies (Collins, Kim, Clay, & Perlstein, 2009; Olsen, 2007; Reisch & Jani, 2012).

Globalization has also been closely linked to emerging demographic trends, including the mass movement of populations in search of employment, primarily from the global south to industrialized nations. In the United States, this has led to the perception of a crisis over immigration, particularly concerning undocumented immigrants. It has also exacerbated existing social and political conflicts, often along ethnic or racial lines. Some of the policy implications of these conflicts will be discussed in following sections.

Poverty, Inequality, and Unemployment

While proponents of globalization frequently tout its benefits for the nation's GNP, its economic impact has been uneven at best. Although median household income in the United States surpasses that of most industrialized nations, the United States has one of the highest poverty rates in the world (Annie E. Casey Foundation, 2012; Brooks, 2011; Luhby, 2011). As of this writing, the official poverty rate in the United States is over 15 percent; more than 46 million people were officially classified as poor in 2011. More than one-quarter of African Americans and Latinos now live below the poverty line and are 2.5 to 3 times more likely than white Americans to be poor.

In contrast to other industrialized nations, children in the United States are the demographic cohort most likely to be poor. Children in poverty "consistently fare worse than children in more affluent families on measures of child well-being, family environment, and sociodemographic risk." They are nearly three times as likely to have fair or poor health and more than twice as likely to have parents who report symptoms of poor mental health (Case, Fertig, & Paxson, 2005; Loprest & Zedlewski, 2006). Child poverty is also a drain on the nation's economy. Five years ago, a study by Holzer, Schanzenbach, Duncan, and Ludwig (2007) concluded that "the costs to the U.S. associated with childhood poverty total about $500 billion per year, or the equivalent of nearly 4 percent of GDP" (p. 1).

The costs are undoubtedly even higher today. Women, particularly elderly women and single parents, are also more likely to be poor at every educational level. The United States has the highest rate of poverty for female-headed households among 22 industrialized nations, about three times higher than average (Buss, 2010). Since the onset of the Great Recession in late 2007, poverty in the United States has spread beyond depressed inner-city neighborhoods and isolated rural areas to the suburbs, particularly in the South and West (Acs & Nichols, 2010).

Many analysts believe that the poverty rate is underestimated by half because it excludes homeless persons, people who are incarcerated, and people "doubled up" and living with family members. It also fails to consider the high cost of living in many metropolitan areas. Three-fourths of Americans have incomes under $50,000 per year, considerably below what it takes to live a minimally decent life in major cities. The official poverty line has not been adjusted to account for increases in real income and changes in living standards since it was formulated nearly 50 years ago. If the poverty line was raised to $25,000, about one-third of the U.S. population (100 million persons) would be considered poor (Buss, 2010).

In the United States, unemployment and wage reductions are the most common cause of poverty. Since the onset of the recession, more than half of all workers have experienced either a pay cut or a layoff, and the percentage of workers facing long-term unemployment (more than 26 weeks) increased from 34 percent to 43 percent. The increase in poverty even among those who are employed and the decline in the proportion of workers with full-time jobs demonstrate the clear connection between unemployment, low wages, and poverty. Without unemployment insurance, an additional 3.3 million people would be counted as poor (Vroman, 2010). Research has demonstrated, however, that the expansion of employment opportunities alone is not sufficient to address these problems unless the jobs that are created pay what is now called a "living wage" (Brooks, 2007; Eisenbrey, Mishel, Bivens, & Fieldhouse, 2011; Holzer & Lerman, 2009).

In addition, the gap between the poverty line and median family income has widened considerably over the past four decades, unlike in European nations, where a relative measure of poverty maintains a standard of 50 percent to 60 percent of median income (Autor, 2010; Center on Budget and Policy Priorities, 2011; National Employment Law Project, 2010). In addition, the U.S. method of determining poverty ignores the enormous socioeconomic changes that have occurred over the past half century in consumption patterns, labor force participation, gender roles, household expenditures, regional shifts in the cost of living, and social policy developments in the areas of health, welfare, and education (Braveman et al., 2011; Cancian, Meyer, & Reed, 2010; Holt, 2011; Iversen, Napolitano, & Furstenberg, 2011; Sherman & Stone, 2010).

Finally, official poverty statistics reveal little about the depth, chronic nature, or likelihood of poverty across the lifespan. They also give no indication of the number of individuals and families who are living just above the official poverty line or of the lasting effects of extended spells of poverty. Poverty has become a deeper and more chronic condition, especially among persons of color and female-headed households. One ominous recent phenomenon is the stark increase in the percentage of low-income families in extreme poverty (i.e., those having incomes 50 percent or less than the poverty line). Nearly 12 percent of African Americans and more than 10 percent of Latinos experience such "deep poverty" (Acs & Nichols, 2010; Buss, 2010). The number of people living in intensive poverty actually increased even before the onset of the Great Recession, particularly among African Americans (U.S. Bureau of the Census, 2006). In addition, African Americans, Latinos, and female-headed household are five times more likely than whites to experience chronic poverty (U.S. Bureau of the Census, 2011).

Nearly half of all individuals who are counted as poor in the United States are now in such extreme or dire poverty (Short, 2011). On average, individuals in poverty have a one in three chance of escaping in a given year, although this probability is much lower among African Americans, Latinos, female-headed households, and larger families. Roughly half of those who escape poverty, however, will become poor again within five years. The psychological and social impact of many people cycling in and out of poverty is profound, with sustained consequences for social services (Acs & Nichols, 2010).

The duration of poverty spells is compounded by the widespread experience of poverty among Americans. Rank (2004) presents startling data demonstrating that more than half of the U.S. population experiences an episode of poverty during their lifetimes of one year or more, and more than three-quarters of the population experiences at least a year of near poverty. Even more striking is his finding that 91 percent of African Americans will experience poverty at some point in their lives. Given our knowledge about the long-term effects of poverty on health, psychological development, and educational attainment, these figures belie the myth of prosperity and widespread well-being in the United States (Edelman, Golden, & Holzer, 2010; Fertig & Reingold, 2008; Lim, Coulton, & Lalich, 2009; Monea & Sawhill, 2010; Pavetti & Rosenbaum, 2010). They also indicate the extent to which large numbers of the U.S. population, particularly in communities of color or immigrant communities, are at risk for a wide range of health, mental health, and social problems (Auerbach & Kellermann, 2011; Galea, Tracy, Hoggatt, DiMaggio, & Karpati, 2011; Inequality.org, n.d.).

The Great Recession underscored how economic globalization and its consequences have increased structural unemployment and underemployment among workers in both developing and industrialized nations. Approximately one-third of the global workforce is now unemployed or underemployed—that is, earning below a living wage (World Bank, 2010). In the United States, the depth and intensity of this phenomenon are often masked by the means used to calculate the official unemployment rate, which has fluctuated between 8 percent and 11 percent since 2008 (Bureau of Labor Statistics, 2009, 2011b). This statistic does not include individuals who are incarcerated, have never entered the workforce (e.g., impoverished inner-city adolescents), have given up looking for work, or are in the military. It also does not include workers who have shifted to part-time employment or taken jobs that pay significantly lower wages and lack healthcare and other fringe benefits (Bureau of Labor Statistics, 2009, 2011a; Van Horn & Zukin, 2011).

Even as U.S. poverty and unemployment statistics increased dramatically in recent years, key indicators of inequality both in the United States and worldwide have soared. Income inequality has nearly tripled in the past half century. The richest 20 percent of the world's population now produces nearly 85 percent of the global GDP, while the poorest one-fifth produces less than 2 percent (Center on Budget and Policy Priorities, 2009; U.S. Bureau of the Census, 2010; Wolff, 2010; World Bank, 2010).

During the past generation, the United States has become the most unequal of all industrialized nations and is more unequal today than at any time since World War II (U.S. Bureau of the Census, 2011). Even before the onset of the current economic crisis, a report published by the Economic Policy Institute and the Center on Budget and Policy Priorities (2006) found that the "incomes of the country's richest families have climbed substantially during the past two decades, while middle and lower-income families have seen only modest increases." Despite the economic booms of the 1980s and 1990s, during the last quarter of the 20th century the lower 60 percent of U.S. households experienced a decline in their share of all income, while the top quintile saw its share increase over 38 percent, and the top 1 percent increased its share by nearly 120 percent. The top 1 percent of all households had as much income to spend as the bottom 40 percent, the largest share of after-tax income since 1979. The top 1 percent of all households earned 22 times as much as the bottom 20 percent in 1979. Today, they earn 70 times as much.

In addition, the share of national assets owned by the richest 1 percent of households has grown from one-fifth to over one-third of all private wealth, the most unequal distribution of the nation's wealth since 1928—the eve of the Great Depression. Inequality has increased for several reasons, including the decline in unions, outsourcing of jobs, stagnation of wages, a decline in the value of public assistance benefits, and changes in the nation's occupational structure and corporate culture (Sherman & Stone, 2010). Although the U.S. economy has begun a slow, if sluggish recovery, as measured by growth in the gross domestic product (GDP), "the triumph of the market has eroded most Americans' standard of living" (Blau, 1999, p. 22).

The long-term implications of these developments are dire. Today, a majority of adult Americans are at economic risk in terms of their levels of literacy and education. More than 50 million Americans lack health insurance and millions more have inadequate coverage. The infant mortality rate in the United States is higher than in some developing nations, and the U.S. life expectancy ranks near the bottom among comparable industrialized countries. While in neighboring Mexico 90 percent of all children under 5 are immunized against childhood diseases, in some U.S. cities the rate is below 50 percent (Children's Defense Fund, 2006).

The primary reasons for increased income inequality are the erosion in wages, particularly for unskilled and undereducated workers, the decline in the purchasing power of the federal minimum wage, which has remained at $7.25 per hour since the middle of the Bush administration, and regressive trends in the overall burden of taxation. Another factor is the impact of new technology and deindustrialization, which have significantly reduced the number of unskilled and semi-skilled entry-level jobs in the workforce, and created what is termed a "dual labor market" (Autor, 2010; Burtless & Looney, 2012; Eisenbrey et al., 2011; Holzer & Lerman, 2009; Mishel & Shierholz, 2011). An additional factor is the impact of foreign competition, particularly from China and India, which is reflected in the United States' burgeoning trade deficit and is exacerbated by the outsourcing of both manufacturing and service jobs. Finally, the declining power of unions has made resistance to these developments more difficult and increased pressure on workers to renegotiate decades-old wage and benefit packages (Reisch, 2009).

The consequences of globalization, however, are not uniformly distributed in the United States. Certain regions have prospered even in times of economic stagnation, whereas others remain mired in recession-like conditions. It is important, therefore, to distinguish between aggregate and distributional data when assessing the extent and nature of economic growth and change. There are also significant differences in poverty, unemployment, and welfare rates among and even within states, often based on the demographic differences of their populations (Annie E. Casey Foundation, 2012; Food Nutrition Service, 2011; Johnson, Oliff, & Williams, 2011; Reisch, 2011).

Policy devolution has exacerbated these trends by reducing the role of the federal government in ameliorating these effects where they are most needed and making state governments responsible for addressing conditions that they did not create. Many states and municipalities now confront the dilemma of responding to increased demands for social and health services in the face of eroding tax bases. Ironically, those states with chronic fiscal crises, such as Michigan and California, are precisely those that need the greatest infusion of resources to address the effects of globalization and demographic changes (Center on Budget and Policy Priorities, 2009; Edelman, Golden, & Holzer, 2010; Hobbie & Barnow, 2011; Sherman & Stone, 2010).

In an analogous fashion, the same contradictory situation confronts families who are experiencing chronic poverty, low-wage work, and unemployment. Although the American dream of upward mobility has some validity, it has largely become a myth, especially for low-income and working-class Americans, who are disproportionately persons of color and immigrants. As educational attainment and job skills become increasingly important determinants of economic success in the global market, children from lower socioeconomic status backgrounds face mounting obstacles resulting from the inadequacy of the schools most of them attend (Allard, 2009; Blank & Kovak, 2008; Collins & Mayer, 2010; Economic Policy Institute, 2012; Wacquant, 2009).

Racial and class gaps in education, particularly in regard to workforce preparation at the secondary school level, create especially acute problems for African American, Latino, and Native American youth. These problems are even more serious for the children of recent immigrants, documented or undocumented, and for children in single-parent, female-headed households. African American and Latino children in these households are at greater risk for poverty and its social consequences because of their parents' lower wages and higher rates of unemployment (Bureau of Labor Statistics, 2010; Collins & Mayer, 2010; Wacquant, 2009).

Thus, data on poverty and economic inequality in the United States are complicated further by the persistence of widespread racial inequality. Throughout U.S. history, race has played a significant role in the development of welfare policies (Brown, 1999; Collins & Mayer, 2010; Jansson, 2005; Katz, 2001; Lieberman, 2005; Patterson, 2001; Soss, Fording, & Schram, 2011; Ward, 2005). Even during periods of social reform, such as the Progressive era, the 1930s, and the 1960s, persons of color faced discrimination in the application of eligibility standards and the distribution of social benefits; they also suffered the effects of white backlash against the modest gains they received. Over the past 40 years, the perpetuation of racial stereotypes in the mass media and the use of racial codes for partisan political purposes reduced public support for welfare programs as a whole (Lieberman, 2005; Quadagno, 1994; Soss, Fording, & Schram, 2011).

In combination with persistent discrimination and the rollback of affirmative action programs, this has produced widening racial gaps in income and assets, which, in turn, result in growing racial disparities in health and education (Abel & Chaudry, 2010; Bates & Swan, 2010; Braveman et al., 2011; Families USA, 2009; Koh, Graham, & Glied, 2011; Lin & Harris, 2008; Lui, Robles, & Leondar-Wright, 2006; Murphy, Bond, Warren, & Maclin, 2008; Reiman & Leighton, 2010; Soss, Hacker, & Mettler, 2007; Twill & Fisher, 2010).

These developments, therefore, are not merely the consequence of uncontrollable global economic forces. They are also the result of conscious policy decisions made during the past quarter century. From the late 1950s through the 1970s, a full-time worker earning the minimum wage could maintain a family of three at or above the poverty level. Since 1981, however, because of the stagnation of minimum wage laws, the same worker's wages have been steadily below this level. The current value of the minimum wage in constant dollars is barely above what it was a half century ago (Economic Policy Institute, 2012; Mishel & Shierholz, 2011).

Today, because of the resistance of policy makers to the expansion of government-subsidized healthcare or health insurance, the majority of working poor families with children lack health benefits. Since the passage of welfare reform in 1996, the proportion of families eligible for public assistance who are now receiving benefits dropped from 80 percent in 1996 to 27 percent in 2009 (Blank, 2002; Schott, 2011; Urban Institute, 2006). At the same time, the percentage of low-income, single-parent families with an employed parent has increased substantially over the past 10 years. Efforts to reform welfare have also exacerbated the problem of children aging out of the foster care system and increased the cost of child welfare programs to states, which bear a disproportionate share of their fiscal burden (Annie E. Casey Foundation, 2012; Collins et al., 2009; Holzer et al., 2007; Johnson et al., 2011).

Demographic Changes: Racism and Immigration

In December 1880, at an informal meeting in New York City, the Committee on Immigration of the National Conference of Charities and Corrections concluded that there was an urgent need for "Federal action to regulate immigration, supervise and protect immigrants, and to guard against the shipment to this country of criminals, and of lunatic, idiotic, crippled, and other infirm alien paupers" (Hoyt, 1881, p. 217). Similar attitudes about immigrants persisted throughout the early 20th century. In a 1901 letter to Homer Folks, a national leader in the field of charities and child welfare, Prescott Hall, the Secretary of the Immigration Restriction League—whose board members included Robert Treat Paine and other leaders of the Charities Organization movement—asked for Folks's support of Congressional legislation, which would

> exclude the more undesirable elements of our present immigration, . . . [specifically those who are] destitute of resources either in money or still more in ability and knowledge of the means to support [themselves]; [those who are] generally ignorant; [those who have] criminal tendencies; [those who are] adverse to country life and congregate in our city slums; [those who have] a low standard of living and little ambition to seek a better life, and [those who have] no permanent interests in this country.
>
> (Hall, 1901)

Hall's language would not seem out of place today on some anti-immigration websites or recently enacted state statutes.

During this period, policy makers focused on two primary concerns about immigrants: their impact on the nation's economy and their effect on a variety of social conditions, including crime and delinquency, public health, family life, and the demographic and cultural balance of the nation (Bowen, 1909; Fishberg, 1906; Hart, 1896; Hugo, 1912; Marshall,

1906; McMurtrie, 1909). Opinions on the former ranged widely, although there was widespread awareness that economic, rather than political, motivations were spurring mass immigration from Europe and Asia. Proponents of immigration like Phillip Garrett (1888) argued that "it is surely conducive to the industrial well-being of the United States that a constant healthy flow of immigration should pour into this continent" (p. 188). Critics cited the threat of "industrial saturation," which would increase unemployment and depress wages, and an increase in undesirable interracial competition. Others commented on the danger of exploitation, particularly of young women and children (Coletti, 1912; Gates, 1909; Sulzberger, 1912; Taylor, 1913; U.S. Industrial Commission on Immigration and Education, 1901; Wald, 1909; Weyl, 1905).

Views about the social impact of unrestricted immigration reflected similar differences. Opponents of unrestricted immigration spoke of the need "to rid ourselves of aliens who are a burden to our people or a menace to our peace and welfare," cited the challenges of linguistic and cultural assimilation, and discussed the menace of growing numbers of "foreign quarters" in U.S. cities (Antwerp, 1890; Guenther, 1896, p. 305). Legislative proposals included deportation of immigrants who became dependents, tighter regulation of entry into the United States to screen out "convicts, lunatics, idiots, or others likely to become a public charge," and more stringent state residency laws (Gates, 1898; Hoyt, 1887; Hoyt, Sanborn, & Dana, 1886; Sanborn, 1886).

These attitudes about immigrants, particularly non-European immigrants, have persisted throughout U.S. history since colonial times. In the modern era, they have shaped restrictive federal legislation (most notably in 1882 and 1924), forced the repatriation of Mexican immigrants in the 1920s and 1930s, justified the incarceration of Japanese Americans during World War II, led to the passage of discriminatory state laws, such as Proposition 187 in California, and spurred the current militarization of the United States–Mexico border. Even within the social welfare field, repeated concerns have been expressed about the alleged criminality of immigrants, their demands on the social service system, and, particularly in times of economic distress, their impact on the workforce (Barrabee, 1954; Bowler, 1931; Hopkins, 1932; Kohler, 1931; Lamb, 1942; Larned, 1930; MacCormack, 1934; Powell, 1943; Snyder, 1930; Warren, 1933). It was not until the post–World War II era that concerns about the quality of services to immigrants and migrants began to be discussed in earnest (Douglass, 1955; Hoey, 1947; Rawley, 1948). These concerns recurred in the 1970s and 1980s in the aftermath of the Vietnam War, with an increased emphasis on improving the scope of substance of programs addressing these issues (Blum, 1978, 1981; Finch, 1982–1983; Jones, 1981; Palmieri, 1980).

On the whole, however, U.S. policies have been fueled by persistent myths about the economic and social impact of immigrants. These include such myths as the following:

- *There are too many immigrants*. This myth is especially powerful when the immigrants are from different races, ethnicities, and religions and when the proportion of immigrants in urban areas equals or exceeds that of the native-born population. This situation existed in Chicago and New York at the turn of the 20th century and is present today in New York, California, Florida, and Texas. This myth is often coupled with other myths, such as that most immigrants are poor and uneducated and are disproportionately involved in crime.

- *Immigrants take jobs from U.S. citizens and decrease the standard of living*. This myth is particularly prevalent today among low-income whites and African Americans. It is usually most powerful during periods of economic insecurity or stagnation and in regions with high rates of poverty and unemployment.

- *The influx of immigrants will destroy the nation's cultural heritage and undermine its civilization*. The roots of this nativist sentiment go back at least as far as the creation of the Know-Nothing Party of the 1840s, perhaps even to the colonial period. At one time or another, the specter of cultural decline has been raised in the aftermath of Irish, Italian, Eastern European, Chinese, and Mexican immigration. Today, it is reflected in attacks on bilingual education, in support for English-only ballot initiatives, and in the anti-immigrant laws being debated in Congress.

- *Immigrants do not pay taxes—or pay insufficient taxes—and drain government resources by placing excessive demands on health and social services*. This myth persists, despite numerous studies to the contrary, and the discriminatory pattern of policy implementation toward immigrants (Borjas, 2002; Capps, Fix, Ost, Reardon-Anderson, & Passel, 2004; Chapin Hall, 2011; Chow, Osterling, & Xu, 2005; Drachman, 1995; Foner, 1987; Jensen & Chitose, 1994; Muller, 1993; Rand Corporation, 2006; Tumlin & Zimmerman, 2003; Ward, 2005).

The persistence of these myths obscures many of the real issues that immigrants confront, such as increased juvenile delinquency among second-generation immigrant youth, and the wide variation in the experiences, problems, and needs of different groups. By viewing all immigrants through the same lens, it also masks the role of race, regional, and religious differences among immigrants, even those from the same country (Bean & Stevens, 2003; Borjas, 2002; Capps et al., 2004; Carlson, 1994; Gold, 1989; Karoly & Gonzalez, 2011; Kirmani & Leung, 2008; Kissane, 2010; Layzer & Burnstein, 2007; Lee & DeVita, 2008; Neidell & Waldfogel, 2009). In addition, myths about immigration make it harder to distinguish the effects of immigration and internal migration, among both immigrants and the native-born population, and to examine the relationship between these phenomena (Office of Planning, Research, and Evaluation, 2011; Portes, 1990; Waldinger, 2001; Yang, 1995).

Historically, internal migration has occurred for several different reasons in patterns that are frequently repeated among different immigrant groups. One cause of migration is the natural resettlement process of immigrants from the coasts to the heartland, which occurs largely for economic reasons. A second is an intergenerational diaspora, which coincides with broader trends in geographic and economic mobility in the United States. A third explanation is the migration of agricultural workers for employment, which is a cyclic and ongoing process. Finally, throughout U.S. history there have been periods of internal migration because of economic depression, agricultural failures, or political repression. These have included the Great Migration of African Americans in the early 20th century, the movement of dustbowl "Okies" in the 1930s, and the influx of Puerto Ricans to the U.S. mainland in the 1950s (Takaki, 1994).

These periods of internal migration differ from the experiences of immigrants who came to the United States to flee political or religious persecution. Among the latter have been Germans in the mid-19th century; Eastern European Jews in the late 19th and early 20th centuries; Filipinos in the early 20th century; Cubans in the 1920s, 1960s, and 1980s; German and Polish Jews in the 1930s and 1940s; Soviet Jews and Southeast Asians in the 1970s and 1980s; Central Americans in the 1980s; Haitians in the 1980s and 1990s; and Iraqis in the early 21st century (Takaki, 1994; Waldinger, 2001). Today, however, as a result of economic globalization, the lines between immigration and migration have been blurred, as have the distinctions between the economic, social, and political reasons for large population movements (Bates & Swan, 2010; Browne & Braun, 2008; Duncan, 1998; Ferrera, 2005; Penna, Paylor, & Washington, 2000).

Throughout U.S. history, immigrants and migrants have been at greater risk than native-born Americans of living in poverty. In recent decades, this trend has been exacerbated by the general decline in the wage scale particularly for unskilled and semi-skilled labor, changing occupational patterns, and cuts in public school funding and other social supports. Immigrants from Latin America and parts of the Caribbean are particularly vulnerable because of their lack of education and higher birth rates, although the poverty rate among Asian and Pacific Island immigrants is also higher than that of whites (U.S. Bureau of the Census, 2011). These immigrants are increasingly concentrated not only in traditional coastal urban enclaves but also in heartland metropolises such as Minneapolis, Memphis, Denver, and Kansas City. Their presence has produced enhanced intergroup tensions and competition with other low-income communities and, in an era of policy devolution, has intensified pressures on local and state governments to create responsive social policies at the same time as they are struggling with the realities of fiscal austerity (Sherman & Stone, 2010).

As these changes have intensified the need for structural responses to the consequences of unregulated economic transformation, a variety of other demographic factors have made the policy and political environment increasingly complex. The following sociodemographic changes have taken on particular importance:

• *The aging of the population, especially the rapid increase in the so-called old-old population (i.e., those above 85).* This already has had a dramatic impact on the cost of healthcare and has precipitated a fiscal "time bomb" in Medicare funding, which the nation's policy makers have, to date, failed to address (Aaron, 2011). Less frequently discussed, but no less significant consequences of this change have occurred in housing and employment patterns (e.g., for caretakers) and the stability of family systems.

- *The dramatic shifts in the racial and ethnic composition of the United States, particularly in large cities and major states like California, Florida, Texas, and New York*. In several states and many large cities, former minorities are now the demographic, if not the political, majority (U.S. Bureau of the Census, 2011). This transformation underscores the existence of persistent disparities between population distribution and the distribution of resources, power, and status (Chow, Johnson, & Austin, 2005). It also alters intergroup dynamics and complicates growing intergroup tensions in unprecedented ways (i.e., from a simple majority-minority racial/ethnic dichotomy to a complex network of interlocking alliances and conflicts).

- *Changing patterns of household size, including the growth of single-person households, particularly among women, and variations in these patterns among different ethnic groups and regions*. Significant variations in birth and mortality rates also have critical implications for social policy and will shape what issues, in what areas, and through what means the United States will spend finite resources (Allard, 2009; Baruah, 2010; Buss, 2010; DeParle & Tavernise, 2012; U.S. Bureau of the Census, 2011).

- *The transformation of the family, including new gender roles, variations in family size by class, ethnicity, and religion, emerging patterns of intergenerational relationships and responsibilities, and new definitions of what constitutes a family* (Annie E. Casey Foundation, 2012; U.S. Bureau of the Census, 2011). These cultural and social changes have significant implications in such policy areas as healthcare, child welfare, and employment.

- *The depopulation of certain regions of the country (e.g., rural areas, the plains) and the increased density of urban areas* (U.S. Bureau of the Census, 2011). This trend is particularly important in an era of policy devolution.

- *The economic decline of older, "inner-ring" suburbs, which are increasingly populated by persons of color, the elderly, and new immigrants* (Diez-Roux & Mair, 2010; Harvey, 2009; Sassen, 2012). Unless regional approaches to social and economic problems are developed, these communities will find it difficult to break out of their current downward spiral.

- *Changing attitudes about sexual orientation*, which affect social policies as wide ranging as legal definitions of marriage, laws regarding child custody and adoption, domestic partner benefits, and guardianship rights of nonmarried couples (Black, Sanders, & Taylor, 2007). These issues have generated intense political and cultural controversy in the past decade and have been resolved differently (and through different means) in different parts of the nation.

Implications for Social Policy

In combination, these profound economic and demographic changes raise several critical questions about the direction of U.S. social policy in the 21st century. These include:

- Which groups should bear the social and economic costs of these changes?
- What values and goals will guide the development of future social policies?
- What roles should the public, nonprofit, and private sectors play in policy development and implementation to address these problems?

Developing answers to these questions is more difficult in the United States because of the unique way in which its social welfare system evolved. Unlike most other industrialized nations, social policies in the United States have been driven largely by pragmatic, rather than ideological, considerations (at least, until recently), and the nation has consistently relied more on the private sector and less on government than its European counterparts (Jansson, 2005; Katz, 2001; Patterson, 2001; Stern & Axinn, 2012). U.S. social policies have tended to have more limited goals and a looser, more decentralized organizational structure. The United States also has confronted far greater demographic diversity than other industrialized nations.

For the latter reason, some critics argue that despite its pragmatic appearances, U.S. policy choices were deliberately designed to maintain racial, gender, and class hierarchies (Brown, 1999; Lieberman, 2005; Piven, 2002; Reisch, 2005). Nevertheless, since the 19th century, government intervention in the economy and society has expanded gradually. The creation of publicly funded social policies in the 20th century diminished somewhat the negative effects of the market by collectivizing what Kapp (1972) called the "social costs of private enterprise." Unlike most European welfare states, however, U.S. social policies have focused primarily on reducing poverty, rather than inequality, and such efforts have been modest, at best, even in periods of reform such as the 1930s and 1960s (Katz, 2001; Patterson, 2001).

There are several explanations for this so-called American exceptionalism, which have implications for how the United States will respond to contemporary economic and demographic developments. One is the deep-seated American tendency to emphasize individualism and self-reliance and resist seeing problems or their solutions in group terms. Ironically, there has also been a contradictory tendency to attach labels to populations at risk, which attribute their common condition to the possession or absence of particular cultural characteristics or behaviors. The "culture of poverty" thesis and the concept of a welfare "underclass" are just two examples of this phenomenon (Collins & Mayer, 2010; Soss et al., 2011). In combination, these tendencies have reinforced the values of dominant cultural groups and maintained the social and economic status quo. The relative weakness of working-class and left-wing political parties and the absence of sustained interracial social justice movements have also made it difficult for alternative policy proposals to obtain or sustain legitimacy (Reisch, 2005).

As a result of recent economic and demographic transformations, long-standing conflicts between charitable and social justice perspectives on social policy have now emerged in a different context. Throughout the 20th century, social policy debates focused on the extent to which the government should establish rights or entitlements, engage in institutionalized redistribution, or promote various forms of compensation or redress (Katz, 2001). These principles are now under attack by the logic of a world market system that regards social investment as an impediment to capital growth. A neoliberal "post-Fordist" regime has replaced the Keynesian-style system of social policies that first appeared in the 1930s. The new regime requires significant alterations in the institutional fabric of policy making to abet "the pursuit of a competitive edge in a global economy" (Jessop, 1999, p. 353). Consequently, in nearly all advanced welfare states, social policies are increasingly designed to enhance corporate rather than individual, family, or community well-being (Collins & Mayer, 2010; Smith, Stenning, & Willis, 2008). Piven (2002) argues that

> what the American example actually suggests is not a model of a country adapting to globalization, but rather the impact of politics—class politics specifically, the impact of a business class moving to use public policy to shore up private profits. (p. 21)

Welfare Reform as a Policy Illustration

For decades, proponents of so-called welfare reform inflated the costs of welfare programs and focused on a minority of recipients—African American adolescent mothers—to promote the myth of welfare failure. By creating a wedge issue based on symbolic appeals to racial and, to a lesser extent, gender bias, anti-welfare propagandists undermined the foundations of the U.S. welfare system. Many of the myths disseminated as facts at the height of the welfare reform debate reflected a deliberate misinterpretation about the nature of human need in modern industrial society. Over the past several decades, welfare reform can best be understood as the spearhead of a broader campaign to reduce government's role in addressing the economic and demographic problems generated or exacerbated by globalization (Abramovitz, 2006; Collins & Mayer, 2010; Wacquant, 2009).

In this context, welfare reform has served several interrelated purposes. First, it helps lower the wage scale by increasing competition for unskilled jobs. This conforms to the logic of globalization by reducing the costs of production and making U.S. industries more competitive in the global market system. Second, it strengthens the drive for greater workforce discipline and compliance, particularly in the service sector of the economy. Third, it promotes a general reduction in the role of government, which has significant implications beyond the social welfare arena, in such areas as trade, banking, and environmental regulations. Finally, by calling into question the legitimacy of welfare entitlements and government's effectiveness in administering social programs, it creates an enormous opportunity for the private sector to acquire new and vast resources of capital—the Social Security Trust Funds—as the recent political offensive by Congressional conservatives demonstrates (Reisch, 2011).

The effects of welfare reform, however, have been decidedly mixed. Its supporters point to the dramatic (nearly 50 percent) decline in welfare caseloads as evidence of success (DeParle, 2012). Critics, however, argue that caseloads began to decline in the mid-1990s and continued to decrease throughout the decade because of economic growth. Second, they claim that the poverty rate is a better indicator of families' well-being and, as discussed previously, not only has the poverty rate significantly increased during the past five years, but the depth and chronic nature of poverty have also increased, particularly for persons of color. Nearly 4 percent of U.S. households with children live on less than $2 per person per day, and the number of female-headed families in deep poverty is the highest in 18 years (DeParle, 2012).

In addition, families on welfare are hardly well off. Before welfare reform, AFDC benefits lifted 62 percent of children who would otherwise have been in deep poverty. A decade later, that proportion dropped to 21 percent (Schott, 2011). Even in the most generous states, the combined benefits of TANF and Food Stamps never reach 80 percent of the poverty threshold (U.S. Department of Health and Human Services, 2012). Sixteen states have cut their welfare rolls since the start of the Great Recession, eleven by 10 percent or more. Nationally, only 30 percent of the TANF block grants that states receive is spent on cash assistance (DeParle, 2012). During the same period, however, food stamp usage has soared by nearly 50 percent (U.S. Department of Agriculture, 2012).

Third, states have not been able to keep track of former TANF recipients. There is no way to determine, therefore, whether these families left welfare for employment or, if they did, whether they are still employed. Recent evidence indicates that many TANF recipients remain employed for only brief periods, are employed in low-wage jobs, which often lack benefits, or simply drop out of sight and are discouraged from reapplying for TANF because of the program's restrictions (Bartik & Houseman, 2008; DeParle, 2012; DeParle & Gebeloff, 2010; Heinrich & Scholz, 2009; Iversen et al., 2011).

The consequences of welfare reform have been particularly severe for particular demographic segments of U.S. society. As a result of welfare reform, the myth that African Americans constituted the largest portion of benefit recipients has become a reality. The five-year time limit on benefits has had a disproportionate impact on persons of color, including those of Asian descent. Increasingly, low-income families (whether on or off welfare) are concentrated in high-poverty neighborhoods, with deleterious effects on employment and educational opportunities, health and mental health status, and children's prospects for the future. Finally, the growth of anti-immigration sentiment in parts of the United States has led to an overall backlash against the provision of social welfare services to persons of color, including legal immigrants (Collins & Mayer, 2010; Fairbanks, 2009; Wacquant, 2009). These developments have planted the seeds for future conflict over the resolution of major policy issues.

Conclusion

The significance of welfare reform, therefore, has not been confined to its effects on beneficiaries and their families. In an environment of economic globalization and increasing demographic complexity, such policy changes should also be assessed in regard to their impact on the underlying philosophy of U.S. social welfare; the respective roles of government, nonprofits, and the for-profit sector in 21st-century policy making; and the distribution of policy responsibilities among federal, state, and local governments. Welfare reform also illustrates the interlocking nature of economic and demographic changes. By terminating the entitlement to cash assistance and placing severe restrictions on the receipt of benefits, welfare reform undermined the concept of public aid that was at the core of the 1935 Social Security Act. This has increased the vulnerability of other entitlement programs, such as old age assistance, Medicare, and Medicaid, to political and ideological attacks. The fate of these social safety net programs will be particularly critical in the years ahead as the population ages and the economic and demographic effects of globalization mount.

Finally, the confluence of these developments makes it clear that the United States can no longer separate debates over issues like welfare, health care, and education from those over employment and immigration policy. By the mid-21st century, the United States will have a growing population of elderly people, two-thirds of them white, being supported by fewer workers, about half of whom will be persons of color. Not long after 2050, the majority of American workers will be persons of color, as will nearly 60 percent of the nation's children.

This contrast has profound implications for such issues as intergenerational responsibility and equity, the determination of funding priorities, and the management of social conflict in an increasingly diverse society. It creates difficult fiscal choices in an era of chronic budget deficits. For example, should we spend finite healthcare dollars today on the elderly or on children, their future benefactors?

Such questions have real-world implications. In less than 40 years, just to maintain Social Security benefits at their current levels, the United States will have to provide educational and social supports for today's children to enable them to earn an average wage that is 1.5 times more than at present. Without dramatic improvements in such supports, particularly for children of color, low-income children, and those from immigrant families, by the middle of the 21st century they will be economically worse off and unable to sustain our current health and income support systems for the elderly. As Martha Ozawa (1997) argued eloquently and prophetically 15 years ago, unless current trends in social welfare spending are reversed, the United States is on a self-destructive econo-demographic course that could transform the American dream into a nightmare.

Key Terms

economic globalization   *inequality*   *migration*
welfare capitalism   *unemployment*

Review Questions for Critical Thinking

1. Should funding for healthcare for seniors be reduced and redirected toward expanding services to children and youth?

2. How has the growth of diverse, immigrant population groups impacted the development of the American welfare system?

3. Is the so-called safety net strong, broad, and secure? Explain your answer.

4. How does economic globalization impact the American welfare system and the development of social policies?

Online Resources

U.S. Government Bureau of Labor Statistics: www.bls.gov

U.S. Government Census Bureau: www.census.gov

U.S. Department of Agriculture: www.fns.usda.gov

Center on Budget and Policy Priorities: www.cbpp.org

Inequality.org: www.inequality.org

References

Aaron, H. J. (2011, April 28). How not to reform Medicare. *New England Journal of Medicine*, *364*(17), 1588–1589.

Abel, L., & Chaudry, A. (2010, April). *Low-income children, their families, and the Great Recession: What next in policy?* Paper prepared for the Georgetown University and Urban Institute Conference on Reducing Poverty and Economic Distress after ARRA, Washington, DC.

Abramovitz, M. (2006). Welfare reform in the United States: Gender, race and class matter. *Critical Social Policy*, *26*, 336–364.

Acs, G., & Nichols, A. (2010, February). Changes in the economic security of American families. *Low Income Families Paper 16*. Washington, DC: Urban Institute.

Allard, S. (2009). *Out of reach: Place, poverty, and the new American welfare state*. New Haven, CT: Yale University Press.

Annie E. Casey Foundation. (2012). *City KIDS COUNT: Data on the well-being of children in large cities*. Baltimore, MD: Author.

Antwerp, J. H. (1890). Report of the committee on immigration. In *Proceedings of the National Conference of Charities and Corrections* (pp. 279–281). Boston, MA: Press of Geo. H. Ellis.

Auerbach, D., & Kellermann, A. (2011, September). A decade of health care cost growth has wiped out real income gains for an average U.S. family. *Health Affairs*, *39*(9), 1630–1636.

Autor, D. (2010). *The polarization of job opportunities in the U.S. labor market: Implications for employment and earnings*. Washington, DC: Center for American Progress and the Hamilton Project, Brookings Institution.

Barrabee, P. (1954). How cultural factors affect family life. In *Proceedings of the National Conference of Social Work* (p. 17). Chicago, IL: University of Chicago Press.

Bartik, T. J., & Houseman, S. N. (Eds.). (2008). *A future of good jobs? America's challenge in the global economy*. Kalamazoo, MI: W. E. Upjohn Institute for Employment Research.

Baruah, B. (2010). Gender and globalization. *Labor Studies Journal*, *35*(2), 198–221.

Bates, K. A., & Swan, R. S. (Eds.). (2010). *Through the eyes of Katrina: Social justice in the United States* (2nd ed.). Durham, NC: Carolina Academic Press.

Bean, F. D., & Stevens, G. (2003). *America's newcomers and the dynamics of diversity*. New York, NY: Russell Sage Foundation.

Bergman, L. R., & Lundberg, O. (2006). Perspectives on determinants of social welfare: Introduction and commentary. *International Journal of Social Welfare*, *15*(Supp. 1), 52–54, 549–552.

Black, D. A., Sanders, S. G., & Taylor, L. J. (2007). The economics of lesbian and gay families. *Journal of Economic Perspectives*, *21*(2), 53–70.

Blank, R. (2002). Evaluating welfare reform in the United States. *Journal of Economic Literature*, *40*(4), 1105–1166.

Blank, R., & Kovak, B. (2008). The growing problem of disconnected single mothers. *Working Paper Series #07-28*. Ann Arbor, MI: National Poverty Center.

Blau, J. (1999). *Illusions of prosperity: America's working families in an age of economic insecurity*. New York, NY: Oxford University Press.

Blau, J., with Abramovitz, M. (2010). *The dynamics of social policy* (3rd ed.). New York, NY: Oxford University Press.

Blum, M. D. (1978). Service to immigrants in a multicultural society. In *Proceedings of the Annual Forum of the National Conference on Social Welfare* (pp. 216–233). New York, NY: Columbia University Press.

Blum, M. D. (1981). Refugees and community tension. In *Proceedings of the Annual Forum of the National Conference on Social Welfare* (pp. 115–130). New York, NY: Columbia University Press.

Borjas, G. (2002). *The impact of welfare reform on immigrant welfare use*. Washington, DC: Center for Immigrant Studies.

Bowen, J. T. (1909). The delinquent children of immigrant parents. In *Proceedings of the National Conference of Social Work* (pp. 255–260). Chicago, IL: University of Chicago Press.

Bowler, A. (1931). Recent statistics on crime and the foreign born. In *Proceedings of the National Conference of Social Work* (pp. 479–494). Chicago, IL: University of Chicago Press.

Braveman, P. A., Kumanyika, S., Fielding, J., LaVeist, T., Borrell, L. N., Manderscheid, R., & Troutman, A. (2011). Health disparities and health equity: The issue is justice. *American Journal of Public Health*, *101* (S.1), 149–156.

Brooks, F. (2007). The living wage movement: Potential implications for the working poor. *Families in Society*, *88* (3), 437–442.

Brooks, R. (2011, November 7). Office poverty measure (again) underestimates a growing crisis. Retrieved on March 7, 2012, from The Demos Blog, www.policyshop.net/home/2011/11/7/official-poverty-measure

Brown, M. (1999). *Race, money, and the American welfare state*. Ithaca, NY: Cornell University Press.

Browne, C. V., & Braun, K. L. (2008). Globalization, women's migration and the long-term care workforce. *The Gerontologist*, *48* (1), 16–24.

Bureau of Labor Statistics. (2009). How the government measures unemployment. Retrieved on March 11, 2012, from http://data.b.s.gov/cgi-bin/print.pl/cps/cps_htgm.htm

Bureau of Labor Statistics. (2010). *Unemployment rates by age, sex, race, and Hispanic or Latino ethnicity*. Washington, DC: Author.

Bureau of Labor Statistics. (2011a). *Alternative measures of labor underutilization*, Table A-15, www.bls.gov/news.release/empsit.t15.htm

Bureau of Labor Statistics. (2011b). *The employment situation—June 2011*. Washington, DC: U.S. Government Printing Office.

Burtless, G., & Looney, A. (2012, January 13). *The immediate jobs crisis and our long-run labor market problem*. Washington, DC: Brookings Institution.

Buss, J. A. (2010). Have the poor gotten poorer? The American experience from 1987–2007. *Journal of Poverty*, *14* (2), 183–196.

Cancian, M., Meyer, D. R., & Reed, D. (2010). Promising antipoverty strategies for families. *Poverty & Public Policy*, *2* (3), 151–169.

Capps, R., Fix, M., Ost, J., Reardon-Anderson, J., & Passel, J. (2004). *The health and well-being of young children of immigrants*. Washington, DC: Urban Institute.

Carlson, A. W. (1994). America's new immigration: Characteristics, destinations, and impact, 1970–1989. *Social Science Journal*, *31* (3), 213–236.

Case, A., Fertig, A., & Paxson, C. (2005). The lasting impact of childhood health and circumstance. *Journal of Health Economics*, *24* (2), 365–389.

Censky, A. (2011, February 14). The new normal unemployment rate: 6.7%. Retrieved on March 7, 2012, from http://money.cnn.com/2011/02/14/news/economy/fed_unemployment

Center on Budget and Policy Priorities. (2006, January 26). *Income inequality grew across the country over the past two decades*. Washington, DC: Author.

Center on Budget and Policy Priorities. (2009, September 8). Top 1 percent reaped two-thirds of income gains in last economic expansion. Retrieved on March 27, 2012, from www.cbpp.org/cms/index.cfm?fa = view&id = 2908

Center on Budget and Policy Priorities. (2011, November 28). *A guide to statistics in historical trends in income inequality*. Washington, DC: Author.

Chapin Hall. (2011). *Foreign-born and U.S. families: Who takes up supports?* Retrieved on March 29, 2012, from www.chapinhall.org/research/inside/foreign-born-and-us-born-families-who-takes-supports

Children's Defense Fund. (2006). *Statistics on child poverty in the United States*. Washington, DC: Author.

Chow, J. C., Johnson, M. A., & Austin, M. J. (2005). The status of low-income neighborhoods in the post-welfare environment: Mapping the relationship between poverty and place. *Journal of Health and Social Policy*, *21*(1), 1–32.

Chow, J. C., Osterling, K. L., & Xu, Q. (2005, Summer/Fall). The risk of timing out: Welfare-to-work services to Asian immigrants and refugees. *AAPI Nexus*, *3*(2), 85–104.

Coletti, U. (1912). The Italian immigrant. In *Proceedings of the National Conference on Social Work* (pp. 249–254). Chicago, IL: University of Chicago Press.

Collins, M. E., Kim, S. H., Clay, C., & Perlstein, J. (2009). Addressing issues of globalization in the training of public child welfare workers: Lessons from a training program in the USA. *International Social Work*, *52*(1), 72–83.

Collins, J. L., & Mayer, V. (2010). *Welfare reform and the race to the bottom in the low-wage labor market*. Chicago, IL: University of Chicago Press.

DeParle, J. (2012, April 7). Welfare left poor adrift as recession hit. *The New York Times*, p. A1.

DeParle, J., & Gebeloff, R. M. (2010, January 2). Living on nothing but food stamps. *The New York Times*, p. A1.

DeParle, J., & Tavernise, S. (2012, February 18). Unwed mothers now a majority in births in 20's. *The New York Times*, p. A1.

Diez-Roux, A., & Mair, C. (2010). Neighborhoods and health. *Annals of the New York Academy of Science*, *1186*, 125–145.

Douglass, J. H. (1955). Migration. In *Proceedings of the National Conference on Social Welfare* (pp. 160–173). New York, NY: Columbia University Press.

Drachman, D. (1995, March). Immigration statuses and their influence on service provision, access, and use. *Social Work*, *40*(2), 188–197.

Duncan, L. (1998). The role of immigrant labor in a changing economy. Retrieved on March 15, 2005, from www.nelp.org/docUploads/duncan%2Epdf

Economic Policy Institute. (2010). *Wages and compensation, 2011*. Retrieved on April 12, 2012, from www.stateofworkingamerica.org/articles/view/9

Economic Policy Institute. (2012). *The state of working America*. Washington, DC: Author.

Edelman, P., Golden, O., & Holzer, H. (2010). *Reducing poverty and economic distress after ARRA: Next steps for short-term recovery and long-term economic security*. Washington, DC: Urban Institute.

Eisenbrey, R., Mishel, L., Bivens, J., & Fieldhouse, A. (2011). *Putting America back to work: Policies for job creation and stronger economic growth*. Washington, DC: Economic Policy Institute.

Fairbanks, R. P. (2009). *How it works: Recovering citizens in post-welfare Philadelphia*. Chicago, IL: University of Chicago Press.

Families USA. (2009). Health coverage in communities of color: Talking about the new census numbers: Fact sheet from Minority Health Initiatives. Retrieved on March 18, 2012, from Families USA, www.familiesusa.org/assets/pdfs/minority-health-census-sept-2009.pdf

Ferrera, M. (2005). *The boundaries of welfare: European integration and the new spatial politics of social protection*. New York, NY: Oxford University Press.

Fertig, A. R., & Reingold, D. A. (2008). Homelessness among at-risk families with children in twenty American cities. *Social Service Review*, *82* (3), 485–510.

Finch, J. (1982–1983). Voting with their feet: Secondary migrations of Indochinese refugees. In *Proceedings of the Annual Forum of the National Conference on Social Welfare* (pp. 101ff). New York, NY: Columbia University Press.

Fishberg, M. (1906). Ethnic factors in immigration: A critical view. In *Proceedings of the National Conference of Social Work* (pp. 304–314). Chicago, IL: University of Chicago Press.

Foner, N. (1987). *New immigrants in New York*. New York, NY: Columbia University Press.

Food Nutrition Service. (2011, September 1). *SNAP monthly data*. Retrieved on April 2, 2012, from www.fns.usda.gov/pd/34SNAPmonthly.htm

Galea, S., Tracy, M., Hoggatt, K. J., DiMaggio, C., & Karpati, A. (2011). Estimated deaths attributable to social factors in the United States. *American Journal of Public Health*, *101* (8), 1456–1465.

Garrett, P. (1888). Immigration to the United States: Report of the Committee on Immigration. In *Proceedings of the National Conference of Charities and Corrections* (pp. 185–192). Boston, MA: Press of Geo. H. Ellis.

Gates, W. A. (1898). Alien and non-resident dependents in Minnesota. In *Proceedings of the National Conference of Charities and Corrections* (pp. 276–282). Boston, MA: Press of Geo. H. Ellis.

Gates, W. A. (1909). Oriental immigration on the Pacific coast. In *Proceedings of the National Conference of Social Work* (pp. 230–232). Chicago, IL: University of Chicago Press.

Gold, S. (1989, January). Differential adjustment among new immigrant family members. *Journal of Contemporary Ethnography*, *17* (4), 408–434.

Guenther, R. (1896). United States legislation respecting immigration. In *Proceedings of the National Conference of Charities and Corrections* (pp. 302–307). Boston, MA: Press of Geo. H. Ellis.

Hall, P. F. (1901, October 19). *Letter to Homer Folks*. Boston, MA: Immigration Restriction League.

Hart, H. (1896). Immigration and crime. In *Proceedings of the National Conference of Charities and Corrections* (pp. 307–313). Boston, MA: Press of Geo. H. Ellis.

Harvey, D. (2009). *Social justice and the city* (rev. ed.). Athens: University of Georgia Press.

Heinrich, C. J., & Scholz, J. K. (Eds.). (2009). *Making the work-based safety net work better: Forward-looking policies to help low-income families*. New York, NY: Russell Sage Foundation.

Hobbie, R. A., & Barnow, B. S. (2011). *Early implementation of the American Recovery and Reinvestment Act: Workforce development and unemployment insurance provisions*. Washington, DC: National Association of State Workforce Agencies.

Hoey, J. M. (1947). Adequate public social services for migrants. In *Proceedings of the National Conference on Social Welfare* (pp. 163–175). New York, NY: Columbia University Press.

Holt, S. (2011). *Ten years of the EITC movement: Making work pay then and now*. Washington, DC: Brookings Institution.

Holzer, H. J., & Lerman, R. I. (2009). *The future of middle skill jobs*. Washington, DC: Brookings Institution.

Holzer, H. J., Schanzenbach, D. W., Duncan, G. J., & Ludwig, J. (2007, January 24). *The economic costs of poverty in the United States: Subsequent effects of children growing up poor*. Washington, DC: Center for American Progress.

Hopkins, E. (1932). The police and the immigrant. In *Proceedings of the National Conference of Social Work* (pp. 509–519). Chicago, IL: University of Chicago Press.

Hoyt, C. S. (1881). Report on immigration. In *Proceedings of the Conference of Charities and Corrections* (pp. 217–218). Boston, MA: A. Williams & Company.

Hoyt, C. S. (1887). Alien paupers, insane, and criminals in New York. In *Proceedings of the National Conference of Charities and Corrections* (pp. 197–206). Boston, MA: Press of Geo. H. Ellis.

Hoyt, C. S., Sanborn, F. B., & Dana, M. M. (1886). Report on the standing committee on immigration and migration. In *Proceedings of the National Conference of Charities and Corrections* (pp. 251–252). Boston, MA: Press of Geo. H. Ellis.

Hugo, E. (1912). Desertion of wives and children by emigrants to America. In *Proceedings of the National Conference of Social Work* (pp. 257–260). Chicago, IL: University of Chicago Press.

Hulme, D. (2010). *Global poverty: How global governance is failing the poor*. London and New York: Routledge.

Inequality.org. (n.d.). Inequality and health. Retrieved on March 28, 2012, from http://inequality.org/inequality-health/

Iversen, R. R., Napolitano, L., & Furstenberg, F. F., Jr., (2011). Middle-income families in the economic downturn: Challenges and management strategies over time. *Longitudinal and Life Course Studies*, *2*(3), 286–300.

Jansson, B. (2005). *The reluctant welfare state* (5th ed.). Pacific Grove, CA: Brooks/Cole.

Jensen, L., & Chitose, Y. (1994, Winter). Today's second generation: Evidence from the 1990 U.S. census. *International Migration Review*, *28*(4), 714–735.

Jessop, B. (1999). The changing governance of welfare: Recent trends in its primary functions, scale, and modes of coordination. *Social Policy and Administration*, *33*, 348–359.

Johnson, N., Oliff, P., & Williams, E. (2011, February 9). *An update on state budgets*. Washington, DC: Center on Budget and Policy Priorities.

Jones, J. M. (1981). Thursday's children: Foster home services for Cuban refugees. In *Proceedings of the National Conference on Social Welfare* (pp. 131ff). New York, NY: Columbia University Press.

Kapp, J. W. (1972). *The social costs of private enterprise*. New York, NY: Schocken.

Karoly, L. A., & Gonzalez, G. C. (2011). Early care and education for children in immigrant families. *Future of Children*, *21*(1), 71–101.

Katz, M. (2001). *The price of citizenship: Redefining the American welfare state*. New York, NY: Henry Holt.

Kim, M. (2009). The political economy of immigration and the emergence of transnationalism. *Journal of Human Behavior in the Social Environment*, *19*(6), 675–689.

Kirmani, R., & Leung, V. (2008). *Breaking down barriers: Immigrant families and early childhood education in New York City*. Retrieved on March 12, 2012, from www.cacf.org/resources_publications.html#breakingthebarriers

Kissane, R. J. (2010). 'We call it the badlands': How social-spatial geographies influence social service use. *Social Service Review*, *84*(1), 3–28.

Klein, N. (2007). *The shock doctrine: The rise of disaster capitalism*. New York, NY: Henry Holt & Co.

Koh, H. K., Graham, G., & Glied, S. A. (2011). Reducing racial and ethnic disparities: The action plan from the Department of Health and Human Services. *Health Affairs*, *30*(10), 1822–1829.

Kohler, M. (1931). Enforcing our deportation laws. In *Proceedings of the National Conference of Social Work* (pp. 495–505). Chicago, IL: University of Chicago Press.

Krugman, P., & Wells, R. (2011, July 14). The bust keeps getting bigger. Why? *The New York Review of Books*. Retrieved on February 12, 2012, from www.nybooks.com/articles/archives/2011/jul/14/busts-keep-getting-bigger-why/?pagination = false

Lamb, R. (1942). Mass relocation of aliens I. In *Proceedings of the National Conference on Social Work* (pp. 186–194). New York, NY: Columbia University Press.

Larned, R. (1930). The tangled threads of migrant family problems. In *Proceedings of the National Conference of Social Work* (pp. 469–477). Chicago, IL: University of Chicago Press.

Layzer, J. I., & Burnstein, N. (2007). *National study of child care for low-income families: Patterns of child care use among low-income families*. Retrieved on April 1, 2012, from www.acf.hhs.gov/programs/opre/cc/nsc_low_income/reports/patterns_cc_exsum/patterns_cc_execsum.pdf

Lee, A., & De Vita, C. J. (2008). *Community-based nonprofits serving ethnic populations in the Washington, DC metropolitan area*. Retrieved on April 3, 2012, from www.urban.org/publications/411675.html

Lieberman, R. C. (2005). *Shaping race policy: The United States in comparative perspective*. Princeton, NJ: Princeton University Press.

Lightman, E., Mitchell, A., & Herd, D. (2008). Globalization, precarious work, and food banks. *Journal of Sociology and Social Welfare*, *35* (2), 9–28.

Lim, Y., Coulton, C. J., & Lalich, N. (2009). State TANF policies and employment outcomes among welfare leavers. *Social Service Review*, *83* (4), 525–555.

Lin, A. C., & Harris, D. R. (2008). *The colors of poverty: Why racial and ethnic disparities exist*. The National Poverty Center Series on Poverty and Public Policy. New York, NY : Russell Sage Foundation.

Loprest, P., & Zedlewski, S. (2006). *The changing role of welfare in the lives of low-income families with children*. Washington, DC: The Urban Institute.

Lorenz, W. (2006). *Perspectives on European social work: From the birth of the nation state to the impact of globalization*. Opladen, Germany: Barbara Budrich.

Luhby, T. (2011, November 7). Poverty rate rises under alternate Census measure. Retrieved on March 7, 2012, from http://money.cnn.com/2011/11/07/news/economy/poverty_rate/index.htm

Lui, M., Robles, B., & Leondar-Wright, B. (2006). *The color of wealth: The story behind the U.S. racial wealth divide*. New York, NY: New Press.

MacCormack, D. W. (1934). The New Deal for the alien. In *Proceedings of the National Conference of Social Work* (pp. 465–472). Chicago, IL: University of Chicago Press.

Marshall, L. C. (1906). Race effects of immigration. In *Proceedings of the National Conference of Social Work* (pp. 314–324). Chicago, IL: University of Chicago Press.

McDonald, C., & Reisch, M. (2008). Social work in the workfare regime: A comparison of the U.S. and Australia. *Journal of Sociology and Social Welfare*, *35* (1), 43–74.

McMurtrie, D. C. (1909). The immigrant and public health. In *Proceedings of the National Conference of Social Work* (pp. 247–250). Chicago, IL: University of Chicago Press.

Mishel, L., & Shierholz, H. (2011, March 14). The sad but true story of wages in America. *Issue Brief #297*. Washington, DC: Economic Policy Institute.

Monea, E., & Sawhill, I. (2010). *A simulation on future poverty in the United States*. Washington, DC: Urban Institute.

Mourre, G. (2009). *Wage compression in Europe: First evidence from the Structure of Earnings Survey 2002*. CEB Working Paper No. 09/051. Brussels, Belgium: Solvay School of Economics and Management.

Muller, T. (1993). *Immigrants and the American city*. New York, NY: New York University Press.

Murphy, F. G., Bond, T. M., Warren, R. C., & Maclin, S. D., Jr., (2008). Twenty-first century globalization: Impact of gentrification on community health. *American Journal of Health Studies*, *23*(2), 66–75.

National Employment Law Project. (2010, August 27). *Where the jobs are: A first look at private industry job growth and wages in 2010*. New York, NY: Author.

Neidell, M., & Waldfogel, J. (2009). Program participation of immigrant children: Evidence from the local availability of Head Start. *Economics of Education Review*, *28*(6), 704–715.

Office of Planning, Research, and Evaluation. (2011). Design for migrant and seasonal Head Start survey. Retrieved on April 3, 2012, from www.acf.hhs.gov/programs/opre/hs/migrant_mshs/reports/migrant_design.pdf

Olsen, G. M. (2007). Toward global welfare state convergence? Family policy and health care in Sweden, Canada and the United States. *Journal of Sociology and Social Welfare*, *34*(2), 143–164.

Ozawa, M. (1997). Demographic changes and social welfare. In M. Reisch and E. Gambrill (Eds.), *Social work in the 21st century* (pp. 8–27). Thousand Oaks, CA: Pine Forge Press.

Palley, T. I. (2012). *From financial crisis to stagnation: The destruction of shared prosperity and the role of economics*. New York, NY: Cambridge University Press.

Palmieri, V. H. (1980). International and domestic policies regarding refugees. In *Proceedings of the Annual Forum of the National Conference on Social Welfare* (pp. 121ff). New York, NY: Columbia University Press.

Patterson, J. (2001). *America's struggle against poverty in the 20th century*. Cambridge, MA: Harvard University Press.

Pavetti, L., & Rosenbaum, D. (2010, February 25). *Creating a safety net that works when the economy doesn't: The role of the food stamp and TANF programs*. Washington, DC: Center on Budget and Policy Priorities.

Penna, S., Paylor, I., & Washington, J. (2000). Globalization, social exclusion and the possibilities for global social work and welfare. *European Journal of Social Work*, *3*(2), 109–122.

Piven, F. F. (2002). Welfare policy and American politics. In F. F. Piven, J. Acker, M. Hallock, & S. Morgen (Eds.), *Work, welfare and politics: Confronting poverty in the wake of welfare reform* (pp. 19–33). Eugene: University of Oregon Press.

Portes, A. (1990). *Immigrant America: A portrait*. Berkeley: University of California Press.

Powell, J. (1943). America's refugees: Exodus and diaspora. In *Proceedings of the National Conference of Social Work* (pp. 301–309). New York, NY: Columbia University Press.

Quadagno, J. (1994). *The color of welfare: How racism undermined the war on poverty*. New York, NY: Oxford University Press.

Rand Corporation. (2006). Small fraction of spending on health goes to undocumented immigrants. Retrieved on November 30, 2006, from http://content.healthaffairs.org/current.shtml

Rank, M. R. (2004). *One nation underprivileged: Why American poverty affects us all*. New York, NY: Oxford University Press.

Rawley, C. (1948). Adjustment of Jewish displaced persons in an American community. In *Proceedings of the National Conference of Social Work* (pp. 317–323). Chicago, IL: University of Chicago Press.

Rehbein, B. (Ed.). (2011). *Globalization and inequality in emerging societies*. New York, NY: Palgrave MacMillan.

Reiman, J., & Leighton, P. (2010). *The rich get richer and the poor get prison: Ideology, class, and criminal justice* (9th ed.). Boston, MA: Allyn & Bacon.

Reisch, M. (2005). American exceptionalism and critical social work: A retrospective and prospective analysis. In I. Ferguson, M. Lavalette, & E. Whitman (Eds.), *Globalisation, Global Justice and Social Work* (pp. 157–171). London, England: Routledge.

Reisch, M. (2009). Social workers, unions, and low wage workers: An historical perspective. *Journal of Community Practice*, *17*(1–20), 50–72.

Reisch, M. (2011). Social services in the U.S.A. *Neue Praxis*, *2*(3), 217–227.

Reisch, M. (2012). Community practice challenges in the global economy. In M. Weil, M. Reisch, & M. Ohmer (Eds.), *Handbook of Community Practice* (2nd ed.). Thousand Oaks, CA: Sage.

Reisch, M., & Jani, J. S. (2012, in press). The new politics of social work: Understanding context to promote change. *British Journal of Social Work*.

Sanborn, F. B. (1886). Migration and immigration. In *Proceedings of the National Conference of Charities and Corrections* (pp. 253–259). Boston, MA: Press of Geo. H. Ellis.

Sassen, S. (2012). *Cities in a world economy* (4th ed.). Thousand Oaks, CA: Sage.

Schott, L. (2011, July 6 revision). *An introduction to TANF*. Washington, DC: Center on Budget and Policy Priorities.

Sherman, A., & Stone, C. (2010, June 25). *Income gaps between very rich and everyone else more than tripled in last three decades, data show*. Washington, DC: Center on Budget and Policy Priorities.

Short, K. (2011, November). *The Research Supplemental Poverty Measure: 2010*. Washington, DC: U.S. Census Bureau, Economics and Statistics Administration, and U.S. Department of Commerce.

Smith, A., Stenning, A., & Willis, K. (Eds.). (2008). *Social justice and neoliberalism: Global perspectives*. New York, NY: Palgrave MacMillan.

Snyder, P. F. (1930). Social considerations in deportability: The legal background and new legislation. In *Proceedings of the National Conference of Social Work* (pp. 495–501). Chicago, IL: University of Chicago Press.

Soss, J., Fording, R. C., & Schram, S. F. (2011). *Disciplining the poor: Neoliberal paternalism and the persistent power of race*. Chicago, IL: University of Chicago Press.

Soss, J., Hacker, J. S., & Mettler, S. (Eds.). (2007). *Remaking America: Democracy and public policy in an age of inequality*. New York, NY: Russell Sage.

Stern, M., & Axinn, J. (2012). *Social welfare: A history of the American response to need* (8th ed.). Boston, MA: Pearson.

Sulzberger, C. L. (1912). Immigration. In *Proceedings of the National Conference of Social Work* (pp. 239–249). Chicago, IL: University of Chicago Press.

Takaki, R. (1994). *From distant shores: Perspectives on race and ethnicity in America*. New York, NY: Oxford University Press.

Taylor, G. (1913). Distribution and assimilation of immigrants: Report for the committee. In *Proceedings of the National Conference of Social Work* (pp. 26–36). Chicago, IL: University of Chicago Press.

Titmuss, R. M. (1963). *Essays on the welfare state*. Boston, MA: Beacon Press.

Tumlin, K. C., & Zimmerman, W. (2003). *Immigrants and TANF: A look at immigrant welfare recipients in three cities*. Washington, DC: The Urban Institute.

Twill, S., & Fisher, S. (2010). Economic human rights violations experienced by women and children in the United States. *Families in Society: The Journal of Contemporary Social Services*, *91* (4), 356–362.

Urban Institute. (2006, July). *Government work supports and low-income families: Facts and figures*. Washington, DC: Author.

U.S. Bureau of the Census. (2006). *Poverty in the United States*. Washington, D. C.: U.S. Government Printing Office.

U.S. Bureau of the Census. (2010). Share of aggregate income received by each fifth and top 5 percent of households, Table 2. Retrieved on March 29, 2012, from www.census.gov/hhes/www/income/data/historical/household/index.html

U.S. Bureau of the Census. (2011). *Poverty in the United States*. Washington, DC: U.S. Government Printing Office.

U.S. Department of Agriculture. (2012). *Participation in the Supplemental Nutrition Assistance Program*. Washington, DC: U.S. Government Printing Office.

U.S. Department of Health and Human Services. (2012). *TANF recipients and their families*. Washington, DC: U.S. Government Printing Office.

U.S. Industrial Commission on Immigration and Education. (1901). *Report of the Commission*, XV (pp. 319–322). Washington, DC: U.S. Government Printing Office.

Van Horn, C. E., & Zukin, C. (2011). *The long-term unemployed and unemployment insurance: Evidence from a panel study of workers who lost a job during the Great Recession*. New Brunswick, NJ: Rutgers University, John J. Heldrich Center for Workforce Development.

Vroman, W. (2010, July). *The Great Recession, unemployment insurance, and poverty—Summary*. Washington, DC: Urban Institute.

Wacquant, L. (2009). *Punishing the poor: The neoliberal government of social insecurity*. Durham, NC: Duke University Press.

Wald, L. P. (1909). The immigrant young girl. In *Proceedings of the National Conference of Social Work* (pp. 261–265). Chicago, IL: University of Chicago Press.

Waldinger, R. (Ed.). (2001). *Strangers at the gates: New immigrants in urban America*. Berkeley: University of California Press.

Ward, D. E. (2005). *The white welfare state: The racialization of U.S. welfare policy*. Ann Arbor: University of Michigan Press.

Warren, G. (1933). Assistance to aliens in America. In *Proceedings of the National Conference of Social Work* (pp. 578–589). Chicago, IL: University of Chicago Press.

Weyl, W. E. (1905). Immigration and industrial saturation. In *Proceedings of the National Conference of Social Work* (pp. 363–375). Chicago, IL: University of Chicago Press.

Wolff, E. (2010, March). Recent trends in household wealth in the United States. *Levy Economics Institute Paper #589*. Annandale-on-the-Hudson, NY: Bard College.

World Bank. (2010). *Global Monitoring Report 2010*. Goal 1: Eradicate extreme poverty and hunger. Washington, DC: Author.

Xu, Q. (2007). Globalization, immigration, and the welfare state: A cross-national comparison. *Journal of Sociology and Social Welfare*, *34* (2), 87–106.

Yang, P. (1995). *Post-1965 immigration to the United States*. Westport, CT: Praeger.

Chapter 8
The U.S. Patriot Act: Implications for the Social Work Profession

Stan Stojkovic

> At what point should people be willing to give up or have some of their basic rights reduced in scope for the greater good? Will such limitations codify discrimination and segregation against certain groups of people? How does the Patriot Act reflect social justice as promoted by the social work profession?

Introduction

September 9, 2001 (9/11) will always be remembered as the day the United States, and the world, was changed forever. People remember where they were and what they were doing when they first learned that a plane had crashed into one of the World Trade Center towers. Almost 50 years prior, another generation of people remembers where they were and what they were doing when they learned that U.S. President John Fitzgerald Kennedy had been assassinated. And almost 25 years prior in December 1941, another generation of people could remember where they were and what they were doing when they first learned of the air attacks on Pearl Harbor. Sadly, we know that future generations will also experience horrific events that will be forever seared into their psyches.

Just like Pearl Harbor, 9/11 resulted in significant policy changes that limited individual and human rights: Following Pearl Harbor, the U.S. government ran three basic types of facilities, including civilian assembly centers (temporary residence), relocation centers (aka internment camps), and detention centers; approximately 110,000 Japanese American citizens who lived on or near the Pacific Coast were interned in relocation centers/internment camps. Here, they lost their property and their basic rights guaranteed by the U.S. Bill of Rights. Now, the Patriot Act is in place to "secure the homeland" against future terrorist attacks.

On September 11, 2001, as two hijacked planes crashed into the twin towers of the World Trade Center, and a third plane attacked the Pentagon in Washington, D.C., the typical American was left with much fear and uncertainty as to the future. The post-terrorist attack investigation revealed that a small group of foreign terrorists, armed and financed by a terrorist network known as al-Qaeda, headed by a mastermind named Usama bin Laden, had begun their initial planning for the attack years before. In fact, the World Trade Center was attacked by fellow terrorist Ramzi Yousef in February 1993, and the tragedy of 9/11 was only one event in a long series of events intended to bring down the American government and to fulfill a *fatwa* that demanded all Muslims kill Americans in any location of the world because of American occupation in Islam's holy lands and aggression against Muslims (The 9–11 Commission, 2004).

In response, the U.S. Congress passed the "Uniting and Strengthening America by Providing Appropriate Tools Required to Intercept and Obstruct Terrorism Act," or the USA PATRIOT Act, Public Law 107–56. The U.S. Patriot Act, passed with virtually no public debate and signed into law six weeks after the tragedy of 9/11, redefined the public's response to terrorism. In addition, the act gave broad and sweeping powers to the federal government, through its various law enforcement agencies, to investigate, apprehend, and detain suspected terrorists. These powers, somewhat unprecedented in American history, even though similar acts and practices were created during times of strife in the country's past—such as the Alien Act of 1798, the suspension of habeas corpus by President Lincoln during the Civil War, and the Espionage Act of 1917—forced all social institutions to examine how they responded to the terrorist threat. Unlike previous attempts directed toward the nation's enemies, the Patriot Act was directed toward an unknown target: would-be terrorists.

Coupled with advancing technologies, terrorists have many tools to pursue bombings, kidnappings, and mass destruction. The 19 men, for example, who attacked the World Trade Center were from all over the world, and the extremists that they worked for in planning the attack were headquartered in Afghanistan, an initial target of U.S. forces in response to the 9/11 tragedy. Yet, questions still remain regarding homeland security, and the ability of the federal government to prevent attacks and to pursue terrorists both in this country and around the world. The U.S. Patriot Act is designed, according to its supporters, to give law enforcement more effective weapons to address domestic terrorism and secure the homeland.

For the purposes of this chapter, we will show how the U.S. Patriot Act, through its implementation over the past 10 years, has changed the nature of the relationship between the federal government and the citizenry. This change is most directly felt within the thousands of agencies that represent the criminal justice system. These organizations—police, prosecution, courts, and corrections—have all been directly or indirectly affected by the U.S. Patriot Act. The most significant change has occurred in law enforcement, especially federal law enforcement, where broad powers have been given to investigate, detect, apprehend, prosecute, and detain terrorists and other criminals. These changes have had a profound impact on the quality of life for Americans and immigrants alike. Through our zeal to protect the homeland, we have passed laws and allowed criminal justice agencies to enter our lives in more invasive and insidious ways. Law enforcement agencies, like the terrorists they are pursuing, also have the power of modern technologies at their fingertips. The ability to observe and detect suspicious movements of criminals and terrorists is remarkably accurate and frightening at the same time. Cities across the country have adopted practices and employed technologies that allow government agencies to watch over citizens without them even knowing about it and outside of public review and possible criticism (American Civil Liberties Union, 2003). Most importantly, with the passage of the U.S. Patriot Act, we have created two systems of justice in this country, one that is transparent in its operations and one that is not transparent in its operations.

This chapter shall examine the U.S. Patriot Act. This law has led to the creation of many questionable practices in pursuit of terrorist suspects. Additionally, we will show how these practices, for all intents and purposes, have produced a subterranean system of justice that is antithetical to the very core values of a democracy and the social work profession. Through the U.S. Patriot Act, the potential for abuse by government officials is very high, and the cost to average citizens is the liberty interest that we all have in a democracy. This chapter contends that in the final analysis the U.S. Patriot Act has eroded fundamental freedoms that citizens have vis-à-vis their government and has not made us safe from terrorist attacks. The chapter concludes with some thoughts on the impact of the U.S. Patriot Act on vulnerable populations, an audience that human service professionals deal with on a daily basis. This discussion will focus on what social work professionals can do to respond to the U.S. Patriot Act and to protect and advocate for those people whom this law has had and will continue to have deleterious consequences.

The U.S. Patriot Act: Significant Activities and a New System of Justice

The 324-page document that makes up the U.S. Patriot Act, which was signed into law by President George W. Bush on October 26, 2001, has many provisions that affect the law enforcement community. Much of the language of the act provides specific direction to the Federal Bureau of Investigation (FBI). Section 215, for example, provides authority to the Director of the FBI to make application for the production of "any tangible things" for an investigation and serves as a supplement to the Foreign Intelligence Surveillance Act (FISA) of 1978. Prior to the passage of the U.S. Patriot Act, and under the old law, the FBI could only obtain records, but under the current law they can seize any material that is pertinent to an investigation regarding "international terrorism or clandestine intelligence activities" (ACLU, 2003). We will examine how the U.S. Patriot Act has created a separate system of justice in this country based on activities that are outside public review. These activities include the detention of noncitizens, military tribunals, fingerprinting of immigrants, and domestic spying.

Detention of Noncitizens

One of the more frightening provisions of the U.S. Patriot Act is the ability of the government to detain noncitizens. Immediately following the September 11, 2001 attacks, the government began rounding up large numbers of immigrants, most of whom who were of Arab or South Asian origin. The American Civil Liberties Union (ACLU), along with other organizations, filed suit under the Freedom of Information Act to determine who these detainees were and the bases of their detention (ACLU, 2003). Much controversy surrounded the detention of noncitizens, who were being held largely at Guantanamo Bay in Cuba and in Afghanistan. The U.S. Congress responded by passing the Military Commissions Act, which contained definitions of both lawful and unlawful "enemy combatants."

The term *enemy combatant* is problematic, as its definition is left up to great ambiguity and broad interpretation. The issue of what legal rights enemy combatants possessed came to a head in the case of *Boumediene v. Bush* (2008). The Supreme Court ruled that the Military Commissions Act (2006) could not remove the rights of Guantanamo Bay captives' access to the federal courts. Somewhat surprisingly, subsequent to the Bush presidency, President Barack Obama sought to preserve President Bush's view of what an enemy combatant is as he addressed the rights of detainees held in Afghanistan. In the end, the Obama administration abandoned the term "enemy combatant, arguing it is inconsistent with democratic values" (Holder, 2009). To date the government has been slow in providing details on who is being detained and what they are being charged with by the government. In its zeal to seem responsive to terrorism, the government, through the Department of Justice, has embarked on a strategy that is nothing short of racial profiling, targeting largely young Arab men.

The impact of this mass herding of suspected terrorists is not new in our history. Similar strategies were used by the government in the past, most notably during the era of the Palmer Raids. This name is derived from the infamous A. Mitchell Palmer, who was attorney general and used the raids as a technique against immigrants who were viewed as a threat to the social order. It is suspected that more than 5,000 "Bolsheviks" were arrested, illegally detained with no charges brought against them, and in some cases deported for being suspected of violating the Espionage and Sedition Acts of 1917 and 1918, even though most charges were later dropped and Palmer's efforts criticized (Powers, 1987). The 2011 film *J. Edgar* portrayed the life and times of the infamous FBI director J. Edgar Hoover (played by the actor Leonardo DiCaprio) and his inquisitor zeal against immigrants and men of color. The current situation with young Arab men post-9/11 is no different.

Attempts to understand the scope and magnitude of the detention of noncitizens are barely discernible. The only accounts are typically from journalists, and very little research has been directed toward this topic.

Operating under a siege mentality, the government has done what it always has done under difficult circumstances: arrest the usual suspects. In this case, the usual suspects are young Arab men who in a majority of cases have broken no laws nor have any interest in attacking the United States. The problems for law enforcement agencies in this detention process are numerous, particularly when they are asked to detain suspected terrorists as well as typical criminals. Some have even suggested that the increase in homeland security has drained local law enforcement budgets to a breaking point and that "(W)e've spent five years on homeland security. Now we need to focus on a little hometown security (Barrett, 2006)."

The consequences of this specious detention of noncitizens is that local law enforcement agencies, typically police and prosecution, are being asked to reorganize to focus on the activities of suspected terrorists at a time when resources are dwindling and local agencies have neither the time nor the inclination to investigate them. Additionally, these same law enforcement agencies are being asked to work with federal law enforcement agencies at a time when they are being criticized for racially profiling citizens, particularly African American and Hispanic citizens (Stojkovic, Kalinich, & Klofas, 2012). The end result is that usually nothing of substance gets accomplished, and even when pursued in an earnest fashion, it is not clear that the detention of these noncitizens makes us safer. What we do know is that, through the U.S. Patriot Act, we have instituted actions that run counter to our existing laws and the laws of the international community.

Under the current Patriot Act, the government can detain noncitizens for an indefinite "reasonable" period of time. In this country and according to the International Covenant on Civil and Political Rights (the United States is a signatory to this covenant), the period of detention prior to being brought in front of a judge or magistrate is 48 hours or a few days, but under the Patriot Act this could be for months, and there have been cases where people were detained for months without access to a lawyer (Fainaru, 2002, as cited in ACLU, 2002). For most citizens, such a practice strikes at the heart of our democracy, especially when there is no discernible benefit and when it actually makes things worse. In the first 10 years of its implementation, the U.S. Patriot Act and the provision to detain noncitizens has produced no demonstrable effects in the protection of the homeland or the global war on terrorism. If anything, this activity has actually produced onerous and burdensome costs on law enforcement agencies and no actual increase in the safety of citizens. More pernicious, however, has been the effect of this activity on the quality of life for many persons, most of whom are foreign-born immigrants from Arab countries.

Military Tribunals

Another disturbing activity emanating from the U.S. Patriot Act is the creation of military tribunals. In November 2001, President Bush, as Commander-in-Chief, granted himself unprecedented authority to create and operate military tribunals for suspected terrorists. These tribunals would be outside the purview and review of civilian courts. Suspected terrorists would be detained, and in some cases, defined as "enemy combatants," ultimately tried and convicted through the rubric of the military system of justice. The exact language of the presidential order also provides that ordinary rules of court procedure would not apply (e.g., unanimity for jurors only required in capital cases, trials would be held in secret, and no review of the courts' actions would be allowed). While these provisions of the U.S. Patriot Act do not apply to American citizens, they do impact the more than 18 million foreign-born legal residents of the United States (ACLU, 2003).

Some of these secret trials were held at the infamous detention center at Guantanamo Bay, Cuba, because if they were held in the United States suspects would have the right to habeas corpus review, a right inherent with our system of justice. Habeas corpus protections are required and cannot be suspended, as dictated by the U.S. Constitution, if trials are held in the country. Because the trials are held in Cuba—or any other place the government wishes to try suspected terrorists—the rule of habeas corpus does not apply. The Supreme Court (*Boumediene v. Bush*, 2008) addressed the denial of habeas corpus as articulated in the Patriot Act and implemented by President Bush, and under current law, detainees must be afforded constitutional protections such as access to the federal courts. This decision was a major victory for advocates of due process rights for noncitizens. Additionally, as noted earlier, there is much debate as to whether or not military tribunals adequately protect the country or combat the war on terrorism. As with other legislation passed in the late 1990s and post 9/11, such as the Antiterrorism and Effective Death Penalty Act of 1996, the presumed benefits of these activities on terrorism or crime in general are suspect at best (Cole & Smith, 2007).

Moreover, the image of the United States as the longest-running democracy has been tarnished by the presence of secret military tribunals. More often than not, suspects defined as terrorists or enemy combatants are neither, and as an intelligence-gathering tool, detention facilities and the threat of facing a military tribunal have limited or no value. The questions of fundamental fairness and due process must be raised under such a secretive process. For those who work in the civilian court system, the notion of military tribunals and secretive processes are antithetical to our system of justice. This practice, under the auspices of the U.S. Patriot Act, has raised the ire of both critics and citizens alike. How does a civilian system of justice survive when it has to operate parallel to a military system of justice that allows no review, limited due process, and no accountability?

Most interesting is that of the hundreds of noncitizens detained by the U.S. government since the passage of the Patriot Act in 2001, only two persons have been actually convicted at trial, and five detainees have plead guilty as part of tribunals that were being held at Guantanamo Bay. President Obama has been thwarted by Congress to close Guantanamo

Bay and move the trials of noncitizen detainees to federal civilian courts (Sutton, 2012).

Fingerprinting of Immigrants

While the civilian system of justice has spent the past decade trying to end the practice of racial profiling by criminal justice agencies, the federal government has created its own nefarious system of racial profiling by targeting men of Arab and Latino descent and requiring them to submit to fingerprinting. The obvious purpose is to have a record of who they are and what they are doing. No one has a problem with identifying would-be criminals and terrorists, but we don't allow people to do this outside the purview of the law and without rationale. In the civilian justice system, this is accomplished by having law enforcement agencies show *probable cause* that a crime has been committed or is about to be committed. Without this standard, no person can be pursued and ultimately arrested.

When tactics are used by law enforcement to investigate ordinary criminals without probable cause and subsequent arrests are made, the judiciary typically invalidates such arrests. It is well known that in many cases, when such tactics are employed by law enforcement personnel, there is usually a *pretextual* basis for the stop that cannot meet the probable cause standard. Again, this has been found to be a common practice among police who are conducting racial profiling among African American and Hispanic citizens (Engel & Calnon, 2004). A broken taillight, for example, becomes the pretext to justify a stop and ultimately conduct a search of someone's car when there is no probable cause to stop him or her (see a fascinating description of this practice by theologian Cornell West, 1993).

The tragedy is that we are now doing this same practice with persons of Arab origin and doing so with impunity. Immediately following the 9/11 attacks, the federal government rounded up thousands of Arab men with no cause, fingerprinted them, and provided no justification for their arrest and detention. The net result of such a practice was that ill will was engendered among young Arab men, and virtually nothing was gained to aid in the investigation of the 9/11 attacks nor credible information generated that would lead to other terrorist suspects (ACLU, 2002). With this practice, as with the other practices described, we are seeing the development of a separate system of justice that is beyond public review, where accountability is limited and injustices enhanced.

In 2007, we saw the practice of fingerprinting immigrants rise to another level. In many communities across the country, a federal initiative, called "Secure Communities," allowed persons who had been booked into any jail for any crime to have their fingerprints forwarded to the Department of Homeland Security to determine who was in the country illegally. While this practice was intuitively attractive to some people, for others it is another example of the government collecting information on immigrants that can be used against them for nefarious purposes (Moreno, 2010).

Domestic Spying

Prior to the passage of the U.S. Patriot Act, there was a clear distinction between intelligence agencies and traditional law enforcement. The Central Intelligence Agency (CIA), for example, was not allowed to conduct traditional law enforcement, nor was it allowed to employ intelligence-gathering strategies used in the foreign sector domestically. Yet, section 203 of the U.S. Patriot Act does allow for foreign intelligence information gathered as a result of a domestic investigation to be shared with the intelligence community. As expected, the definition of "foreign intelligence information" is very broad, and under such a broad rubric, the potential for abuse and harassment of ordinary citizens is very high. Coupled with eased restrictions on wiretaps and surveillance techniques, a system of justice has been created that is outside the domain of traditional public review and comment.

Former Attorney General John Ashcroft rewrote sections of federal guidelines subsequent to the 9/11 attacks to provide broad powers to the FBI in the domestic spying arena. The original guidelines, written during the 1970s, were created to limit the activities of the CIA and FBI in the domestic spying arena, and were a response to serious abuses by the government in its surveillance and harassment of civil rights leaders, such as Martin Luther King, Jr. during the 1960s (ACLU, 2002). The new rules have broadened the powers of agencies like the FBI to spy on ordinary citizens with very little oversight.

Taken together, sections 203, 206, 213, 216, 217, and 218 of the U.S. Patriot Act provide enormous power to governmental agencies to spy on American citizens and to provide no or limited accounting or basis for such activity (Podesta, 2002). Additionally, through the Patriot Act, in practice, we are seeing a separate system of justice evolving that is only accountable to managers and bureaucrats of the various agencies of the federal government and the executive branch of government. This type of system of justice is counter to the core values of a democracy, where transparency and openness are essential to good government.

The controversy that ensued subsequent to 9/11 centered on the creation of warrantless surveillance by the U.S. National Security Agency (NSA). The NSA was authorized by executive order of President Bush to monitor, without warrants, phone calls, Internet activity, text messaging, and other communication by any party believed by the NSA to be engaged in terrorist activities and outside the United States, even if the messaging originated in the United States. In 2007, two lawsuits were brought against the government alleging that the actions of President Bush were unconstitutional and deserving of greater judicial oversight.

One lawsuit involved the telecommunications giant AT&T, and another lawsuit came from an Islamic charity foundation. In the former case, a class-action lawsuit was brought on behalf of customers of AT&T and alleged that the company provided substantial information and records to federal authorities regarding their phone usage and other electronic communications (Liptak, 2007). In the latter case, a federal court found the

NSA's program of surveillance to be illegal and supported the government paying civil court damages to the Islamic charity foundation (Savage & Risen, 2010).

Additionally, there have been many other legal challenges to the Patriot Act and congressional actions to define more clearly the legality of the NSA surveillance program. In 2008, the United States Foreign Intelligence Surveillance Court of Review affirmed the constitutionality of the NSA surveillance program. We should expect to see further legal challenges to the domestic spying program of the government as more people are placed under surveillance. The problem is that we do not have good data as to the extent of the surveillance, and as such, it will be difficult to question the legality of it. This is how a clandestine system of justice evolves, predicated on secrecy and limited transparency.

The U.S. Patriot Act and the Social Work Profession

While Congress acted in haste to pass the U.S. Patriot Act, it did do something that allowed for further review of the law once it was implemented by the various agencies of the federal government. The law had a sunset provision that allowed for greater review four years after its implementation. In the fall of 2005 and into early 2006, Congress did review many of the law's provisions and made some modifications to provide greater public oversight and protections of primarily First and Fourth Amendment rights of citizens. Yet, critics argue that the passage of H.R. 3199, the Patriot Act Improvement and Reauthorization Act, does very little to curb the powers granted to federal law enforcement agencies, like the FBI, and the potential infringement of citizens' rights under the First and Fourth Amendments are still present.

The ACLU has sued the FBI over the release of subscriber information by an Internet service provider. While the government has acceded to the ACLU's demand, not forcing the provider to divulge sensitive information about its users, it still holds in place a gag order that does not allow providers to speak publicly about the order and does it through a "national security letter" (ACLU, 2006).

So, what does all this mean for the social work professional, and how can you deal with the consequences of the U.S. Patriot Act? There are some very clear steps for the social work profession that must be taken so that the harm of the aforementioned activities does not further threaten the vulnerable populations we serve. These actions fall into three areas: advocacy, protection, and activism and reaffirmation.

Advocacy

The social work profession has had a long history of advocacy for those whom society has disregarded or abused. As social work professionals, we must work with others to address the abuses that the U.S. Patriot Act has created among vulnerable populations. The most glaring example of these abuses has been how men and women of Arab descent have been treated by the practices described previously in the implementation of the U.S. Patriot Act. The social work profession has to continue to work with the victims of the U.S. Patriot Act. This means working with the legal community to petition the government when it is wrong and acting unjustly. This means speaking out against injustices and pursuing our traditional goal of social justice.

More importantly, this means sharing information with others and speaking out against the oppression of the minority by the majority under a specious law. The U.S. Patriot Act is in violation of the social work code of ethics, which compels us to act against injustices and not practice any form of discrimination against someone based on national origin. This advocacy must be viewed as part of our mission and purpose as social workers. We cannot sit back idly while others are oppressed under the false pretense of security and safety, especially when we know that the implementation of the U.S. Patriot Act has not made us any more safe and ultimately less free than we were prior to its implementation.

As a collective voice, we as social work professionals must join with other groups to support a dissenting view when it comes to the U.S. Patriot Act. The ACLU (2006) reports that more than 400 communities and seven states have taken a stand, demanding meaningful reform of the U.S. Patriot Act. While Congress has been slow to react, there has been a groundswell of voices and professional organizations who have asked for changes in the law. As social workers, we should consider ourselves as part of the voice of dissent, because, like others, we have a long history of advocating for those who have no one to advocate for them. If we don't take on this advocacy role to change the U.S. Patriot Act, we not only violate our own code of ethics, but more perniciously, we silently condone the mistreatment of vulnerable populations.

Protection

We must work with other like-minded organizations to protect vulnerable populations and victims of the U.S. Patriot Act. As we have done in the past, for example, with children who have been abused, women who have been battered, and the elderly who have been mistreated, we must assist those who need our aid in the wake of the implementation of the U.S. Patriot Act. The central thesis of this chapter has been that the U.S. Patriot Act created two separate systems of justice. This new clandestine system of justice has many victims. One of the more nefarious consequences of the sweeping power of the U.S. Patriot Act is the misidentification or mislabeling of suspected terrorists and the mass rounding up of people who look like terrorists (e.g., young Arab men). Who protects these people against the ravages of the U.S. Patriot Act?

In many urban centers across this country, young Arab men are being singled out for arrest, prosecution, and detention with no ability to protect and advocate for themselves. Just like the suspected Bolsheviks of the 1920s, the new boogey-man is the young Arab male. Similar to his counterpart of the 1920s, he is being denied rights to an attorney, secretly detained and interrogated in unknown locations, tried in some cases, and sentenced to military prisons. While we do not have accurate numbers on how many people are being placed in this secret system of justice, because the government refuses to reveal the numbers, who protects the potential victims of this abuse? Who comes to their aid when it looks like no one will? Again, the social work profession has a role in working with other professional associations to aid in the protection of these persons by demanding an accounting, and where appropriate, the opportunity to intervene.

The greatest protection is promoting greater visibility regarding the plight of persons being unjustly persecuted by the government. Chief Justice Oliver Wendell Holmes once stated that "sunlight is the greatest disinfectant." We need more sunlight on the workings of the government when implementing the U.S. Patriot Act. More people need to know what is going on in the name of democracy and freedom, and as social workers we need to protect those who are being ensnarled in the government's web of bureaucracies created to enforce the provisions of the U.S. Patriot Act. The scope of this web reaches well beyond the domain of young Arab men.

When the government is able is spy on its citizens, detain them with no cause, fingerprint and interrogate citizens at will, and conduct secret military tribunals, it is a short leap to wiretapping homes, invading privacy rights of citizens, conducting searches of homes, and chilling free speech. Through the various activities done under the authority of the U.S. Patriot Act, the government has made us all less free. For the social work field, which is predicated on informed choice, such a law is in opposition to everything we stand for as a profession dedicated to assisting others and promoting the greatest freedom allowable within the context of a democratic nation. If we don't protect the vulnerable, who will? The British philosopher Edmund Burke once stated, "The only thing necessary for the triumph of evil is that good men do nothing." Doing nothing is not a social work option when addressing the consequences of the U.S. Patriot Act.

Activism and Reaffirmation

Our best chance of addressing the wrongs of the U.S. Patriot Act is through good old-fashioned activism. We must become more involved in the political process and protect those vulnerable populations that are being targeted unjustly. This activism must be rooted in the belief that if people do not stand up and confront oppression, injustice, and continued abuse, all being committed under the rubric of law, it will continue unabated. As a profession, social work has a long tradition of promoting the dignity of the individual vis-à-vis government-sponsored oppression and social justice. In our short glorious history, we have been called upon to address wrongdoing when we see it and to affirm the principles on which this country and our professional code of ethics are buttressed.

According to the preamble of the National Association of Social Workers (2008) code of ethics, we as social work professionals are committed to the core value of social justice. Social justice demands that we as professionals work with others to change the existing U.S. Patriot Act. As described in this chapter, the government has particiapted in numerous activities that produce irreparable harm to individuals and provide them with minimal recourse to defend themselves against government agencies. As vulnerable populations, men and women of Arab origin are being persecuted and unjustly labeled, all under the notion of homeland security and rooting out suspected terrorists. The evidence is that the country is not safe against future terrorist attacks as a result of the creation of the U.S. Patriot Act. In fact, it may be hypothesized that we are actually less safe and less free simultaneously because of the U.S. Patriot Act.

Case law has attacked many of the premises and activities of the government under the U.S. Patriot Act. Take, for example, the case of *Doe I, II v. Gonzales* (2006), in which the government sought to enforce a provision of the U.S. Patriot Act that compelled the divulging of information from Internet service providers regarding their subscribers' activities, and more nefariously, imposing a gag order that prevented them from telling anyone that they had been served a dubious "national security letter." In September 2004, a district court struck down the U.S. Patriot Act provision that allowed the government to demand such information from Internet providers and declared the gag order rule unconstitutional. The situation, however, did not end there.

The government appealed the decision of the district court to the Second Circuit Court of Appeals, but before a decision could be issued, the U.S. Congress amended the specific provision of the U.S. Patriot Act to allow for greater judicial review when someone receives a national security letter. As a response, the FBI withdrew its national security letter, the second time it had done this when facing judicial review. The appellate court sent the case back to the district court to rule on the constitutionality of the amended law.

As we head into 2012, we have more certainty regarding the amended law. In the summer of 2007, the New York American Civil Liberties Union and the American Civil Liberties Union went to court arguing that the amended law should be deemed unconstitutional. Similarly, in 2007, a federal judge in Oregon ruled that certain provisions of the Patriot Act were unconstitutional, specifically noting one provision that allowed agencies to "sneak and peek" into records of alleged terrorists and conduct searches of their homes and property (Keller, 2007). In early 2008, the ACLU and the Electronic Frontier Foundation filed suit against the modifications made in the amended law as well.

In 2010, a federal district court judge ruled that the actions of the NSA were illegal, and the government was liable to pay damages to victims (Savage & Risen, 2010). Finally in 2011, a federal appeals court ruled in *Jewel v. National Security Agency* that a lower court erred when it determined that the plaintiff—Carolyn Jewel (and other similarly situated persons harmed by the NSA surveillance program)—lacked standing in the court. The appeals court ordered the case remanded back to the lower court for another trial, questioning what the government refers to as the "state secrets privilege," a privilege granted to the government when it is asked to divulge information that it deems to be sensitive and its release detrimental to the security of the country. Whether or not the state secrets privilege will be held up in this case and other similarly situated cases remains to be seen.

It is no doubt that in the future many parts of the Patriot Act will continue to be questioned by the courts. The net effect of these court decisions is that the government no longer can issue national security letters (over 30,000 a year!) and conduct questionable searches and seizures without allowing persons to whom the letters and the searches and seizures are directed to address the particulars in open court.

The courts have stated that abuses of power by the government under the auspices of the U.S. Patriot Act will not be tolerated. Further legal developments will continue to challenge the constitutionality of the U.S. Patriot Act. As social workers, we will have to work with others to check governmental actions that engender social injustice and oppression of vulnerable populations. To stay true to our mission and purpose, activism and reaffirmation of the social work values means that we speak truth to power and voice our opposition to any activity that further oppresses disadvantaged populations, especially actions that are done in our name as citizens and are wrongfully institutionalized through our laws.

Conclusion

The purpose of this chapter was to reveal the many practices that are being conducted by governmental officials under the aegis of the U.S. Patriot Act. We examined these practices—detention of noncitizens, military tribunals, fingerprinting of immigrants, domestic spying—to show how a separate, secret system of criminal justice is evolving that is antithetical to the values and principles of a democracy and the social work profession. Such practices are damaging on many levels, because they are done under the authority of law. The U.S. Patriot Act, passed in the frenzied times after 9/11, has changed the way the dispensation of justice is achieved in this country and the relationship that citizens have with their government.

As social work professionals, we have to recognize that we have a role and *obligation* to address and confront wrongful activities conducted under the authority granted by the U.S. Patriot Act. As advocates for the oppressed, protectors of freedom, fairness, and due process, and activists for change, we as a social work profession must align ourselves with other similarly minded organizations to protect these values and principles that are coming under attack by the government through the U.S. Patriot Act. We have always shown up when the vulnerable and oppressed needed us. They, again, need us to confront the evils and injustices pursued by a clandestine system of justice created by the U.S. Patriot Act.

In his book *Why We Can't Wait* (1964), the Reverend Dr. Martin Luther King, Jr. defended his actions of peaceful protest and economic boycott by saying he could no longer wait for others to come forward and speak out against injustices toward vulnerable and oppressed populations. He could no longer wait for justice to happen; he decided to *make* justice happen. So, we as social work professionals must not wait for justice to happen in our current situation. We must remain ever vigilant to our mission and values of assisting those who have to carry the burden of government oppression as expressed through the U.S. Patriot Act. To do anything less would be inimical to our profession, the people we serve, and the democracy we cherish.

Key Terms

Patriot Act   *police state*   *privileges*
homeland security   *rights*

Review Questions for Critical Thinking

1. Does the Patriot Act in effect open the door for the U.S. government to spy on people?

2. Do you believe it is fair that the U.S. government can maintain wiretaps on multiple phones and spy on non-Americans even though they have no prior or current connection to a terrorist group? Are you concerned that the U.S. government, without informing you, can gather reports of books you took out of your college library or purchased at the bookstore? And is this an infringement of your rights and confidentiality?

3. Should someone from a Middle Eastern country or a person who is Muslim by faith be treated differently from an American Christian citizen by the U.S. government?

4. Does the Patriot Act give too much power to government?

5. What should the social work profession's role be with implementing the full intent of the Patriot Act?

Online Resources

U.S. Department of Justice: www.justice.gov

U.S. Department of Homeland Security: www.dhs.gov

National Commission on Terrorist Attacks Upon the United States: www.9-11commission.gov

American Library Association: www.ala.org

American Civil Liberties Union: www.aclu.org

References

American Civil Liberties Union. (2002). *Insatiable appetite: The government's demand for new and unnecessary powers after September 11: An ACLU report*. New York, NY: Author.

American Civil Liberties Union. (2003). *Freedom under fire: Dissent in post-911 America*. New York, NY: Author.

American Civil Liberties Union. (2006). FBI drops another Patriot Act demand but keeps gag on internet service provider. Retrieved on November 22, 2006, from www.aclu.org

Barrett, T. (2006). Quoted in K. Kingsbury, The next crime wave. *Time*, *168*(24), 70–77.

Boumediene v. Bush, 553 U.S. 723 (2008).

Cole, G., & Smith, C. (2007). *The American system of criminal justice* (11th ed.). Belmont, CA: Wadsworth/Thomson.

Doe I, II v. Gonzales, 05-0570-cv (L), 05-4896-cv (CON) (2006).

Engel, R., & Calnon, J. (2004). Examining the influence of drivers' characteristics during traffic stops with police: Results from a national survey. *Justice Quarterly*, *21*, 49–90.

Fainaru, S. (2002). Suspect held 8 months without seeing judge. *The Washington Post*, June 12, 2002, as cited in American Civil Liberties Union. (2002). *Insatiable appetite: The government's demand for new and unnecessary powers after September 11: An ACLU report*. New York, NY: Author.

Holder, E. (2009). Cited in US retires 'enemy combatant,' keeps broad right to detain. *The Washington Post*, March 14, 2009, pp. 3–14.

Jewel v. National Security Agency, No. 10–15616 D.C. Nos. 3:08-cv-04373-VRW M:06-cv-01791-VRW (2011).

Keller, S. J. (2007). Judge rules provisions in Patriot Act to be illegal. *The New York Times,* September 27, 2007.

King, M. L., Jr. (1964). *Why we can't wait*. New York, NY: Harper & Row.

Liptak, A. (2007). U.S. defends surveillance to 3 skeptical judges. *The New York Times*, August 16, 2007.

Moreno, I. (2010). Illegal immigration fingerprint program, secure communities, has advocates up in arms. The Associated Press.

National Association of Social Workers. (2008). *Code of ethics of the National Association of Social Workers*. Washington, DC: Author.

Podesta, J. (2002). USA Patriot Act: The good, the bad, and the sunset. *Human Rights Magazine*, Winter 2002.

Powers, R. (1987). *Secrecy and power: The life of J. Edgar Hoover*. New York, NY: Free Press.

Savage, C., & Risen, J. (2010). Federal judge finds N.S.A. wiretaps were illegal. *The New York Times*, March 31, 2010.

Stojkovic, S., Kalinich, D., & Klofas, J. (2012). *Criminal justice organizations: Administration and management* (5th ed.). Belmont, CA: Wadsworth/Cengage Learning.

Sutton, J. (2012). Former U.S. resident convicted at Guantanamo of murder. *Chicago Tribune* Online, February 29, 2012.

The 9–11 Commission. (2004). The 9–11 Commission report: Final report of the National Commission on Terrorist Attacks Upon the United States. Executive Summary.

West, C. (1993). *Race Matters*. Boston, MA: Beacon Press.

Chapter 9
Social Justice in a World of Anywhere Access?

Paul R. Raffoul

> As you read this chapter, consider the human implications of the evolving technologies; to what extent are human rights downplayed and lost in the emerging social media? Similarly, think through how technology can be used as an empowering tool that people can use to create change. Finally, reflect on the nature of technology: Is it really worth it in the long run?

Introduction

Technology has evolved and will continue to evolve in almost unimaginable ways. Our way of working, living, and relating with others has dramatically changed since the Internet became available to the public in 1990. Information that was once scarce to come by is easily accessible on the Internet and, as a result, creates opportunities for individuals, groups, organizations, and governments to develop innovative change strategies. Thomas Friedman—in his best-selling 2005 book *The World Is Flat*, which was revised in 2007 and retitled *The World Is Flat 3.0*—argued that globalization, through technology, essentially "leveled the playing field" between the north, south, east, and west, which has resulted in a flattened world. But is the world really flat? What of those countries and peoples who barely have drinkable water, never mind no electricity or access to technology; have they been set further aside into deeper valleys? Technology has created and opened many possibilities for some, but what of the human toll? Research shows that young people today prefer texting friends over having face-to-face conversations, essentially dramatically shifting human interaction to a new paradigm.

There is a lot of discussion about the new digital revolution that has been taking place since the early 80s when the Information Age began. The latest slogan, as stated by Microsoft founder Bill Gates, is a "World of Anywhere Access." This comes on the heels of Friedman's book, in which he traces the recent history of the 21st century using the developments in technology as the model for moving from the information revolution to the digital revolution. He identified 10 information "flatteners," beginning with the release of Microsoft Windows, version 3.0 (1990), to make the world of information flat:

> *The diffusion of the PC, fax machines, Windows and dial-up modems connected to a global network all came together in the late 80s and early 90s to create the basic platform that started the global information revolution.*
>
> *Quoted by Craig J. Mundie, Chief Tech Officer for Microsoft, in Friedman (2005), p. 53*

How has this burgeoning technology influenced social policy? What are the implications of this technological revolution for the future of social policy? As the title of this chapter suggests, the big question is: Can social justice exist (or be increased) in a world of anywhere access? This chapter addresses this question by reviewing where we have come with technology and how technology has influenced social policy. The final section will begin to answer the title question about social justice and technology over the next 10 years.

Twenty years ago, people did not have cell phones, PDAs, iPods, or iPads. The Internet was just beginning to change the ways in which people access information. E-mail was beginning to alter the ways people communicated both at work and at play. The business community was still struggling to find a standard combination of hardware and software to fit their particular work environment. The policy issues of privacy, confidentiality, and security of information had yet to become a reality. Personal identity was not yet at risk of theft or misrepresentation.

Today, these devices have become ubiquitous. Since being introduced in 2010, the iPad has been Apple's fastest-selling product ever, selling more than 55 million units. Conversely, it took Apple 22 years to sell the same number of Mac computers, five years to sell that many iPods, and three years to sell that many iPhones (*Houston Chronicle*, February 29, 2012, p. D-1-2).

What is the place of these growing technologies in everyday life? They have become a common denominator for people around the world. Wherever one travels, it is common to see people walking down the street working an iPod, or they have some cords dangling from their ears, or some other electronic device hanging onto the outside of one ear.

For whatever reason, people must be connected 24/7. Cell phone use and texting are commonplace, yet their intrusiveness into everyday life raises significant safety issues. As of April 2012, handheld cell phone use while driving is banned in 10 states, and 37 states ban texting while driving. Not to be outdone by these growing restrictions, new technologies quickly emerged to allow for hands-free operation while driving a motor vehicle. Federal, state, county, and city courthouses are banning cell phone use; cell phones and other electronic devices must be turned off when going through most countries' customs and immigration offices at airports for security purposes; and corporations are developing policies on where, when, and what type of devices can be brought to the workplace, again because of security concerns.

Employees complain that they cannot work as effectively if their e-mail or business network is down and not working. More importantly, the productivity of an individual decreases considerably when the technology they rely upon to do their work or conduct their lives is not working. A 2005 survey found that an employee considers 17 hours of employment each week to be "wasted," though technology helps increase their personal productivity (Microsoft News Center, 2005). A test of a newspaper editor revealed he could not go without his cell phone for more than just a couple of days; he lost his temper, his productivity decreased, and eventually he succumbed to tears because he could not be contacted on his cell phone by people he deemed important. Quite clearly, people are seeking a social balance as to where and when cell phones are acceptable.

The issues of privacy and security are uppermost in the minds of employers, and personal identity theft has become a major source of illicit revenue. Identity theft is no longer an unusual occurrence. According to a 2005 survey released jointly by the Better Business Bureau and Javelin Strategy and Research, although identity fraud no longer seems to be increasing, 9.3 million American adults became victims of identity fraud during the past 12 months. The total U.S. annual identity fraud cost was $56.2 billion, a figure that has remained essentially unchanged since a Federal Trade Commission (FTC) survey in September 2003 (Better Business Bureau, 2005). If this trend in the use of technology and the products derived from technology continues, what will happen in the next 10 years? How will technology influence social policy, and will social justice be any more attainable than it is today? Several critical themes will be discussed to begin to answer these questions in this chapter.

Globalization

Globalization is advancing rapidly today throughout our society, both in the workplace and in our personal lives. With the increased use of digital technology, the world has become a smaller place, with fewer barriers to communication and greater access to everyone, wherever they are in the world, for whatever information they want to know. Geography is no longer a barrier to communication; people from all over the world can organize around issues of mutual interest and have access to information that is available to all:

> A revolution in technology has enabled any work that can be digitized to be performed virtually anywhere on the globe. Highly skilled employees in Bangalore, Beijing, and other distant places are able to communicate with colleagues in American companies just as if they were working down the hall.

> (Bok, 2006, pp. 4–5)

Social justice takes on a new meaning when the common frame of reference is humankind, not just our own society. Will this globalization trend make the achievement of social justice more possible, or will it make for increased discrepancies and injustices?

Societal Acceptance and Utilization of Technology

With this diffusion of technology throughout the world has come the societal acceptance of technologies that enables more human behavior to be visible, albeit in digital form. Today, it is commonplace to see a video recording posted on YouTube or some other form of social media; the private space and time of the person is virtually lost in the 24/7 technology world.

The search engine Google and its phenomenal growth exemplifies the worldwide acceptance and utilization of technology. It is reported that Google is now processing more than 1 billion searches per day, up from 200 million just two years ago. Who are the people asking these questions? What are they using this information for?

Tracking Google searches has become a new way to gain insight into cultures and societies. Google Correlate, for example, correlates searches with each other. This unique innovation started in 2008 with the growing flu pandemic. At that time, Google was able to discern that the activity of certain search terms were good indicators of actual flu activity. Based on this finding, Google Flu Trends was created to provide timely estimates of flu activity in 28 countries.

However, tools that provide access to search data, such as Google Trends or Google Insights for Search, were not designed with this type of research in mind. Rather, these systems were created so an individual could search a specific term to determine if there was an emerging trend. Researchers were able to enter words or phrases that reflected a growing trend and conclude which search terms best matched that trend. In other words, a system like Google Trends but in reverse. This is now possible with Google Correlate (May 25, 2011), which allows users to upload their data series and create a list of search terms whose popularity best corresponds with that real-world trend.

Use of Social Media

The expansion of social media networking sites such as Facebook and Twitter has increased the use of information and communication technologies dramatically. Most people over the age of 12 have at least one social network that they maintain regularly. This use of social media is a dual-edged sword: personal empowerment on the one hand and potential loss of privacy on the other.

Social Media and Empowerment

With the availability of information to everyone comes personal empowerment and community development. All participants share equally in information, which leads to more informed decision making and, hopefully, better planning. While the validity and reliability of information is not always known, it is equally available to all and provides a shared beginning for groups with similar and special interests. It also establishes, builds, and maintains relationships without geographic, ethnic, and social boundaries. The so-called digital divide does not include clear, discernible access to valid information but rather the divide between credible information and bogus or spurious information. The challenge for policy makers is to ensure that credible information is made available as soon as possible to all constituents. The bottom line is that just because something is reported on the Web does not make it correct or accurate information.

Social Media and Privacy Issues

Personal identity, confidentiality, and security issues have become especially important as we have moved more into a digital world. This potential violation of personal freedom(s) has led to many inconveniences and delays in implementing a truly digital environment in all areas of our lives. From passwords required to gain access to one's personal computer, network, work computer, and work network and to access a variety of sites on the Internet, all access points have become vulnerable to hacking by unauthorized persons and have created numerous security risks, with often considerable financial consequences. The common protocol is to register with a site, select a password, and authenticate oneself in order to conduct business in any way on the Internet. Such passwords are measured for security based on the configuration of letters, numbers, and symbols—the more complicated the password, the greater the security. Even with these increased precautions, private sites, such as credit cards or government records, are frequently hacked into, jeopardizing an individual's personal financial security and private life.

From a social policy standpoint, the question is where to draw the line between freedom of information with that of individual information confidentiality and identity security. For example, how does an organization, be it public or private, provide information about human needs without jeopardizing an individual's privacy rights?

A common issue concerning privacy concerns is prospective employers who are requiring job applicants to provide their social media passwords as part of the hiring process. Essentially, the posting of statements or photos on a social media site is viewed as public information, so employers see such information as providing insight into a potential employee's character. Yet, there are ethical and legal questions swirling around the use of such information: Is this an invasion of one's privacy that should be limited or eliminated, or is a personal posting on a website considered part of the public domain and therefore not protected by privacy laws? (Another Voice, 2012).

Information Access and Authenticity

The proliferation of the Web now makes information universally available; yet, this universality does not suggest or imply that the presentation is accurate (valid), consistent (reliable), or useful. Critical analysis, reading, and synthesis are often required in order to access the most useful, current, and accurate information available on the Web. This is not an innate skill but rather one that requires critical thinking and practice in order to maximize one's efficiency in terms of time and effort. Learning how to skillfully apply a search engine (e.g., Google, Yahoo!, MS Search, Bing) requires a basic understanding of logic and assessment.

Information made available on the Internet takes on a life of its own and never disappears. It is, if you will, a technological tattoo. Stories are developed, websites are linked with each other, and new sites are created. An initial website or set of data will live on forever, and it eventually becomes a source of outdated information.

Personal information is also easily accessible on the Web. One can enter a person's name and find basic contact information, including a local address, phone number, and e-mail alias. For a small fee, generally less than $20, a background check can be obtained, criminal records checked, and credit reports generated, as well as copies of motor vehicle registrations, marriage certificates, and divorce decrees. There are clearly unanswered ethical issues around the use of this personal information, but once it is on the Internet it is publicly available and beyond the control of the individual user.

A recent letter to the *New York Times Sunday Magazine* ethicist, Randy Cohen, highlights the ethical dilemma yet to be resolved, for a high school graduate seeking admission to a college in which an admissions reviewer had read their personal information on the Internet and asked about the ethics of including this information in their admission review materials. Mr. Cohen's answer was,

> *You would not read someone's old-fashioned pen-and-paper diary without consent... regard a blog similarly.... Many unwisely regard... blogs as... semiprivate.... So befogged are students about online postings.... Universities commonly devote a portion of freshman orientation to wising them up.... Such online info is unreliable, even when posted by the person himself.*
>
> *http://www.nytimes.com/2007/03/11/magazine/11wwlnethicist.t.html?_r=1)*

An example of how information can be changed on the Internet is the user-contributed online encyclopedia Wikipedia. This so-called people's encyclopedia allows users to directly edit any Web page on their own from their home computer. This allows the reader the ability to track the status of articles, review individual changes, and discuss issues and functions as social software. The check and balance for accurate information comes from the users themselves. Any person can add or modify content, while others confirm the information by allowing it to remain on the page, essentially reaching a common ground of information (Friedman, pp. 92–93). There is one problem with sites such as Wikipedia: The validity and reliability of such information is inconsistent and subject to change over time. No controls are in place to attest to the credibility and expertise of the individual poster or the online readers who contribute to an entry. Again, the cautionary note with Wikipedia and other similar Web-based informational sources is: buyer beware.

Ensuring Diversity and Cultural Differences

As we become one with the world, it is important to retain our individual identities, including the cultural, ethnic, and geographic differences that make up our global society. Just because we all have access to the same information doesn't mean that we will all use it in the same way. There is a tendency to assume that with everyone having access to the same information, there is one big digital melting pot of information that is available and applicable to everyone in the same way.

There is another side to informing that people are going to have to get used to, and that is other people's ability to inform themselves about you from a very early age. Search engines flatten the world by eliminating all the valleys and peaks, all the walls and rocks, that people used to hide inside of, atop, behind, or under in order to mask their reputations or parts of their past. In a flat world, you can't run, you can't hide, and smaller and smaller rocks are turned over. Live your life honestly, because whatever you do, whatever mistakes you make, they will be searchable one day. The flatter the world becomes, the more ordinary people become transparent—and available (Friedman, p. 158).

Influencing the Development of Social Policy

Technology provides the means for greater participation in the development of social policy for more people than ever before. With the availability of information, increased access and communication, and consensus building comes the potential to have an increasingly greater impact on the development of new social policies, which can benefit more people. The ability to achieve greater social justice for everyone is now available to more people than ever before. Whether people are willing to take advantage of this technology remains to be seen.

In the first empirical report of the extent of e-mail use by agency-based direct service social workers, Finn (2006) found that while e-mail use is common practice among 75 percent of the social workers in his convenience sample (n = 384), policy and practice on the use of e-mail in social work agencies is not uniform. Only 50 percent reported that their agency has a written e-mail policy, and only one-third indicated that the agency attaches a confidentiality statement to their e-mails. Finn reported that "it appears that practice has outpaced policies and infrastructure at many social work agencies that use e-mail" (p. 15).

Unintended Consequences of Technology and Social Policy

Major societal change as a result of the influence of technology will take time. Some changes brought about by technology have already begun, as we can see from the last 25 years. We must remember that the World Wide Web only made its way to the public in 1990, and the desktop computer with Internet capability was only beginning to become a common workplace fixture by the end of the 20th century.

Some changes have occurred relatively quickly, as seen in the way that the younger generation has taken to the Apple iPod and made it the world's best-selling range of digital audio players and one of the most popular consumer brands worldwide. New technologies are now commonplace, with new versions of the iPad, iPod, iPhone, and Windows coming forth on what seems to be an annual basis. These changes will continue at ever-increasing speeds. The challenge is to develop social policies that control how these new, emerging, faster technologies will be applied in daily life and how to protect the individual's confidentiality and privacy.

One example has to do with people's attitudes and beliefs about using technology in their professional practice. Take direct service social workers, for example. Jerry Finn's (2006) study suggests that

> e-mail is becoming common among social workers, and is beginning to be used between social workers and consumers as well. As electronic communication becomes increasingly integrated into agency life, new opportunities for providing efficient, effective, and convenient services will arise. These opportunities may be underutilized or undermined, however, by social workers' negative attitudes and lack of information about the therapeutic and supportive use of e-mail with consumers.

> Social workers are concerned about the quality of their relationship with consumers of services. If they believe that e-mail is not an effective therapeutic medium and that lack of confidentiality can occur when e-mail is used, they are not likely to support online services. Policies and infrastructure that promote e-mail safety and confidentiality will need to become standard practice. Attitude change and policy development will require well-conceived and comprehensive research efforts to further define, assess, and examine e-mail use in order to inform agency training and practice. (p. 18)

Who will be the master: technology or social policy? How we define social policies about technology in the future will determine how quickly societal changes will take place. It will also determine, in large part, how attainable social justice will become in the future. Technology is a double-edged sword: It can be the motivator to change for the better or it can be the divider between the haves and the have-nots.

In retrospect, the explosion of technology has led to the reformulation of social policies. That is, policies have been developed in response to technology rather than in anticipation of technological changes. Identity theft, loss of personal information, spamming, phishing, and so on have created the need for new policies and procedures to protect personal information from being exploited by others. Laws have been passed to control these behaviors as technology has made information more available.

A Look Ahead to the Year 2022

What will the social work workplace look like when the world of anywhere access is part of our day-to-day living? Will there be a need for people to work in a central office building? Will there be actual office hours built around a 9-to-5 schedule? Will social work client contacts be face-to-face? Will there be a new technology therapy to work with the upcoming "I" generation, just as play therapy was created for communicating with children? To think our work will not change in form and structure is avoiding the obvious: Technology is transforming every part of our lives.

Given the rapid deployment of technology throughout our society and the world, it is highly probable that the centralized, single, unitary workplace will be a commodity of the past. Social workers will probably be working wherever they are physically located, with access to their office databases, clients' records, and the clients themselves via digital technology, either in real time (live video) or in recorded time. Just as centralized, stationary, desktop computing in universities is being transformed today into a learning commons, with access to multiple forms of computing (i.e., from desktops to laptops, with digital media equipment, photographic equipment, graphics, images, etc. all available in a common environment), so too will the workplace of social workers be transformed. Social workers will most likely not be geographically located with their clients, but with technology they will have the ability to communicate instantly with clients in real time. Clients will no longer have to come to the office to initiate contact, complete applications, and sit in waiting rooms; in the future, clients will have access, via the Internet, to all the forms they need to complete the application process before meeting, probably face-to-face via some form of technology such as Skype, with an intake worker.

Online therapy (e-therapy) has already begun to appear on the Internet; a recent Google search found more than 32 million websites under that category alone. E-therapy is not psychotherapy and should not be compared to traditional, face-to-face therapy; however, e-therapy is an alternative source of help when traditional therapy is not accessible. It may be conducted as a single consultation to answer a question or as an ongoing conversation via e-mail, chat, video, or even Internet phone (voice-over-IP). A client can text, call, or video stream with the worker; a client, for example, may need last-minute reassurance before a meeting with his supervisor, and a quick e-therapy intervention will help.

A 1999 Surgeon General's *Report on Mental Health* notes that 20 percent of Americans have a diagnosable mental illness, although nearly two-thirds do not seek treatment for their illness (*Mental Health*, 1999). The use of online therapy will help expand usage as the availability and simplicity to access services changes, and in particular as more social workers and mental health providers recognize and learn to use e-therapy. As this new practice arena evolves, research is necessary to monitor, evaluate, and develop best practice strategies for online therapy.

Digital technology has also birthed a new, vibrant world of virtual reality (VR), which can be used to simulate a variety of clinical and behavioral situations. VR software is being used to educate children with disabilities, parents of children with disabilities, persons with dependency issues, people undergoing smoking cessation interventions, and the like. Online, some 12 million VR websites have been identified.

In the VR world, a digital image can be adapted to be seen as if it were in a real-world environment. Responses and behaviors in the VR simulation are cued to the individual, which allows for unique, client-specific scenarios to emerge. Through the VR experience, a client is able to role play situations, which in turn creates and reinforces appropriate behavioral responses. VR simulations can be used in teaching as well; envision a VR scenario for a student in which she is meeting with an angry client, an angry family, or working with a dysfunctional committee. Simulation training is commonplace in medicine (see www.harvardmedsim.org/), and these experiences can easily be translated to social work education.

Reliance on all facets of technology will continue to increase as more people become comfortable with the use of digital media while the costs decrease. The range of possible applications of this technology seems endless and unlimited, but this now opens the door to another set of questions: Who should be responsible for educating children in the use of this technology? What responsibility should public schools have for teaching young people about the uses and abuses of technology? And for the social work profession, educators and practitioners alike must consider how this growing world can increase social justice for all persons.

So, where we will be in 2022 with technology and social policy is difficult to say with certainty, but it surely will be a different place than where we are today. In 1990, few people could even imagine the scope of change that would result in our communities because of technologies. No matter how technology continues to evolve and change our work habits and interpersonal relationship styles, the social work profession must keep social justice clearly in mind to build, form, and guide all types of social policies and interactions.

Key Terms

technology and social policy

anywhere access

globalization and technology

information access and authenticity

social justice

social media

Review Questions for Critical Thinking

1. What are the positive benefits of technology's influences on social work practice, both clinical and macro?

2. What are the negative attributes of technology's influences on social work practice, both clinical and macro?

3. Why do people feel they must be connected 24/7?

4. How will technology influence social policy, and will social justice be any more attainable than it is today?

5. Will the results of technology's influence on globalization make the achievement of social justice more possible, or will we see increased discrepancies and injustices? In other words, is the world really flat or are the mountains getting taller and the valleys deeper?

Online Resources

Online Social Justice: www.onlinesocialjustice.com/sites-on-the-web/

Center for Medical Simulation: www.harvardmedsim.org/

Institute for Ethics and Emerging Technology: www.ieet.org/

Virtual Reality Medical Institute: www.vrphobia.eu/

Online Therapy Institute: www.onlinetherapyinstitute.com/

References

Another Voice (*The Philadelphia Inquirer*). (March 31, 2012). Passwords and privacy, editorial in *Houston Chronicle*, p. B-6.

Better Business Bureau. (2005). Retrieved on March 2, 2007, from http://www .bbbonline.org/idtheft/consumers.asp

Bok, D. (2006). *Our underachieving colleges: A candid look at how much students learn and why they should be learning more*. Princeton, NJ: Princeton University Press.

Cohen, R. (March 11, 2007). Retrieved on March 13, 2007, from www.nytimes.com/ 2007/03/11/magazine/11wwlnethicist.t.html?_r = 1

Finn, J. (2006). An exploratory study of email use by direct service social workers. *Journal of Technology in Human Services*, 24 (4), 1–20.

Friedman, T. (2005). *The world is flat: A brief history of the twenty-first century.* New York, NY: Farrar, Straus & Giroux.

Mental Health: A report of the Surgeon General. (1999). Available online from www.surgeongeneral.gov/library/mentalhealth

Microsoft News Center. (March 15, 2005). Survey finds workers average only three productive days per week. Retrieved on April 20, 2012, from www.microsoft.com/en-us/news/press/2005/mar05/03-15ThreeProductiveDaysPR.aspx

New iPad announcement is March 7, but when can you buy one? (2012, February 29). *Houston Chronicle*, p. D-1–2.

Author Index

Aaron, H. J., 149
Abel, L., 144
Abramovitz, M., 11–12, 119, 136, 151
Acs, G., 121, 140, 141
Adelantado, J., 86
Administration for Children & Families, 121, 122
Ahmadi, N., 84, 85, 89
Albelda, R., 122
Allard, S., 144, 149
American Civil Liberties Union (ACLU), 167, 168, 169, 171, 172, 173, 174
Annie E. Casey Foundation, 139, 143, 145, 149
Another Voice, 186
Antwerp, J. H., 146
Appleby, J., 34
Auerbach, D., 141
Austin, M. J., 149
Australian Association of Social Workers, 9
Autor, D., 140, 143
Axinn, J., 22, 34, 119, 136, 150

Baker, D., 85
Baker, P., 73
Barker, R., 5, 6
Barnow, B. S., 143
Barrabee, P., 146
Barrett, T., 169
Bartik, T. J., 152
Baruah, B., 149
Bates, K. A., 144, 148
Baumheier, E. C., 5
Bean, F. D., 147
Beckgield, J., 86
Bergman, L. R., 137
Berkowitz, E., 58
Bernard, T. S., 16
Better Business Bureau, 183
Bivens, J., 140
Black, D. A., 150
Blank, R., 144, 145
Blau, J., 136, 143

Bloom, D., 123
Blum, M. D., 146
Boaz, A., 13
Bok, D., 13, 183
Bond, T. M., 144
Borjas, G., 147
Bostrom, M., 126
Bowen, J. T., 145
Bowler, A., 146
Boyer, P., 32
Brady, D., 86–87
Braun, K. L., 148
Braveman, P. A., 141, 144
Brody, D., 43
Brooks, F., 140
Brooks, R., 139
Brown, K., 15
Brown, M., 144, 150
Browne, C. V., 148
Bureau of Labor Statistics, 137, 138, 142, 144
Burnstein, N., 147
Burtless, G., 138, 143
Buss, J. A., 140, 141, 149

Calderón, E., 86
Calnon, J., 171
Canadian Association of Social Work, 8
Cancian, M., 141
Capps, R., 147
Carafano, J. J., 74
Carlson, A. W., 147
Case, A., 140
Censky, A., 138
Center on Budget and Policy Priorities, 137, 140, 142, 143
Chan, R. K. H., 107
Chan, W. T., 107
Chan-Tibergian, J., 84, 85
Chapin Hall, 147
Chatterjee, P., 5
Chaudry, A., 144
Chen, C., 85

Children's Defense Fund, 143
Chitose, Y., 147
Chow, J. C., 147, 149
Clay, C., 139
Cloward, R. A., 119
Cohen, N., 75
Colby, Ira, 1–19
Cole, G., 170
Coletti, U., 146
Collins, J. L., 144, 151, 153
Collins, M. E., 139, 145
Commission on Human Security, 71
Congressional Budget Office, 118
Coulton, C. J., 141
Council on Social Work Education, 8
Creamer, R., 69

Dana, M. M., 146
Daniels, N., 24
Davis, J., 71
Davis, K., 25
Deacon, B., 87
Dear, R. B., 5
Declaration of Alma-Ata, 2
D'Emilio, J., 47
DeNavas-Walt, C., 122
DeParle, J., 149, 152
Derthick, M., 119
DeVita, C. J., 147
Diez-Roux, A., 149
DiMaggio, C., 141
DiNitto, D., 5
Douglass, J. H., 146
Drachman, D., 147
Duncan, G. J., 130, 140
Duncan, L., 148
Dye, T., 5
Dyer, T., 40
Dzieza, J., 12

Economic Policy Institute, 139, 144, 145
Edelman, P., 141, 143

Edsall, T., 58
Eichler, A., 2
Eisenbrey, R., 140, 143
Elder, L., 13
Engel, R., 171

Fainaru, 169
Fairbanks, R. P., 153
Falk, G., 121
Families USA, 144
Ferrera, M., 136, 148
Fertig, A., 140, 141
Fieldhouse, A., 140
Finch, J., 146
Findlay, M., 82, 84, 86
Finn, J., 188
Fishberg, M., 145
Fisher, A., 13
Fisher, S., 144
Fix, M., 147
Foner, N., 147
Food Nutrition Service, 143
Fording, R. C., 144
Fors, M., 83
Friedlander, W., 5
Friedman, L., 37
Friedman, T., 15, 181–182, 187
Furstenberg, F. F., Jr., 141

Galea, S., 141
Galewitz, P., 75
Garrett, P., 146
Gates, W. A., 146
Gebeloff, R. M., 152
Genschel, P., 86, 87
Gilbert, N., 5
Gilens, M., 125, 126
Gish, M., 121
Glied, S. A., 144
Gold, S., 147
Golden, O., 141, 143
Goleman, D., 129
Gonzalez, G. C., 147
Gordon, L., 37, 118
Graham, G., 144
Guenther, R., 146
Guillén, M. F., 82
Guttal, S., 82, 85

Hacker, J., 52, 58, 144
Hagen, J., 3
Hall, P., 145
Halloran, P., 34
Haq, M., 66
Harris, B., 34
Harris, D. R., 144

Hart, H., 145
Hartz, L., 58
Harvey, D., 149
Hataley, T. S., 74
Haub, C., 73
Hay, C., 82
Haynes, K., 4, 12
Healy, L. M., 82
Hedges, C., 77
Heinrich, C. J., 152
Herd, D., 138
Hirsch, A. E., 119
Hobbie, R. A., 143
Hoey, J. M., 146
Hoffman, M. L., 129
Hoggat, K. J., 141
Holder, E., 168
Holt, S., 141
Holzer, H., 130, 140, 141, 143, 145
Hopkins, E., 146
Houseman, S. N., 152
Hoyt, C. S., 145, 146
Hugo, E., 145
Hulme, D., 138

Inequality.org, 141
International Association of Schools of Social Work, 9
International Council on Social Welfare, 8
International Federation of Schools of Social Work, 8, 9
International Federation of Social Workers, 9
Irving, Z., 88
Iverson, R. R., 141, 152

Jani, J. S., 139
Jansson, B., 3, 21–64, 136, 144, 150
Jensen, L., 147
Jessop, B., 151
Johnson, M. A., 149
Johnson, N., 138, 143, 145
Jones, J. M., 146

Kalinich, D., 169
Kapp, J. W., 137, 150
Karoly, L. A., 147
Karpati, A., 141
Katz, M., 123, 144, 150, 151
Kawachi, I., 24
Keller, S. J., 176
Kellerman, A., 141

Kilty, K. M., 123
Kim, M., 138
Kim, S. H., 139
Kimes, M., 70
King, C. T., 121
King, M. L., Jr., 178
Kirmani, R., 147
Kissane, R. J., 147
Klein, N., 137, 138, 139
Klofas, J., 169
Koh, H. K., 144
Kohler, M., 146
Kovak, B., 144
Kraev, E., 85
Krasner, S. D., 68
Krugman, P., 138
Kwok, J., 93–115

Lalich, N., 141
Lamb, R., 146
Larned, R., 146
Layzer, J. I., 147
Lebeaux, C., 9, 11
Lee, A., 147
Lee, C. H., 122
Leff, M., 44
Leiby, J., 22
Leighninger, L., 5
Leighton, P., 144
Leondar-Wright, B., 144
Lerman, R. I., 140, 143
Leuchtenburg, W. E., 130
Leung, V., 147
Levin, H., 22, 34
Lieberman, R. C., 144, 150
Lightman, E., 138
Lim, Y., 141
Lin, A. C., 144
Liptak, A., 172
Loeb, P. R., 129
Looney, A., 138, 143
Loprest, P., 121, 140
Lorenz, W., 136
Ludwig, J., 130, 140
Luhby, T., 139
Lui, M., 144
Lundberg, O., 137

MacCormack, D. W., 146
Maclin, S. D., Jr., 144
Mair, C., 149
Mama, R. S., 81–91
Marshall, L. C., 145
Maruyama, I., 106
Matsui, R., 104, 106
Mayer, D. R., 141

Mayer, V., 144, 151, 153
McClelland, A., 84
McCormack, J., 82, 84, 86
McDonald, C., 136
McMurtrie, D. C., 146
McQuaid, K., 58
McWilliams, C., 37
Mencius, 95
Mennel, R., 32
Mental Health, 190
Mettler, S., 144
Mickelson, J., 4, 12
Microsoft News Center, 183
Miller, D., 6
Mishel, L., 139, 140, 143, 145
Mitchell, A., 138
Monea, E., 141
Morales, A., 5
Moreno, I., 171
Morris, R., 5, 6
Mourre, G., 137
Mueser, P. R., 121
Muller, T., 147
Mundie, C. J., 182
Murphy, F. G., 144

Napolitano, L., 141
Nash, G., 29
National Association of Social
        Workers (NASW),
        8, 176
National Employment Law
        Project, 137, 140
National Poverty Center, 74
Neidell, M., 147
Nichols, A., 140, 141
Nossal, K. R., 74
Nozick, R., 7, 8

O'Donnell, P. S., 68
Office of Planning, Research,
        and Evaluation, 147
Oliff, P., 138, 143
Olsen, G. M., 139
Osterling, K. L., 147
Ozawa, M., 154

Palley, T. I., 138
Palmieri, V. H., 146
Parrott, S., 121, 123
Passel, J., 147
Patterson, J., 123, 144, 150
Paul, R., 13
Pavetti, L., 141
Pawson, R., 13
Paxson, C., 140

Paylor, I., 148
Penna, S., 148
Pérez de Cuéllar, J., 88
Perlstein, J., 139
Perry, D. A., 102
Peters, G., 4
Peterson, M., 29
Pierson, P., 60
Piven, F. F., 119, 150, 151
Podesta, J., 172
Popple, P., 5
Portes, A., 147
Powell, J., 146
Powers, R., 168
Proctor, B. D., 122

Quadagno, J., 144

Raffoul, Paul R., 181–192
Rand Corporation, 147
Rank, M. R., 141
Rawley, C., 146
Rawls, J., 6–7, 14
Reamer, F., 3
Reardon-Anderson, J., 147
Reed, D., 141
Rehbein, B., 137
Reiman, J., 144
Reingold, D., 141
Reisch, M., 135–163
Report of the Workshop on
        Human Security, 76
Risen, J., 173, 176
Robinson, D., 24
Robles, B., 144
Roemer, J. E., 95
Rohrbough, M., 33
Rosenbaum, D., 141
Roth, J. K., 7, 15
Ryan, W., 10–11

Sachs, J., 30
Sanborn, F. B., 146
Sanders, S. G., 150
Sassen, S., 149
Savage, C., 173, 176
Sawhill, I., 141
Schanzenbach, D. W., 130, 140
Scholz, J. K., 152
Schorr, A. L., 5
Schott, L., 145, 152
Schram, S. F., 144
Seeleib-Kaiser, M., 86
Segal, Elizabeth, A., 117–133
Sehrt, M., 83
Sellers, C., 33

Shalev, M., 58
Shapiro, I., 123
Sharma, O. P., 73
Sheafor, B., 5
Sherman, A., 121, 141, 142, 143,
        148
Shierholz, H., 139, 143, 145
Short, K., 141
Skocpol, T., 25, 58
Smith, A., 151
Smith, C., 170
Smith, J. A., 74
Smith, J. C., 122
Smith, R., 30
Snell, K., 29
Snyder, P. F., 146
Social Security Administration,
        121
Solomon-Fears, C., 121
Soss, J., 144, 151
Specht, H., 5
Stenning, A., 151
Stern, M., 136, 150
Stevens, G., 147
St. John, S., 84
Stoesz, D., 16
Stojkovic, Stan, 165–179
Stone, C., 141, 142, 143, 148
Stout, M., 129
Sulzberger, C. L., 146
Super, D., 123
Sutton, J., 171
Swan, R. S., 144, 148

Takaki, R., 48, 148
Tateoka, A., 106
Tavernise, S., 149
Taylor, G., 146
Taylor, L. J., 150
Thelen, D., 38
Titmuss, R., 5, 11–12, 98, 136
Tracy, M., 141
Trattner, W., 22, 119
Tsang, D., 97
Tumlin, K. C., 147
Twill, S., 144
Tyrell, I., 32

UNDP, 94
UNESCO, 84
United Nations, 2, 102
UN Trust Fund for Human
        Security, 72
Urban Institute, 145
U.S. Census Bureau, 15, 125,
        139, 141, 142, 148, 149

U.S. Department of Agriculture, 152

U.S. Department of Health and Human Services, 118, 120, 152

U.S. Industrial Commission on Immigration and Education, 146

U.S. Office of Management and Budget, 21

Van Horn, C. E., 142
Villegas, A., 75
Vroman, W., 140

Wacquant, L., 144, 151, 153
Walby, S., 84
Walch, T., 25
Wald, L. P., 146

Waldfogel, J., 147
Waldinger, R., 147, 148
Ward, D. E., 144, 147
Warren, G., 146
Warren, R. C., 144
Washington, J., 148
Watson, J. C., 129
Weinstein, J., 39
Weisbrot, M., 85
Wells, R., 138
West, C., 171
Weyl, W. E., 146
Wilensky, H., 9, 11
Williams, E., 138, 143
Williams, Jody, 65–80
Willis, K., 151
Wilson, G., 86
Wilson, W. J., 123
Witte, J., 52
Wolff, E., 142

Wong, W. P., 100
Wood, G., 28, 29
Woolley, J., 4
World Bank, 2, 94, 137, 142
World Health Organization (WHO), 2
The Writings of Benjamin Franklin, 3

Xu, Q., 136, 147

Yang, P., 147
Yeates, N., 88
Young, P., 88

Zedlewski, S., 140
Zimmerman, S. L., 5
Zimmerman, W., 147
Zukin, C., 142

Subject Index

Accountability, corporate, 69
Accretion, 56–57
ACLU (American Civil Liberties Union), 168, 173, 176
Activism, social workers', 175–177
Addams, Jane, 39
Adolescence, 136
Adoption Assistance and Child Welfare Act, 50
Advocacy, social worker, 173–174
Affirmative action, 47, 144
Afghanistan, 67, 168
African Americans, 45, 46. *See also* Slaves/slavery
  during and after the Civil War period, 35–37
  and discrimination, 47
  gaps in education, 144
  and poverty, 139, 141
  during Progressive era, 40
  and racial profiling, 171
  and welfare reform, 153
Aging population, 60, 136, 148–149
Agricultural Adjustment Agency (AAA), 41
AIDS/HIV, 2, 47
Aid to Dependent Children (ADC), 117, 119–120
Aid to Families with Dependent Children (AFDC), 42, 51, 57
  changed from ADC, 120
  converted from entitlement to block grant, 54
  devolution of, 52
  and welfare reform, 118
Aid to the Blind, 42
American Civil Liberties Union. *See* ACLU (American Civil Liberties Union)
Americans with Disabilities Act, 48
Annan, Kofi, 67, 72

Anthony, Susan B., 34
Anti-discrimination laws, 47–48, 97
Anti-federalists, 30
Anywhere access, 181–192
Arab-descent persons, 168, 171, 174–175
Arab Spring, 16, 65, 68, 69
Ashcroft, John, 172
Asia, 93–115
  regional financial crisis, 99–100
Asian Americans, 40, 47, 153
Asian and Pacific Decade of Disabled Persons, 94, 102–103
Asian Development Bank, 106–107, 111
Asia Pacific Disability Forum, 103
Assimilation, 48
AT&T, 172
Attachment, workplace, 97
Authenticity, 186–187
Autonomy, 87
Axworthy, Lloyd, 71

Beneficence, 87
Bias, 13
Bigotry, 101
Bill of Rights, 30
Biwako Millennium Framework, 94, 102–103, 111
"Blaming the victim," 10–11
Block grants, 51, 52, 54, 57
Boumediene v. Bush, 168, 170
Boundaries, political, 139
Brace, Charles, 32
Brown, Pat, Sr., 57
Bureaucracies, state, 57
Bureau of Old Age and Survivors, 119
Bureau of Public Assistance, 119
Bush, George W., 25, 33, 50–54, 127, 172

Canada, 71
Capital gains, 53
Capitalism, 33, 136, 138
Carter, Jimmy, 49
Cash assistance programs, 118, 120, 124
Categorical programs, 51
Cell phones, 83, 182–183
Center for Economic and Policy Research, 85
Center on Budget and Policy Priorities, 142
Central government, 24, 30
Charities Organization movement, 145
Chavez, Cesar, 47
Chicano movement, 47
Childhood diseases, 143
Children:
  low-income, 45
  and poverty, 32, 121–122, 130, 139–140, 152
  underweight, 2
  and welfare, 122–123
Children's Aid Society of New York, 32
Children's Bureau, 40
Children's Health Insurance Plan (CHIP), 54
China, 97, 143
China Disabled Persons' Federation (CDPF), 105
CIA (Central Intelligence Agency), 172
Civic culture, global, 87–88
Civilian Conservation Corps (CCC), 41
Civilian Works Administration (CWA), 41
Civil law, 23
Civil rights, 35, 36–37, 40, 45, 46, 57, 60
Civil Rights Acts, 36, 46, 47
Civil society, 76–77
Civil War period, 34–37, 56
Clinton, Bill, 47, 51–52, 54–56

Cohen, Randy, 186
Colonial period, American, 28–31
Commerce, international, 137
Commission on Human Security, 71
Community-building programs, 22–23
Community-corporate relationships, 137–138
Community workshops, 105, 106
Compassionate conservatives, 127
Competition, international, 82, 143
Comprehensive Employment Training Act (CETA), 50
Computers:
  in developing world, 83
Confidentiality, 185
Conflict resolution, 78, 88
Congress, U.S., 128
Consciousness, globalization of, 84, 88–89
Convention against Torture and Other Cruel, Inhuman or Degrading Treatment or Punishment, 96
Convention on the Elimination of All Forms of Discrimination Against Women (CEDAW), 96
Convention on the Rights of the Child (CRC), 96
Cooperatives:
  of persons with disabilities, 107–108
Corporate-community relations, 69, 137–138
Corporate welfare, 11–12
Corruption, 34, 76
Council on Social Work Education (CSWE), 8
Council on Social Work Educational Policy and Accreditation Standards (EPAS), 8
Court system, 24
Creative thinking, 14
Crime, 138
  organized, 69
Crimes against humanity, 70
Criminal justice system, 97
Criminal law, 22–23
Critical thinking, 13–15
Cultural diversity, 84, 87, 97

Cultural programs, 22
Culture:
  defined, 84
  of poverty, 151
Curative programs, 23

Defense budgets, 66, 70
Deficit Reduction Act, 120
Deindustrialization, 143
Democracy, 88
Democratic Party, 39, 43, 46, 49, 59
Democratization:
  and lack of corporate accountability, 69
Demographics:
  diversity of, in U.S., 150
  and social policy, 135–163
Department of Homeland Security, 171
Dependency, 136
Destitution. *See* Poverty
Devolution, 50–54, 143, 149
Dewelfarization, 123
Diaspora, intergenerational, 148
Digital divides, 83, 185
Digital revolution, 181
Disability-concerned enterprises, 105
Disabled persons, 47, 48, 57, 94
  in Asia, 102–107
  employment of, 104–106
  global movement, 103
  implications for government policy in support of, 110–111
  in Philippines, 107–108
  social capital development for, 111
  in Taipei, Taiwan, 108–110
Disadvantaged groups, 93–115
Discrimination, 36, 45, 144. *See also* Prejudice; Racism
  gender-based, 47
  and national origin, 174
  against people of Arab descent, 174–175
Diseases, 2, 69, 143
Disparity, economic, 68, 69
Distributive justice, 6, 95
Diswelfares, 136
Diversity, cultural, 84, 87, 187
Divorce, 125
Dix, Dorothea, 32, 34
Dodd-Frank Wall Street Reform and Consumer Protection Act, 55

Doe I, II v. Gonzalez, 176
Domestic spying, 172–173
"Don't Ask, Don't Tell" policy, 47
Dual labor market, 143

Early Republic period, 31–34
Earned Income Tax Credit, 50, 52
Economic disparities, 68, 69
Economic opportunity, 107
Economic Opportunity Act, 46
Economic Policy Institute, 142
Economics:
  and globalization, 136–139
  and social policy, 135–163
Education, public, 11, 33, 56, 144
Education for All Handicapped Children Act, 50
Egocentric thinking, 13
Elderly people. *See* Senior citizens
Electronic Frontier Foundation, 176
Elementary and Secondary Education Act, 46
Elizabethan Poor Laws, 28, 31, 126
E-mail, 188
Emotional intelligence, 129
Empathy, 118, 127, 128–129.
  See also Social empathy
Employment:
  becomes insecure, 139
  of persons with disabilities, 104–106
  primary goal of TANF, 120
  of senior citizens, 104
Empowerment:
  and social media, 185
Encyclopedia of Language and Linguistics, 15
Encyclopedia of Social Work, 5
Enemy combatant, 168, 170
Entitlement programs, 49, 54, 59, 127
  devolution of, 51
  and welfare reform, 153
Environmental destruction, 69
Epidemics, 39
Equal Employment Opportunity Commission, 47
Equal opportunity, 97
Equal Pay Act, 47
Equity and privilege model, 12

E-therapy, 189–190
Ethics, 87–88, 172, 174, 176
Evidence-based practice, 13–14
Exceptionalism, 150–151

Fair Labor Standards Act, 42
Fair trade, 76
Faith-based charities, 25, 33
Family, 136, 149
Family and Medical Leave Act, 54
Family Assistance Plan (FAP), 50
Family supplementing programs, 22
FBI (Federal Bureau of Investigation), 167, 172, 173
Fear, freedom from, 71–72, 76, 96
Federal Deposit Insurance Corporation (FDIC), 41
Federal Emergency Relief Administration (FERA), 41
Federal government. See Government, federal
Federalism, 30
Female-headed households, 141, 144, 152. See also Single-parent families
Financial markets, 82
Fingerprinting, 171
Fiscal welfare, 11–12
Five Year Plan, China, 97
Folks, Homer, 145
Food and Agriculture Organization (FAO), 111
Food stamps, 1, 10, 50, 51, 152
Food Stamps Act, 46
Ford, Gerald, 49
Foreign policy, 69, 82
Foreign trade, 138
For-profit agencies, 24
Foster care, 145
Freedom from fear, 71–72, 76, 96
Freedom from want, 71–72, 75, 76, 96
Freedom of Information Act, 168
Freed slaves, 35–37
Free-market libertarian model, 7
Free trade, 137
Frontier, American, 32–33

Gates, Bill, 181
Gay men, 47–48

Gender roles, 136, 149
General Assistance, 10
Gilded Age, 39
Gingrich, Newt, 51–52, 54
Global Diversity Network, 111
Globalization, 26, 68–69
    benefits of, 85
    criticisms of, 85
    cultural dimensions of, 84
    defined, 82
    and economics, 69, 82–83, 136–139, 142
    and ethics, 87–88
    as it relates to policy, 86–87
    political dimensions of, 83–84, 139
    and poverty, 138
    as a process, 85
    and social justice, 89
    and social work, 82–85
    and technology, 181, 183–184
    and world politics influencers, 135
Global warming, 69
Goals, global, 87
Google, 184
Governance:
    civic, 88
    equity in, 97
    global, 87
Government:
    spending in New Deal period, 44
    spending on social welfare programs, 23
    state, 50–54
    during westward expansion period, 34
Great Depression, 40, 119
Greater good, 7, 12
Great Recession, 55, 56, 140, 142
Great Society, 46–49, 57
Greed, corporate, 69
Group rights, 60
Growth:
    economic, 137
    personal, 129
Guantanamo Bay, Cuba, 168, 170–171

Habeas corpus, 170
Handouts, 127
Haq, Mahbub ul, 66
"Hard benefits," 49–50
Harper, Stephen, 71

Head Start program, 10, 60
Health/health care, 144, 149
Health insurance, 45, 143, 145
    corporate deductions for, 52
    national, 59
    and poverty, 75
    public, 46
    reform, 55
    and welfare, 124
Health savings accounts, 53
Higher education, 13
Hispanics. See Latinos
Homeland security, 65, 165–179
Homelessness, 34
Home mortgage deductions, 12, 52
Homosexuality, 47
Hong Kong, 97, 100
Hoover, J. Edgar, 168
Households, size of, 149
Housing, subsidized, 42, 46, 50, 52
Housing and Urban Development, U.S. Department of (HUD), 46
Human rights, 81, 88, 96
    and human security, 76
    and social justice, 96
    and social policy, 106
    violations in colonial period, 31
Human security, 65–80
    criticisms of, 73–74
    definitions, 72
    framework created by UNDP, 67
    fundamentals and roots, 70–75
    and human rights, 76
    and national security, 75
    pillars of, 71–72
Human Security Network, 67, 71, 73–77
Human Security Now (Commission on Human Security), 71
Human trafficking, 69

Identity, personal, 185
Identity theft, 183
Immigrants/immigration, 23–24, 26, 28, 48, 139
    in 1800s, 33
    economic and social impact of, 146–147

Immigrants/immigration
    (*continued*)
    fingerprinting of, 171
    gaps in education, 144
    policy makers' primary
        concerns about, 145–146
    and poverty, 141
    and racism, 145–150
    and social policy changes, 136
    undocumented, 48–49, 139
    and welfare reform, 153
Immigration Reform and Control
    Act, 48
Immorality, 32
Immunizations, 143
Income:
    inequality, 142, 143, 144
    in U.S., 139, 140
Income taxes, 44, 58
India, 143
Indian Self-Determination and
    Education Assistance Act,
    48
Individualism, 10, 84, 127, 150
Individual Retirement Accounts
    (IRAs), 52
Indochina Migration and
    Refugee Assistance Act,
    48
Indonesia, 99
Industrialization, 38–39, 136
*Industrial Society and Social
    Welfare* (Wilensky), 9
Inequality, 61
    income, 142, 143, 144
    poverty and unemployment,
        139–145
    racial, 144
Infant mortality rate, 143
Information:
    access and authenticity,
        186–187
    overload, 14
Instability, economic, 69
Institutional welfare, 9, 11
Institutions, 22
Intelligence gathering, 172
Interest groups, 59–60
Intergenerational equity, 88
International Association of
    Schools of Social Work
    (IA), 8, 82
International Campaign to Ban
    Landmines, 67
International Conference of
    Alma-Ata, 2

*International Convention of the
    Elimination of All Forms
    of Racial Discrimination*
    (CERD), 96
*International Convention on the
    Protection of the Rights of
    All Migrant Workers*
    (MWC), 96
*International Convention on the
    Rights of Persons with
    Disabilities,* 96, 103–104
International Council on Social
    Welfare (IC), 8
*International Covenant on Civil
    and Political Rights*
    (ICCPR), 96, 169
*International Covenant on
    Economic, Social and
    Cultural Rights* (ICESCR),
    96
International Criminal Court, 70
International Federation of
    Social Workers (IF), 8, 82
International Labour
    Organization, 111
International Monetary Fund
    (IMF), 83
International poverty line, 72–73
International social work, 81–91
International trade, 82
Internet, 83, 176, 181
Intervention, humanitarian, 74
Investment, international, 82
Iraq, 67

Japan, 106
Japan Association of
    Community Workshops
    (JACW), 106
*Jewel v. National Security
    Agency,* 176
Jim Crow laws, 36
Johnson, Lyndon B., 4, 45,
    46–49
Justice, 3, 6–8, 65, 87. *See also*
    Social justice
Justice-based policy, 12–15
Justice system, U.S., 167–173
Juvenile delinquency, 147
Juvenile Justice and
    Delinquency Prevention
    Act, 50

Kennedy, John F., 4, 45
Kerr-Mills medical program, 45
Knowledge economy, 83

Labor:
    and corporate management,
        137–138
    organized, 43, 139
Laissez-faire thinking process, 13
Land distribution policies, 29,
    31–32, 56
Landmines, 67, 70, 71
Land-use policies, 22
Languages, 15
Latinos:
    civil rights violations during
        Progressive era, 40
    and discrimination, 47
    gaps in education, 144
    and immigration, 49
    and poverty, 139, 141, 148
    racial profiling, 171
Law, 22–23
Law enforcement agencies,
    166–167, 169
Lean production techniques, 139
Lesbian women, 47–48
"Less government approach," 7
Lewis, David, 130
Libertarianism, 7
Life expectancy, 143
Liquid-asset poor, 2
Living standards, gaps in, 83
Living wage, 140, 142
Local Fiscal Assistance Act, 50
Logic, 13

Malaysia, 99
Management-labor relationship,
    137–138
Manpower Development and
    Training Act, 46
Marginalized groups, 93–115
Market economy, 29
Marriage, 123, 125, 136
Means testing, 10, 45, 46, 51
Medicaid, 10, 46, 49, 51
    devolution of, 51–52
    growth of, 58, 59
Medical services, 22, 57
Medicare, 11, 46, 49
    expenditures in 2011, 118
    growth of, 58, 59
    impact of aging population
        on, 149
Mental health, 25, 45, 140, 190
Mental institutions, 32, 34
Mental Retardation and
    Community Mental
    Health Centers Act, 46

Mercantilism, 28
Metropolitan areas, 140
Mexico, 37
Middle East, 69
Migration, internal, 82, 136,
    147–148
Militarism, 67
Military Commissions Act, 168
Military spending, 44, 51, 66
Military tribunals, 169–171
Millennium Declaration, 2
Mine Ban Treaty, 67
Minimum wage, 143, 144–145
Minmax approach, 7
Minorities:
    becoming demographic
        majority, 149
    and economic opportunity,
        107
    oppression of, 174
    protection of, 88
Morality, 31–34, 39, 87–88
Moral value, 110
Mothers' pensions, 39

National Association of Social
    Workers (NASW), 8, 176
National Federation of
    Cooperatives of Persons
    with Disabilities, 107–108
National Labor Relations Board,
    43
National Recovery
    Administration, 41
National security, 66, 73, 75
National security letters, 176,
    177
National Youth Administration
    (NYA), 41
Nation-states:
    interconnectedness of, 101
    relationship with corporate
        entities, 69
Native Americans, 31, 33, 34,
    48, 144
Negotiation, fairness of, 88
Neighborhood deterioration, 138
Neoliberalism, 86
New Deal, 24, 30, 40–44, 49,
    56, 57
New Dimensions of Human
    Security (UNDP), 66
NGOs (non-governmental
    organizations)
    and Asian and Pacific Decade
        of Disabled Persons, 103

in Hong Kong, 97
    and human rights, 76
    and human security, 75
    role of in civil society, 76–77
9/11. See September 11, 2001
Nixon, Richard M., 45, 49–50
Noncash assistance programs,
    124
Noncitizens, detention of,
    168–169
Nonconformist populations, 23
Nonmalfeasance, 87
North American Free Trade
    Agreement (NAFTA), 137
North Korea, 101
Not-for-profit agencies, 24, 136
NSA (National Security Agency,
    U.S.), 172–173, 176

Obama, Barack, 54–56
Occupational Safety and Health
    Act (OSHA), 50, 57
Occupy Movement, 16, 65, 68
OCHA (UN Office for the
    Coordination of
    Humanitarian Affairs), 72
OECD, 106
Old Age Assistance (OAA), 42
Older Americans Act, 46
Opportunity-enhancing
    programs, 22, 59
Organized crime, 69
Organized labor, 43, 139
Out-of-wedlock births, 123
Outsourcing, 139, 143

Palmer Raids, 168
Parenting, 136
Patient Protection and
    Affordable Care Act, 55
Patriot Act, U.S., 165–179
    and Internet users' activities,
        176
    need for reforms of, 174,
        175–177
    significant activities of,
        167–173
    and social work profession,
        173–177
Payroll taxes, 23
Peace, 65, 76
Peace dividend, 49, 66
Peace of Westphalia, 68
People-centered security, 66
Personal Responsibility and
    Work Opportunities Act,
    52, 54

Personal Responsibility and
    Work Opportunity
    Reconciliation Act
    (PRWORA), 123
Personal rights, 44–49
Persons of color, 45, 141, 144,
    153. See also African
    Americans; Arab-descent
    persons; Asian
    Americans; Latinos;
    Native Americans
Philanthropy, private, 23
Philippines, 99, 107–108
Philosophy, political, 13
Pierce, Franklin, 34
Politics and welfare, 3–4
Poorhouses, 28–29, 32
Population. See also
    Demographics
    aging, 136, 148–149
    changing in urban areas, 149
    distribution, 149
    world, 15
Poverty, 2–3
    addressing, 76
    alleviation, 98, 111
    children living in, 121–122,
        130, 152
    culture of, 151
    and economic globalization,
        138
    extreme, 2, 94
    and family well-being, 152
    gap in experiencing and
        understanding, 127–128
    inequality and
        unemployment, 139–145
    international poverty line,
        72–73
    method of determining,
        140–141
    during New Deal period,
        40–44
    pervasive, 69
    and security, 74–75
    and social capital, 106–107
    and social inequality, 129
    and social well being, 126
    in U.S., 139–141
    and values conflicts, 125–127
    and welfare reform, 123–124
    and women, 140 (see also
        Female-headed
        households)
Prejudice, 13, 24, 40. See also
    Discrimination; Racism

Preventive services, 22
Privacy, 183, 185–186
Privatization, 51, 53–54
Probable cause, 171
Progressive era, 37–40, 56–57
Property ownership, 7
Property taxes, 58
Public assistance, 10, 119, 145
Public education, 11, 33, 56, 144
Public housing programs,
    federal, 42
Public welfare, 11–12
Public Works Administration
    (PWA), 41

Quota systems, 104–105, 108

Racial profiling, 168, 169, 171
Racism, 37, 145–150. *See also*
    Discrimination; Prejudice
Reagan, Ronald, 4, 24, 50–54,
    57
"Real" security, 73–75
Reasoning, 13
Recession of 2009. *See* Great
    Recession
Recreational programs, 22
Refugee Act of 1980, 48
Regulations, 11, 22, 56–57
    established during New Deal
        period, 42
    in Progressive era, 37–40
Rehabilitation Act of 1973, 48
Report on Mental Health, 190
Republican Party, 39, 46
Residual welfare, 9, 10–11
Resilience, 60
Resource distribution, 7, 73, 75,
    95, 149
Responsibility, social, 127
Retirees, 45
Retirement accounts, private,
    52, 53
Retrenchment, 60
Revisionism, 87
Revivalism, Christian, 32
Rights:
    group, 60
    personal, 44–49
Riots, 31
Robber barons, 39
Rome Statute, 70
Roosevelt, Franklin, 4, 30,
    40–44, 119
Roosevelt, Theodore, 39
Roth Retirement Accounts, 52

Safety-net programs, 22, 50
Sales taxes, 58
Schools, inadequacy of, 144
Secure Communities, 171
Securities and Exchange
    Commission (SEC), 41
Security:
    defined, 66
    and deprivation, 74–75
    and global community, 68
    and military and economic
        might, 68
    people-centered, 66
    and privacy, 183
    redefined for 21st century,
        68–70
    and social media, 185
Segregation, 36
Self-sufficiency, 125, 126–127,
    150
Senior citizens, 46, 47, 60–61,
    104, 140. *See also* Social
    Security
"Separate spheres" doctrine, 34
September 11, 2001, 67,
    165–166
    and American foreign policy,
        69
    changes in world since, 77
    militarized response to, 68
    and terrorism in Asia, 101
    and war on terror, 74
Sexual orientation, 136,
    149–150
"Shadow welfare state," 11
Sheltered workshops, 105–106,
    109
Simulation training, 190
Single-parent families, 124, 140,
    144. *See also*
    Female-headed
    households
Single-person households, 149
Slaves/slavery, 30–31, 34–35.
    See also African
    Americans
SNAP (Supplemental Nutritional
    Assistance Program). *See*
    Food stamps
Social capital, 106, 107–111
Social class, 24
Social empathy:
    benefits of, 129–130
    and welfare reform, 117–133
    what it is, 128–129
Social enterprise, 107–111

Social equity, 87, 97
Social goods, 7
Social harmony, 96–98
Social indicators, negative, 138
Social insurance programs, 11,
    119
Social integration, 98
Social justice, 65
    and anywhere access,
        181–192
    Asian perspective, 95–96,
        99–101
    and ethics, 176
    and globalization, 89
    for marginalized and
        disadvantaged groups,
        93–115
    overview, 1
    and Patriot Act, 174
    and social harmony, 96–98
    and social welfare policy,
        1–19
    and the UN, 95
Social media, 16, 184–186
Social policy:
    in Asia, 93–115
    changing, 6
    and Christian morality, 31–34
    defined, 5–6
    and demographic and
        economic changes,
        135–163
    direction in 21st century,
        150–151
    focus on reducing poverty,
        150
    as form of social justice,
        1–19
    future of, 60–61
    from a global perspective,
        81–91
    as instrument of change, 9
    justice-based, 12–15
    and justice theory, 6–8
    neoliberal approach to, 86
    overview, 98–99
    and technology influence,
        181–192
    and values conflicts, 126–127
    what it is, 3
Social problems, globalization
    of, 84
Social programs, federal, 40–44
Social regulation, global, 87
Social responsibility, 127
Social rights, global, 87

Social Security, 9, 50, 57, 117,
    127, 129–130
  establishment of, 42, 119
  expenditures in 2011, 118
  future of, 154
  growth of, 57, 58, 59, 60
  Trust Funds, 152
Social services, 22, 44–49, 57
Social support, 126–127
Social transfer, global, 87
Social wage, 139
Social welfare:
  devolution of federal
      programs, 50–54
  traditional conceptual
      framework of, 9–12
Social well being, 126
Social work:
  and activism, 175–177
  and advocacy, 173–174
  code of ethics, 174, 176
  core competencies for
      practice, 8
  core mission, 1–2
  globalization and policy,
      88–89
  impact of Patriot Act on
      profession, 165–179
  international, 81–91
  policy (see Social policy)
  and policy development,
      4–5
  and politics, 12–13
  in 2022, 189–191
  values and policy, 8–9
Social work centers, 105, 106
Social Work Dictionary (Barker),
    5
Socioeconomic justice, 73
Sociopathic behaviors, 129
South Korea, 99
Spanish-speaking persons, 37.
      See also Latinos
Spying, domestic, 172–173
Stanton, Elizabeth Cady, 34
"State secrets privilege," 177
Stewardship, 87
Stimulus Plan, 55
Street children, 32
Suburbs, 149
Suffrage, universal, 36
Sunday School movement, 32,
    37
Supplemental Security Income
    (SSI), 10, 50
Supported employment, 105

Surveillance, warrantless,
    172–173
Sustainability, 76, 85, 93
Sympathy, 118, 127

Taft, William, 39
Taipei, Taiwan, 108–110
TANF (Temporary Assistance to
    Needy Families), 9, 10,
    52, 54, 57, 117–118
  and children, 130
  comparison between
      recipients and Congress,
      128
  overview of, 120–121
  and welfare reform, 118
  who receives it, 122–123
Taxes, 7, 58
  and affluent persons, 53
  during colonial period, 30
  credits, 23, 50
  cuts in during Reagan years,
      51
  deductions, 12, 52
  expenditures, 21, 23, 52–53,
      57, 58, 59
  during Great Depression, 41
  income, 44, 58
  rebates, 52
  regressive, 143
  revenues during inflation of
      1970s, 49
  subsidies, 12
Tea Party, 55–56, 135
Technology, 181–192
  and cultural diversity, 187
  and globalization, 82–83
  and income inequality, 143
  influence on social policy,
      181–192
  societal acceptance and
      utilization of, 184
  unintended consequences of,
      188–189
Temperance crusaders, 32
Temporary Assistance to Needy
    Families. See TANF
    (Temporary Assistance to
    Needy Families)
Tennessee Valley Authority, 42
Terrorists/terrorism, 166
Thailand, 99
Therapy, on-line, 189–190
Title VII, 47
Trade:
  deficit, 143

foreign, 138
liberalization, 82
openness, 86
Transnational corporations, 138
Truman, Harry, 43

Undocumented workers, 48–49
UNDP. See United Nations
    Development Program
Unemployment/
    underemployment:
  during the Early Republic
      period, 32
  during the Great Depression
      period, 40
  during the Great Recession,
      142
  in Hong Kong, 100
  poverty and inequality,
      139–145
  in U.S., 140
UNESCO (United Nations
    Economic and Social
    Commission), 94
Unfunded mandates, 143
Unintended consequences,
    188–189
Unions, labor, 43, 143
United Farm Workers, 47
United Nations:
  Advisory Board on Human
      Security, 75
  Commission on Human
      Security, 75
  Decade of Disabled Persons,
      102
  Declaration of Human Rights,
      81
  Development Program, 66,
      67, 102
  Economic and Social
      Commission for Asia and
      the Pacific (ESCAP),
      102–103
  Human Security Unit, 72
  Millennium Summit, 71
  Office for the Coordination of
      Humanitarian Affairs
      (OCHA), 72
  Trust Fund for Human
      Security (UNTFHS), 72
  Universal Declaration of
      Human Rights Charter,
      96
United States:
  distrust of, 69

United States (*continued*)
  effects of economic collapse
    in, 74–75
  infant mortality rate, 143
  people without health
    insurance, 143
  poverty in, 139–141
  shifting racial and ethnic
    composition of, 149
  unemployment rate, 140
Universal social programs, 22
UNTFHS. *See* United Nations
    Trust Fund for Human
    Security
Upward mobility, 33, 144
Urbanization, 136, 149
Urban problems, 37–40
Utility, 87

Value, moral, 110
Values and poverty, 125–127
Veil of ignorance, 7, 14
Veterans, 11, 48
Veterans Administration, 45
Vietnam War, 46, 48, 49
Violence, 69, 75, 78
Virtual reality, 190
Voting, 36, 40, 43
Vulnerable populations, 23–24
  during the Great Society
    years, 49
  and Patriot Act, 173–175
  during Progressive era, 39

Wages, 139, 140
Wagner, Robert, 130
Wagner Act, 43, 47
Wagner-Steagall Housing Act, 42
Want, freedom from, 71–72, 75,
    76, 96
War, 77–78
War crimes, 70
*War Is a Force That Gives Us
    Meaning* (Hedges), 77
War on poverty, 4, 46
War on terror, 74
Warrantless surveillance,
    172–173
Wealth distribution, 69, 94, 137,
    142
Weapons, 69, 70, 76
Weapons of mass destruction,
    69

Welfare. *See also* Social welfare
  capitalism, 136
  central question related to, 6
  evolution from 1935 to
    present, 118–120
  expenditures and trade
    openness, 86
  factories, 105
  future in America, 130–131
  political leaders' positions on,
    3–4
  and values conflicts, 125–127
  who receives it, 122–123
Welfare reform:
  and African Americans, 153
  and Asian Americans, 153
  and immigrants, 153
  impact on entitlement
    programs, 153
  impact on underlying social
    welfare philosophy, 153
  inherent contradictions in,
    125
  mixed effects of, 152
  as policy illustration, 151–153
  and poverty, 123–124
  and public assistance, 145
  purposes of, 152
  and social empathy, 117–133
  success of, 121–122
  and values conflicts, 126–127
  why it has failed, 123–124
Welfare state, American:
  during and after the Civil War,
    34–37
  challenges facing historians
    of, 21–28
  during the colonial period,
    28–31
  evolution of, 21–64
  expanding parameters of,
    22–25
  expansion from late 60s
    through 1970s, 49–50
  in full context, 25–26
  and globalization, 86–87
  history in chronological
    segments, 26–56
  within individual states,
    57–58
  surrogates, 25
  why it's grown so much, 59
Welfare-to-work program, 120

Welfare underclass, 151
Well-being, 140, 152
Westward expansion, 33
Wheelchair project, 109–110
"White backlash," 46
Why We Can't Wait (King), 178
Wikipedia, 186–187
Wilson, Woodrow, 39
Women. *See also* Female-headed
    households;
    Single-parent families
  and affirmative action
    programs, 47
  during the colonial period, 31
  and discrimination, 49
  granted voting privileges, 40
  in Hong Kong, 97
  involving in peace building,
    76
  lesbian (*see* Lesbian women)
  and poverty, 140
  and social reform during
    Gilded Age, 39
  and welfare, 122–123
  during westward expansion
    period, 34
Workers:
  in the age of industrialism, 38
  undocumented, 48–49
  unskilled and undereducated,
    143
Working poor, 145
Workmen's compensation,
    39–40
Work-relief programs, 41–42,
    50, 57
Works Progress Administration
    (WPA), 41
World Bank, 83, 106, 111
World Health Organization
    (WHO), 2
The World Is Flat (Friedman),
    15, 181
World Summit for Social
    Development, 98
World Summit on the
    Information Society, 83
World Trade Organization
    (WTO), 83, 88, 101
World War II, 40, 43
World Wide Web, 14

Zoning policies, 22